GREAT AT WORK

THE HIDDEN HABITS OF
TOP PERFORMERS

MORTEN T. HANSEN

SIMON & SCHUSTER PAPERBACKS

NEW YORK LONDON TORONTO SYDNEY NEW DELHI

Simon & Schuster Paperbacks
An Imprint of Simon & Schuster, Inc.
1230 Avenue of the Americas
New York, NY 10020

First Simon & Schuster trade paperback edition September 2019

SIMON & SCHUSTER PAPERBACKS and colophon are
registered trademarks of Simon & Schuster, Inc.

For information about special discounts for bulk purchases,
please contact Simon & Schuster Special Sales
at 1-866-506-1949 or business@simonandschuster.com.

The Simon & Schuster Speakers Bureau can bring authors to your live event.
For more information or to book an event, contact the
Simon & Schuster Speakers Bureau at 1-866-248-3049 or
visit our website at www.simonspeakers.com.

Interior design by Ruth Lee-Mui

Manufactured in the United States of America

3   5   7   9   10   8   6   4   2

Library of Congress Control Number: 2018285536

ISBN 978-1-4767-6562-4
ISBN 978-1-4767-6582-2 (pbk)
ISBN 978-1-4767-6583-9 (ebook)

For Hélène

Contents

PART III

MASTERING YOUR WORK-LIFE

ONE

THE SECRETS TO GREAT PERFORMANCE

After nine grueling interviews, I landed my dream job as management consultant at the Boston Consulting Group in London. I'll never forget how I showed up on my first day, wearing an elegant blue suit bought for the occasion, with Oxford lace-up shoes to match. My girlfriend had given me a sleek, soft briefcase of the sort bankers carried around. As I strode through the front doors of the office in posh Devonshire House, right near Piccadilly, I looked the part, but felt intimidated.

I yearned to make a mark, so I followed what I thought was a brilliant strategy: I would work crazy hours. I didn't have much relevant work experience—heck, I didn't have any. It was my first real job. I was twenty-four years old and had just finished a master's degree in finance from the London School of Economics. What I lacked in experience I would make up for by staying late in the office. Over the next three years, I worked sixty, seventy, eighty, even ninety hours per week. I drank an endless stream of weak British coffee and survived on a supply of chocolate bars I kept in my top drawer. It got to the point where I knew the names of the cleaning staff who arrived at five in the morning. As you can imagine, my girlfriend soon wanted the briefcase back.

One day, as I struggled through an intense merger and acquisition project, I happened upon some slides created by a teammate (I'll call her Natalie). Paging through her analysis, I confronted an uncomfortable truth. Natalie's work was better than mine. Her analysis contained crisper insights, more compelling ideas. Her slides boasted a clean, elegant layout that was more pleasing to the eye and easier to comprehend—which in turn made her analysis even more persuasive. Yet one evening in the office, when I went to look for her, she wasn't there. I asked a guy sitting near her desk where she was, and he replied that she'd gone home for the night. He explained that Natalie never worked late. She worked from 8 a.m. to 6 p.m. No nights, no weekends. That upset me. We were both talented and had the analytical capability required of BCG consultants. She had no more experience in the field than I did. Yet she did better while working less.

Three years later, I left BCG to embark on an academic career. I earned a Ph.D. from Stanford University and went on to become a professor at Harvard Business School. From time to time, I found myself thinking back to what I called the "Natalie Question": Why had she performed better in fewer hours? She must have carried some secrets explaining her results. I began to wonder about performance in general and decided to focus my research on corporate performance.

Starting in 2002, Jim Collins and I spent nine years working on our book *Great by Choice* as a sequel to Jim's *Good to Great*.[1] Both books offer empirically validated frameworks that account for great performance in *companies*. That's nice if you're leading a business, but what about the rest of us? After we finished the project, I decided to develop a similarly validated framework for *individual* performance. It was time to discover why Natalie had done better than I, and more generally, to tackle the big question: why do some people perform great at work while others don't?

Social scientists and management experts explain performance at work by pointing to people's innate gifts and natural strengths. How often have you heard phrases like "She's a natural at sales" or "He's a brilliant engineer"? One influential book titled *The War for Talent* argues that a company's ability to recruit and retain talent determines its success.[2] The popular StrengthsFinder approach advocates that you find a job that taps into your natural strengths, and then focus on developing those further.[3] These talent-based explanations are deeply embedded in our perceptions of what makes for success. But are they right?

Some work experts take issue with the talent view. They argue that an individual's sustained *effort* is just as critical or even more so in determining success.[4] In one variant of this "work hard" paradigm, people perform because they have grit, persevering against obstacles over the long haul.[5] In another, people maximize efforts by doing more: they take on many assignments and are busy running to lots of meetings. That's the approach I subscribed to while at BCG, where I put in long hours in an effort to accomplish more. Many people believe that working harder is key to success.[6]

Talent, effort, and also luck undoubtedly explain why some succeed and others don't, but I wasn't satisfied with these arguments. They didn't account for why Natalie performed better than I, nor did they explain the performance differences I had observed between equally hardworking and talented people.

I decided to take a different approach, exploring whether the *way* some people work—their specific work practices as opposed to the sheer amount of effort they exert—accounts for greatness at work. That led me to explore the idea of "working smart," whereby people seek to maximize *output per hour of work*. The phrase "work smarter, not harder" has been thrown around so much that it has become a cliché. Who wants to "work dumb"? But many people do in fact work dumb because they don't know exactly *how* to work smart. And I don't blame them, because it's hard to obtain solid guidance.

I scanned for existing advice on how to work smarter, and the picture I arrived at was incoherent and overwhelming. Every author seemed to say something different. Prioritize. Delegate. Keep a calendar. Avoid distractions. Set clear goals. Execute better. Influence people. Inspire.

Manage up. Manage down. Network. Tap into passion. Find a purpose. The list went on, more than 100 pieces of advice.

So what is *really* going on? If Natalie worked smarter than I, what exactly did she and other top performers do? What secrets to their great performance do they harbor? I decided to find out. After years of study, what I found surprised me a great deal and shattered conventional wisdom.

THE PERFORMANCE STUDY

In 2011, I launched one of the most comprehensive research projects ever undertaken on individual performance at work. I recruited a team of researchers with expertise in statistical analysis and began generating a framework—a set of hypotheses about which specific behaviors lead to high performance. I considered the scattered findings I had found in more than 200 published academic studies, and I incorporated insights from my previous discussions with hundreds of managers and executives. I also drew on in-depth interviews with 120 professionals and undertook a 300-person survey pilot. In the final step, we tested the emerging framework in a survey study of 5,000 managers and employees.

To organize the vast array of potential "work smart" factors, I grouped them into categories that scholars regard as important for job performance. We can think of work as consisting of job design characteristics (*what* a person is supposed to do), skill development (*how* a person improves), motivational factors (*why* a person exerts effort), and relational dimensions (with *whom* and how a person interacts). Once I had settled on these broad categories, I examined factors within each, identifying those that previous research suggested were key. (The research appendix contains details on our methodology.)

With this initial list of factors in hand, my team and I designed a 96-item survey instrument, piloting it with a sample of 300 bosses and employees. We also tracked how many hours people worked each week, and we measured their performance relative to their peers. That way, we could compare the effects of hours worked and our "work smart" factors on performance. We spent months poring over statistical results from the pilot and our notes from in-depth interviews. We winnowed down the number of plausible factors until we arrived at eight main factors. After some more analysis, we discovered that two were similar, so we combined them into one (see the research appendix for further explanation).

In the end, we discovered that seven "work smart" practices seemed to explain a substantial portion of performance. (It always seems to be seven, doesn't it?) When you work smart, you select a tiny set of priorities and make huge efforts in those chosen areas (what I call the work scope practice). You focus on creating value, not just reaching preset goals (targeting). You eschew mindless repetition in favor of better skills practice (quality learning). You seek roles that match your passion with a strong sense of purpose (inner motivation). You shrewdly deploy influence tactics to gain the support of others (advocacy). You cut back on wasteful team meetings, and make sure that the ones you do attend spark vigorous debate (rigorous teamwork). You carefully pick which cross-unit projects to get involved in, and say no to less productive ones (disciplined collaboration). This is a pretty comprehensive list. The first four relate to mastering your own work, while the remaining three concern mastering working with others.

NOT WHAT WE EXPECTED

These seven practices upend conventional thinking about how you should work. I had thought, for instance, that people who prioritized well would perform well, and they did, but the best performers in our study also did something else. Once they had focused on a few priorities, they *obsessed* over those tasks to produce quality work. That extreme dedication to their priorities created extraordinary results. Top performers did less *and* more: less volume of activities, more concentrated effort. This insight overturns much conventional thinking about focusing that urges you to *choose* a few tasks to prioritize. Choice is only half of the equation—you also need to obsess. This finding led us to reformulate the "work scope" practice and call it "do less, then obsess."

Our findings also overturned another convention. How many times have you heard, "Do what you love"? Find a role that taps into your passion, and you will be energized and do a better job. Sure enough, we found that people who were highly passionate about their jobs performed better. But we also came across passionate people who didn't perform well, and people whose passion led them astray (like the poor guy who pursued his passion for graphics design and ended up running down his retirement account and having no job and no income). "Follow your passion," we found, can be dangerous advice. Our top performers took a different approach: they strove to find roles that contributed value to the organization and society, and then matched passion with that sense of purpose. The *matching* of passion and purpose, and not passion alone, produced the best results.

Our results overturned yet another typical view, the idea that collaboration is necessarily good and that more is better. Experts advise us to tear down "silos" in organizations, collaborate more, build large professional networks, and use lots of high-tech communication tools to get work done. Well, my research shows that convention to be dead wrong. Top performers collaborate *less*. They carefully choose which projects and tasks to join and which to flee, and they channel their efforts and resources to excel in the few chosen ones. They discipline their collaboration.

Our study also disputes the popular idea that the path to top performance lies in practicing a skill for 10,000 hours.[7] Our best performers in the workplace did something else, practicing what I call the "learning loop" at work, as we'll discuss in chapter four.

These and other surprising insights turned out to be critical. The very best people didn't just work smart in a conventional sense, but pursued more nuanced practices, like doing less and obsessing, and matching purpose with passion. Comparing these seven practices, I realized that they all embodied the idea of *selectivity*. Whenever they could, top performers carefully selected which priorities, tasks, collaborations, team meetings, committees, analyses, customers, new ideas, steps in a process, and interactions to undertake, and which to neglect or reject. Yet this more nuanced way of working smart wasn't *just* about being selective. The very best redesigned their work so that they would create the most *value* (a term we will define in chapter three) and then they applied *intense, targeted efforts* in their selected work activities.

Based on these findings, I arrived at a more precise definition of working smart: *To work smart means to maximize the value of your work by selecting a few activities and applying intense targeted effort.*

TESTING THE NEW THEORY

To test our framework of the seven work-smart practices, my team and I modified our survey instrument and administered it to 5,000 managers and employees across a wide range of jobs and industries in corporate America. We sampled bosses and direct reports in addition to employees, so as not to rely on self-reported data only (see the research appendix for details). We surveyed sales reps, lawyers, trainers, actuaries, brokers, medical doctors, software programmers, engineers, store managers, plant foremen, marketers, human resource people, consultants, nurses, and my personal favorite–a Las Vegas casino dealer. Some of these people occupied senior positions, but most were supervisors, office managers, department heads, or employees in low-level positions. The 5,000 people represented 15 industry sectors and 22 job functions. Almost half (45 percent) were women (two of the seven practices revealed a gender difference[8]). Age groups ranged from millennials to those over 50. Education level varied from those with less than a bachelor's degree (20 percent of the sample) to people with a master's degree or higher (22 percent). My aim was to develop, test, and share a smart-work theory that most people could use to improve their individual performance.

We ran our 5,000-person data set through a rigorous statistical method called regression analysis. It turned out that our seven work-smart practices went a long way toward explaining differences in performance. *In fact, they accounted for a whopping 66 percent of the variation in performance among the 5,000 people in our dataset.*[9] We can compare that to other fields to get an idea of how remarkable this effect is. Smoking will kill you, we're told, yet smoking only explains 18 percent of variation in people's average life expectancy in the developed world, according to one study.[10]

Having a good salary is considered crucial for building lifelong financial resources, yet income only explains 33 percent of differences in people's net worth, according to a study of U.S. citizens between ages 18 and 65.[11] The basketball star Stephen Curry is famous for hitting three-point shots twenty-two feet away from the basket, yet he has landed "just" 44 percent of these shots during his professional career.[12] These benchmark numbers from other fields indicate how substantial 66 percent really is in explaining an outcome like individual performance.

By contrast, other factors we tested such as educational background, company tenure, age, gender, and hours worked combined to account for only 10 percent of the differences in performance. Hours worked per week mattered, but as I'll explain in chapter three, the relationship to performance was more complicated than the simple "work harder" view suggests. The other 24 percent of the difference was unexplained and possibly included factors such as luck or talent.

What Explains Individual Performance?

Results from Analysis of 5,000 People in the Study

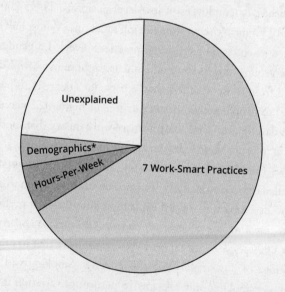

*Gender, age, years of education, company tenure

Think about what these results mean. The talent and effort explanations still play a significant role in determining how individuals perform. *But the real key to individual performance is the seven "work smarter" practices.*

We now have the answer to the "Natalie" question of why some people perform so well, although I will never know what exactly Natalie did to deliver such stellar work. But I know something far more important—a systematic and empirically tested way to lift performance that holds across jobs. By improving on the seven practices, you can boost your performance beyond what it would be if you relied on talent, luck, or the sheer number of hours worked. As the chart below shows, the more a person in our study adopted the seven practices in their work, the better they performed. If you rank in only the 21st percentile in your adoption of the seven practices, your performance is likely to be lackluster—in the bottom 21st percentile (point A in the chart). However, if you crank up your proficiency at these seven practices, jumping to the 90th percentile, your performance is likely to be in the 89th percentile (point B in the chart) according to our predictions. That's becoming a top performer.

HOW TO WORK AT YOUR BEST

For all that has been written about performance, no book to my knowledge has presented an evidence-based, comprehensive understanding of what enables individuals to perform at the highest level at work. *Great at Work* fills this gap. It gives you a simple and practical framework that you can use to work at your best. Think of it as a complement to Stephen Covey's 7 *Habits of Highly Effective People*, updated to reflect the realities of work today, and backed by an unprecedented statistical analysis.[13]

Each chapter presents a "smart" practice and offers concrete advice for how you can include it in your own work. By using the word "practice," I want to emphasize that you can incorporate these ideas into your daily work and make them a habit, just like you would other routines, like grabbing that morning coffee, checking your mail, and exercising. You can start small and build up these routines bit by bit, until you master them.

Lifting Individual Performance

The Positive Effect of the Seven Practices Combined on Individual Performance

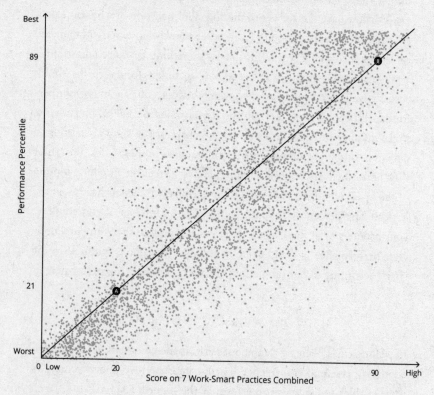

Note:
These 4,964 data points representing people in our study show a pattern: The inserted line represents a statistical regression prediction of how the seven practices combined affect individual performance. Score low on the seven practices (point A in the chart) and your performance likely will be mediocre. Score high (point B) and your performance likely will be excellent (see the Research Appendix for details).

To inspire and guide you in how to apply these ideas, I tell stories of people from all walks of life who have adopted one or more of these practices and achieved outsize results. You'll meet Steven Birdsall, a senior manager who found a way to carve out a new business in the software company SAP. You'll encounter Genevieve Guay, a hotel concierge who infused her work with passion and purpose. I'll introduce you to Greg Green, a principal who accomplished a dramatic turnaround of his failing high school, with inspiration from an unlikely source. You'll encounter an emergency room nurse who found a way for her department to save *more* heart attack patients while doing *less* work. You'll meet a consumer products CEO whose unusual approach to team meetings helped him achieve a top 1 percent performance record. You'll also come across a small business owner, a biotech engineer, a physician, a management consultant, a sushi chef, a salesperson, a factory lineperson, and many others who implemented at least one of the seven practices and boosted their performance. (Throughout the book, we have altered the names and settings for most of the people we interviewed from our dataset.)

HOW YOU CAN LIVE WELL, TOO

You might wonder whether people who work smarter as I've defined it are unhappy with their work. Under the old "work hard" paradigm, high achievers tend to become stressed out, even burned out.[14] You work harder and your performance improves, but your quality of life plummets. I know mine did when I was putting in all those hours at BCG. But our study yielded a surprise. The seven "work smarter" practices didn't just improve performance. They also improved people's well-being at work. As I show in chapter nine, people in our study who worked smarter experienced *better work-life balance, higher job satisfaction, and less burnout.*

I have met so many people who believe that they must make a trade-off between achieving at work and enjoying a happy life. They forgo life outside of their jobs and put in huge amounts of hard work—long hours and maximum effort—to become top performers. Millions of people around the world sacrifice this way because they don't know how to work differently. They don't know *how* to work smart. But now there is a clear answer. As our study shows, you can perform exceptionally well and still have plenty of time to do things you love other than work, like being with your family and friends. *Being great at work means performing in your job, infusing your work with passion and a strong sense of purpose, and living well, too.* How great is that?

Whether you're about to graduate from college or in the middle of your career, whether you're worried about keeping your job or simply want to do it better, I invite you to set aside your preconceived ideas about work and explore the work-smart theory I present in this book. We'll begin with the four practices for mastering your own work, followed by the three practices to help you master working with other people.

PART I

MASTERING YOUR OWN WORK

TWO

DO LESS, THEN OBSESS

Whatever you are, be out and out, not partial or in doubt.

—Henrik Ibsen[1]

In October 1911, two teams were racing to be the first humans to reach the South Pole, the last major place on earth not yet discovered. Royal British Navy Commander Robert Falcon Scott led the first team. A veteran explorer, he had led a previous expedition to Antarctica. That earlier trip had failed to reach the South Pole, but the British public had hailed Scott as a hero. Upon his return, King Edward VII summoned Scott to Balmoral Castle and anointed him commander of the Royal Victorian Order.[2]

The leader of the second team, Norwegian Roald Amundsen, had been the first explorer to navigate the Northwest Passage, the waterborne route connecting the Atlantic to the Pacific through the Arctic Archipelago in northern Canada. Driven to make history, he too had set his sights on the South Pole.

Months after arriving on the continent, having endured an Antarctic winter at their respective camps, Scott and Amundsen readied their teams for the grueling journey south. Each knew of the other's presence, but not the location during the journey. There would be no maps, no communication, no rescue. Just before setting off, Amundsen jotted in his diary: "Not much visibility. Nasty breeze from S. -52°C. The dogs clearly affected by the cold. The men, stiff in their frozen clothes, more or less satisfied after a night in the frost . . . prospect of milder weather doubtful."[3] It would not be easy—or survivable.

The race began. Amundsen took the lead as both teams embarked on their 400-mile journey across the ice barrier, a 10,000-foot climb up a treacherous mountain to the polar plateau. Once there, they would face another 400-mile journey toward the pole, all the while enduring minus 60°F chills, disorienting blizzards, and winds shrieking at 100 miles an hour.

Scaling the mountain, Amundsen and his team struggled across deep crevasses. They survived blizzards. They slaughtered dogs for food. After 52 days, they arrived within 55 miles of the pole. Seeing no sign of Scott, Amundsen pressed on. Two days later, Amundsen and his fellow explorers became the first in history to stand on the South Pole. They planted the Norwegian flag and then journeyed back to their base, reaching it after trudging 1,600 miles.

Scott and his men, exhausted and malnourished, limped to the pole thirty-four days later, only to find the Norwegian flag whipping in the wind. The team slogged homeward, racing against the approaching winter. Starving, frostbitten, exhausted, they pushed forward. Hope faded. A storm pinned them down in their tents. There they would die, only eleven miles from the next depot of food and shelter.

One leader and his team achieved the extraordinary, while the other team perished in the polar night. Why? What made the difference? Over the years, authors have offered several explanations. In our book *Great by Choice*, Jim Collins and I attributed Amundsen's success to better pacing and self-control. Others have pointed to good planning or even luck to explain Amundsen's success and Scott's failure.

However, many accounts neglect one critical part of the dramatic

South Pole race: the scope of the expeditions. One team fielded superior resources: a grander ship, 187 feet vs. 128 feet; a bigger budget, £40,000 vs. £20,000; and a larger crew, 65 vs. 19 men.[4] How could one win against such a mighty foe? It was an unfair race. Except for one thing.

Amundsen's team was the one with the narrow scope. Captain Scott commanded three times the men and twice the budget. He used five forms of transportation: dogs, motor sledges, Siberian ponies, skis, and man-hauling. If one failed, he had backups. Amundsen relied on only one form of transportation: dogs. Had they failed, his quest would have ended. But Amundsen's dogs didn't fail. They performed. Why?

It wasn't just the *choice* to use dogs—Scott took dogs, too. Amundsen succeeded to a large degree because he concentrated *only* on dogs and eschewed backup options. During his three-year trip through the Northwest Passage, he had spent two winters apprenticing with Inuits who had mastered dog sledging. Running a span of dogs is hard. They are unruly animals and sometimes drop down in the snow and refuse to work. Amundsen learned from the natives how to urge dogs to run, how to drive sledges, and how to pace himself.

Amundsen also obsessed over obtaining superior dogs. His research suggested that Greenlander dogs handled polar travel better than Siberian huskies. Greenland dogs were bigger and stronger, and with their longer legs they could better traverse the snowdrift across the ice barrier and the polar plateau.[5] Amundsen traveled to Copenhagen to enlist the help of the Danish inspector of North Greenland. "As far as dogs are concerned, it is absolutely essential that I obtain the very best it is conceivable to obtain," he wrote in a follow-up letter. "Naturally, I am fully aware that as a result, the price must be higher than that normally paid."[6] He sought out expert dog runners to join his team, several more skilled than he. When the star dog driver Sverre Hassel declined, Amundsen didn't look for the next best but kept pursuing Hassel. According to historian Roland Huntford, "Amundsen now exerted all his charm and force of character to coax Hassel, after all, to sail with him. In the end, Hassel, worn down by his persistence, agreed."[7]

Scott, on the other hand, was so busy arranging for five separate transportation methods that he couldn't focus on any of them. Rather than venturing to Siberia to secure ponies, he sent his aide, Cecil Meares. But Meares didn't know about ponies—he was a dog expert.[8] So Scott's team ended up with twenty ill-suited ponies, which slowed the team down in their journey to the pole.

Once moving on the ice, Scott struggled to coordinate his convoy. The motor sledges started first, as they were the slowest. The pony party set out seven days later. The dog sledges, which were the fastest, left last. Each group had to coordinate its departure and speed with the others. Scott got tangled in a complex operation—"a somewhat disorganized fleet," as he noted in his diary.[9] The convoy ended up moving as fast as the slowest method.

Amundsen, meanwhile, had fixated on a single transportation mode and was speeding across the barren landscape. During the first eight weeks, he and his small team of four other experts, with four sledges and 52 superior dogs, averaged 15 miles per day against Scott's 11.[10] Amundsen gained at least four miles on Scott every day on average. By the time Amundsen reached the pole, he was more than 300 miles ahead. Amundsen had chosen one method and mastered it. He had done less, then obsessed.

DO LESS, OBSESS, AND *PERFORM*

The story of the race to the South Pole challenges two common beliefs about work. The first is that we should increase the scope of our activities, pursuing multiple responsibilities and options, like taking five transportation methods to the South Pole. We believe that by taking on more tasks, we accomplish more and improve our performance. "Doing more," as we shall see, is usually a flawed strategy.

The second misconception concerns the idea of focus. Writers like Daniel Goleman and Stephen Covey have argued that people can only perform at their best if they *select* a few items to work on and say no to others.[11] This view is incomplete. It overemphasizes choice, as if that's the only requirement: If you are disciplined enough to *choose* a few priorities, you will succeed. *Picking a few priorities is only half the equation. The other half is the harsh requirement that you must obsess over your chosen area of focus to excel.*

The term "focus" consists of two activities: choosing a few priorities, and then dedicating your efforts toward excelling at them. Many people prioritize a few items at work, but they don't obsess—they simply do less. That's a mistake.

Amundsen didn't win just because he picked dogs. He won because once he had chosen dogs, he applied huge amounts of effort to perfecting that single method of transporting the sledges. Had he shown up with just "good enough" dogs and drivers, he wouldn't have traveled so fast each day, and he might have lost the race.

In our quantitative study of 5,000 people, we found that employees who chose a few key priorities and channeled tremendous effort into doing exceptional work in those areas greatly outperformed those who pursued a wider range of priorities. We asked people to gauge how much they prioritized and how much effort they put into their chosen priorities. We then formed a "do less, then obsess" score for each employee and analyzed the impact on performance. The predicted effect turned out to be substantial. People who were average at other practices but mastered "do less, then obsess" would likely place *25 percentage points higher* in the performance ranking than those who didn't embrace this practice.[12]

Think about that difference. Say you start out as a middling performer—at the 50th percentile of all employees—and then move your "do less, then obsess" score from low (a "do-more" strategy) to high. Your performance now will be at the 75th percentile, meaning that you perform better than 74 percent of employees. That's pretty amazing. *"Do less, then obsess" affects performance more than any other practice in this book.*

Consider the contrast between two people in our study (their names and settings have been altered).[13] One boss gave a low "do less, then obsess" score to Maria, a mortgage specialist in her fifties at a Milwaukee bank. "She gets overwhelmed," the boss said. "When there's too much work, she just tries to do it herself, as opposed to delegating it." Maria landed in the bottom 41 percent on the "do less, then obsess" principle.

It was a different story with Cathy, a fifty-six-year-old quality engineer at a company that manufactures car parts. She could narrow her attention to focus on the most important tasks at hand, and could stick to the priorities she had set. Once, when Cathy had prioritized the product launches of four customers based on start dates, one customer pressured her to do them all at the same time. As she explained, "I had to say no, I'm not going to do this right now. I've got other customers that take priority." Cathy's boss scored her in the top 10 percent on the "do less, then obsess" practice. Cathy placed 15 points higher in the performance ranking than Maria, the difference between excellent and merely good.

Many people we studied struggled to attain this kind of focus at work. Only 16 percent of the 5,000 people in our dataset scored very high on one of our question items, "He/she is extremely good at focusing on key priorities, no matter how much work and how many things he/she has to do." A full 26 percent scored very low.

I had expected that bosses would be better at focusing than low- or mid-level employees. After all, they ought to have more freedom to determine how many tasks, projects, or responsibilities to take on. Yet we found that roughly equal percentages of junior- and senior-level employees excelled at focusing (15 percent and 17 percent, respectively). And only a slightly greater percentage of junior employees were poor at focusing than their senior-level colleagues (28 percent versus 23 percent).

Far more people than we might imagine have at least some latitude in their job to focus their work activities. Of course, some job activities are fixed and cannot be changed. Others, however, are discretionary or can be modified.

To see why you should focus, let's consider some drawbacks of the usual practice of piling on more tasks.

SPREAD TOO THIN

When executive search consultant Susan Bishop opened her own boutique firm in New York City, she had a clear idea of how to succeed. "Our plan was to beat the larger, established competitors through superb execution," she explained. "We accepted every client that called us and tried to make each one as happy as humanly possible."[14]

Bishop believed that putting her clients' happiness first would lead to greater customer satisfaction, which would lead to more business. She was right—up to a point. By saying "yes" to most requests, Bishop found that she reeled in more than enough clients. But she lacked the time and energy to do her job well. Over the next few years, she and her small team undertook searches with low pay, difficult bosses, and in unattractive locations. She expanded beyond her core expertise in media and entered industries she didn't know well, such as financial services and consumer products, and then had to scramble to obtain the necessary background knowledge. With her efforts spread across too many customer areas, her performance suffered. Sales and profits remained flat, even dipping in some years. Her margins languished at about 15 percent, half that of other search firms. "The stress was just horrible," Bishop said. "I felt pulled in a hundred different directions." Her "focus" score in our survey assessment landed her in the bottom 20 percent in our 5,000-person sample.[15]

Like Bishop, many people are quick to say yes. Real estate agents are tempted to cover one more neighborhood; engineers add one more product feature; human resources employees take on one more assignment; marketers agree to help a colleague with a campaign. Before we know it, "taking on more responsibilities" lands us in the same unfortunate situation as Bishop.

But doing more has its advantages, doesn't it? If you work on more tasks, you get more done, and that pleases your boss. Spreading yourself across multiple clients or projects gives you more options. That's why Captain Scott brought five transportation methods to the South Pole. If the motor sledges conked out, Scott could use the dogs. If the dogs failed, he could rely on the ponies. Hedging your bets seems like a smart move, a good way to accomplish more.

There are, however, two big problems with scattering your efforts in this way. The first is the *spread-too-thin trap*. Neither Bishop nor Scott could devote enough time and effort to mastering even one of their tasks. Bishop struggled to keep up with all of her client accounts, and Scott failed to acquire first-rate ponies. We all have a finite supply of attention to devote to our work responsibilities. As economics Nobel-laureate Herbert Simon quipped, "A wealth of information creates a poverty of attention."[16] The more items we attend to, the less time we can allot to each, and the less well we will perform any one of them.

HURT BY COMPLEXITY

A second problem with an increase in the scope of our activities is what I call the *complexity trap*. In racing to the South Pole, Captain Scott not only had to manage many modes of transportation; he also had to deal with their *interrelationships*, which proved difficult as they moved at different speeds.

Coordinating between priorities requires mental exertion. Many regard multitasking as efficient, but research shows that rapidly toggling between two items—reading emails and listening to a colleague's presentation, for example—renders you less effective at both. Each time you switch, your brain must abandon one task and acclimate itself to the other.

A study of 58,280 court cases before Italian judges in Milan found that the judges who handled many cases simultaneously (multitasking) took longer to complete them than those who performed them in sequence. The differences were striking: the slowest judge spent on average 398 days to close the cases, while the fastest took "only" 178 days, or less than half the time. (They all had the same workload and cases were assigned randomly, so their cases were comparable.) The researchers estimated that a 50 percent increase in multitasking led to a nearly 20 percent increase in the number of days to finish cases. Toggling cases slowed them down.[17] Other studies have shown that switching between tasks can decrease your productivity by as much as 40 percent.[18]

The complexity trap wreaks havoc inside companies. In the name of progress, we pile on goals, priorities, tasks, metrics, checkpoints, team members, and so on. But adding these items increases complexity, which we can define in terms of the number of items and the number of connections between them. It's no surprise that in our study, a full 65 percent of people strongly or completely agreed that their organization was "very complex—many departments, policies, processes, and plans that require coordination."

We don't need to add more work activities to excel. There's a better way to work, one that prevents us from falling into the spread-too-thin and complexity traps. If we select just a few items and obsess to excel in those, we can perform at our best. What does obsession look like in the workplace?

MASSAGE THE OCTOPUS

For the past fifty years, ninety-one-year-old Jiro Ono has operated the sushi restaurant Sukiyabashi Jiro, tucked under the underpass of a subway station in Tokyo. The wooden doorway opens off to a corridor that resembles a B-class office space.[19] You might also be disappointed by the menu; there isn't one. Jiro serves twenty pieces of sushi to the ten guests seated at his minute counter. No predinner cocktail, no tempura, no side dishes. Oh, and the bathroom is out in the subway corridor. Sounds like a recipe for failure.

It would be, if the sushi weren't so darn exquisite. Ono is considered the best sushi chef in the world, with not one, not two, but the maximum of three Michelin stars. He has devoted his life to the preparation of twenty pieces of sushi. But *choosing* this tiny set is not what makes him different. It is *how* he focuses that sets him apart.

The marvelous 2011 documentary *Jiro Dreams of Sushi* follows Jiro as he prepares the day's offerings.[20] In the morning, his older son, who has trained with his father for thirty years, heads to the fish market to select a single, superior piece of tuna. Not one of the best pieces. No. The best in the entire market. If Jiro can't have the single best tuna piece, he won't buy any tuna that day. How can you serve superior sushi if you don't have the single best slice of fish?

Then it's time to prepare the octopus. Jiro massages the octopus by hand as part of its preparation to ensure its tenderness. But how long of a massage to give? Jiro used to give his octopus a 30-minute rub, but he discovered that octopus reaches peak tenderness when hand massaged for 40–50 minutes. This task falls to an apprentice.

Another apprentice, who has worked ten years in the restaurant—the first eight spent washing and preparing fish—graduated to the role of preparing the omelet sushi. But Jiro forced him to cook 200 omelet batches—200!—before he was allowed to prepare one that was served to customers. When you make only twenty pieces, you can afford to obsess over each one. Jiro didn't just say, "Let's serve twenty presentable pieces." No. He channeled his full energies into each one. And he spent a lifetime perfecting them.

The obsession to excel can take many forms, depending on your line of work. For the salesperson at Nordstrom, it's calling five other stores to find the exact size and color of the sweater a customer wants, having the sweater delivered to the customer's home, and then calling afterward to ask how it fit. For the real estate agent, it's spending an hour poring through 100 photos of a house she is listing for sale, looking for the single best image to feature on her company's website. For the elementary school teacher, it's preparing for the next day's class by rehearsing his lesson plan one more time, even though he has taught the class for twenty years.

These people strive to produce exceptional quality. Stellar quality—whether it takes the form of a smartphone's intuitive user interface, a retail store's exceptional customer service, or a restaurant's superbly tender piece of octopus—requires both prolonged effort and a fanatic attention to detail.[21] Attaining that quality demands obsession—and focus.

We often disparage obsessions in our daily lives, viewing them as dangerous or debilitating. But obsession can be a productive force.

Greatness in work, art, and science requires obsession over quality and an extraordinary attention to detail. "What many another writer would be content to leave in massive proportions," Ernest Hemingway reflected, "I polish into a tiny gem."[22] Alfred Hitchcock required more than seventy shots to perfect the shower scene in the movie *Psycho*.[23] To create his famous vacuum cleaner, James Dyson created 5,000 prototypes. It took him fifteen years. Now that's obsessing![24]

I wondered if we would find a quantitative link in our dataset between obsessionlike work habits and performance. We plotted the 5,000 people in our study and grouped them into four types, based on their degree of focus and obsession (by measuring their degree of effort). The performance of the four types varied dramatically.

The worst-performing group consisted of people who took on many priorities, but then didn't put in much effort. They were the "accept more, then coast" employees and ranked in the bottom 11th percentile. Ouch.

The second-lowest-performing group, at the 53rd percentile, scored very high on "extremely good at focusing on key priorities," but low on effort. We named this group "Do less, no stress." These were the people in our study who selected a few priorities, but then failed to obsess. Just *choosing* to focus, as work-productivity experts would have you do, does not lead to best performance.

The second best-performing group, at the 54th percentile, consisted of employees who accepted many responsibilities and then became overwhelmed as they worked hard to complete them. They scored low on focus, and high on effort. We called this the "do more, then stress" group. Susan Bishop, the executive recruiter, landed in this category: she took on too many responsibilities (receiving a poor 3 out of 7 "do less" score), yet put in a huge amount of effort (a top score of 7). Notice that this group performed at roughly the same level as the "do less, no stress" group. That is, if you violate either the "do less" or the "obsess" criterion, your performance will remain about average—slightly above the 50th percentile.

Finally, we have the Jiros and Amundsens of the world, those who excelled at choosing a few priorities *and* channeling their obsessionlike effort to excel in those areas. Their performance placed them in the 82nd

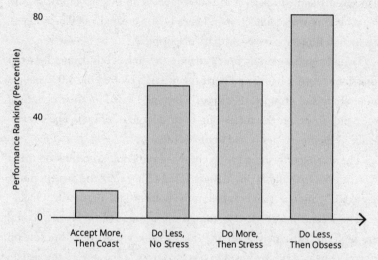

The Link between Focus, Effort, and Performance
The "Do Less, Then Obsess" Category Out-Performed All Others

Note:
These estimates were produced by running a modified regression analysis. We substituted the "do less, then obsess" scale with two variables; one measuring focus (using the item "extremely good at focusing on key priorities, no matter how much work and how many things I have to do") and one measuring effort ("puts a lot of effort into his/her job"). We then ran a regression analysis, converting the variables to percentiles and entering these two variables and their interaction term.

percentile, a whopping 28 percentage points higher than the next category. (And this effect is just for the "do less, then obsess" practice—the other six practices in this book are not taken into account yet.)

So which group do you fall into? Be honest! I confess that I often belong in the "do more, then stress" group. I take on too many tasks and struggle later with the follow-through. But the findings in this chapter have affected me, and I am working hard to move myself into the "do less, then obsess" group. That means saying "no" more often, and directing even more of my energies to the few, remaining priorities.

It also means paying attention to what weakens my focus. We asked people in our study what prevented them from doing less.[25] I assumed most people don't focus because they're distracted. Almost weekly, it seems, an article pops up in the media about how overwhelmed people are by incoming communications, how much time they waste on social media, and how much FOMO (fear of missing out) they feel, causing them to peek at every text, email, or ping. But when our data came back, I discovered that these distractions were only part of the problem. The people in our study cited three main reasons for failing to focus: broad scope of work activities (including having too many meetings and too many work items), temptations (including distractions imposed by others and temptations created by oneself), and pesky, "do-more" bosses (who lack direction and set too many priorities). These three main reasons correspond in turn to three tactics we can deploy to do less and obsess. Let's look at how to narrow your scope.

SLICING AND DICING WITH FRIAR WILLIAM

Today, if you have a heart attack and are rushed to the hospital, you might glance up at the skilled doctors hovering over you and think, "Thank God I made it here in time!" Back in 2005, if you were rushed to a hospital in the Midwest that I'll call Skyline Hospital, you might not have considered yourself so lucky. The hospital had a terrible track record treating heart attacks, especially the most serious form, STEMI attacks. That's when an artery leading to the heart is entirely blocked. The heart muscles will start dying during a STEMI attack, so each minute during and after the attack is critical. Interventional cardiologists must insert a tiny balloon into your artery and inflate it to clear the blockage. If they wait too long, you might not make it.

How long is too long? As John Toussaint and Roger Gerard relate in their insightful book *On the Mend*, the golden rule used to be ninety minutes from entering the hospital to clearing the clog in surgery. That sounds like plenty of time, but a lot needs to happen to diagnose and prepare a patient for surgery.

At Skyline Hospital, the staff only managed the ninety-minute "door-to-balloon" goal in a paltry 65 percent of the cases—much worse

Why People Can't Focus at Work

Main Reported Reasons for Lack of Focus
Among People in Our 5,000-Person Study

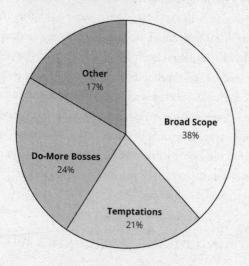

The three main reasons for participants' inability to focus, broken
down by the percentage of people citing each one.

than at the best hospitals. In other words, you had about a one-third chance of clearing your clog *after* ninety minutes had passed. Your risk of dying was much higher than at many other hospitals.[26] Anne (not her real name), a nurse manager in the emergency department whom we interviewed for our study, remarked that she was very frustrated by that number. She had worked in the emergency department for several years and had seen the consequences of the slow process. She felt certain that her department could improve its performance treating heart attack victims. But how?

Anne and a few others in the department, including the emergency room chief physician, began examining what happened when a patient entered the emergency room complaining of chest pain. First, a triage nurse examined the patient, diagnosed a probable heart attack, and rushed the person to a room to perform critical tests, including an EKG. Then the emergency room doctor arrived and proclaimed, "Looks like a STEMI."

They ran more tests. Afterward, a second doctor, a cardiologist, arrived and confirmed the STEMI diagnosis. That could take twenty minutes if the cardiologist was busy with other patients. Finally, the nurses and doctors prepared the patient for surgery.

"We talked about every single step," Anne recalled, "we asked, why do each step at all?" That led the group to suggest a crazy idea: get rid of the expert cardiologist.

The cardiologists could barely contain themselves. *Remove the expert from the process? Are you nuts?* "The cardiologists didn't think the emergency department physicians could be accurate in the diagnosis," Anne recalled. Shouldn't they instead *hire* another cardiologist so that they could speed up the process? But Anne and the team pushed back. If the emergency room doctors improved their knowledge to make the STEMI diagnosis when they first saw the patient, they wouldn't need the expert cardiologist to make a second diagnosis afterward. Why perform the task of diagnosing twice, they asked.

The cardiologists were unconvinced. A break came when they visited another hospital that had already cut out the cardiologist step. The trip itself helped to build trust among the team. "It's amazing how well you get to know each other when you sit in a car together for four hours," Anne reflected. Afterward, the cardiologists agreed to try it without their involvement, but on one condition: the emergency room physicians had to obsess to diagnose right the first time.

Working with the cardiologists, Anne and the team developed a plan that emergency room docs could use to diagnose a STEMI. The emergency room doctors underwent training. Once they tried the new setup, Anne and the team held several meetings in which physicians, nurses, and technicians reviewed the diagnoses on a rolling basis to improve accuracy. Within a year, the emergency department boosted its pitiful 65 percent hit rate to 100 percent. The doctors didn't fail to diagnose a patient who had a STEMI (an omission). And only a handful of patients who were diagnosed with a STEMI didn't have one (a normal occurrence at the best hospitals, too).

Think about this startling result. By doing *less* work—taking away a step in making the diagnosis—Anne and the rest of the team lifted their performance. They didn't add a doctor or expensive equipment to speed it up. They removed a step—freeing up the cardiologist to do other work—and got far better results.

Without realizing it, the team at Skyline Hospital applied a dictum invented 700 years ago by William of Ockham, a European friar, philosopher, and theologian. Ockham is known for a principle called Occam's razor,[27] which stipulates that people should pursue the simplest explanation possible in science and other areas. Applied to the workplace, we can express this idea as follows:

As few as you can, as many as you must.

Instead of asking how many tasks you can tackle given your working hours, ask how many you can ditch given what you *must* do to excel. The Skyline Hospital team changed its approach from "Diagnose then double-check" to "Diagnose once and obsess over doing it right."

Occam's razor at work doesn't say that you should simplify all the way to one. It says you should do everything possible to cull activities—the fewest metrics, the fewest goals, the fewest steps, the fewest pieces of sushi—while retaining everything necessary to do great work. As the French writer Antoine de Saint-Exupéry observed, "Perfection is finally attained not when there is no longer anything to add, but when there is no longer anything to take away."[28]

You can apply Occam's razor to simplify and narrow the scope of your work. When it comes to goals, customers, metrics, procedures, priorities, tasks, emails, words in an email, meetings, conference calls, the number of sign-offs required during decision making, and many other parts of work, go from many to few.

That's precisely how Susan Bishop, the executive search consultant who said yes to all kinds of client requests, turned around her business. Bishop wielded Occam's razor and crafted the following simple rules to shave away her client roster and concentrate on fewer but better clients:[29]

1. She would work only with clients in the media industry, where she had deep expertise. She would eliminate financial services, consumer goods, and retail.
2. She would only conduct senior-level searches that paid a minimum fee of $50,000.
3. She would refuse rush jobs and only take assignments where the positions paid market salaries.
4. She would refuse unreasonable and unpleasant clients.

The idea was to narrow the scope to one client segment—senior searches in media—and to do higher-quality work. *As few segments as she could, as many as she must.*

You can also apply Occam's razor to smaller work tasks. I used to stuff too many slides into my presentations. It gave me a sense of security. Then I met with the CEO of a large European company to discuss a leadership development program we were doing together. His chief of staff asked me to use only one slide in my meeting with the CEO. "One slide?" I asked in disbelief.

"Yes, one slide."

Holy cow! How could I distill fifteen slides into one? I tried shrinking four slides onto one. Then I thought, "What is the key issue?" I applied the razor and cut all my slides except for one: a graphic displaying the program's hourly calendar. Then I obsessed to get that graphic right. I had formerly spent three slides showcasing the program's three topics. Now I conveyed the same information by coloring the calendar segments using three different colors, one for each topic. The visual gave the CEO an immediate understanding of the program's flow.

What a difference Occam's razor made. Since I didn't have to labor through fifteen slides, the CEO and I could spend our forty-five minutes *discussing* the program in greater depth. When we finished, he remarked how productive the meeting had been.

If using Occam's razor is working smarter, you might wonder why most people don't do it. The problem is that we love to keep our options open. Dan Ariely, author of the book *Predictably Irrational*, and his collaborator Jiwoong Shin demonstrated through a series of psychological experiments that people cling to options, even when those options no longer provide any value whatsoever.[30] "We have an irrational compulsion to keep doors open,"[31] Ariely noted. To perform at your best, discipline yourself to shave away any options that you stick with for psychological comfort alone.

WHEN YOU SHOULD NOT FOCUS

There are two circumstances when you may want to "do more" and *not* focus, at least temporarily.

1. *When you need to generate many new ideas.* When we start a new task, we often don't know what the best option will be. In this phase, academic research suggests it's best to generate and consider many ideas. As Wharton professor Adam Grant reports in his book *Originals*, "Many people fail to develop originality because they generate few ideas."[32] At a certain point, you must cull your ideas and zoom in on the one that works best. In our book *Great by Choice*, Jim Collins and I found that the most innovative companies first generated lots of ideas and then killed off the bad ones and obsessed over only a few good ideas.[33] You can do the same in your work.

2. *When you know your options, but are uncertain which to choose.* A manager in one of my executive education programs at the University of California, Berkeley recalled an instance when she had pursued two technological solutions to a product because her team didn't know which one would win in the marketplace. Eventually, she and her colleagues grew confident that one solution would succeed. Only then did they select that solution and ditch the other. "It would have been disastrous for us to select a solution prematurely," she noted. "We might have chosen the wrong one."[34]

TIE YOURSELF TO THE MAST

Twenty-one percent of employees in our study regarded temptations and distractions as key impediments to focusing. The second tactic for focusing and obsessing, then, is to seal yourself off from those distractions. I did that while writing this book. Knowing how hard writing is for me, and how tempted I am to procrastinate, I bought a laptop and got rid of the Internet browser, email, and the instant messaging app—everything except for Microsoft Word. I carried this barren computer to Starbucks for two-hour intervals. Day after day, I sat there with my dark-roast tall coffee (black, no sugar). I felt a terrible urge to check my email—but I couldn't. So I kept writing. Before long, I had completed a manuscript.

What had happened? I had unwittingly adopted a strategy from Greek mythology. Odysseus was terrified of the beautiful island creatures called "sirens" that beckoned sailors on passing ships to their death with their irresistible songs. So he ordered his men to stuff their ears with wax and bind him to the ship's mast. He commanded his sailors not to untie him, no matter how much he begged. When the ship passed the sirens, Odysseus heard the gorgeous melody and implored the men to free him so that he could rush to the sirens' side. Instead, they tightened the knots some more, and Odysseus escaped temptation. By using a special computer that I'd disconnected from the Internet, I tied myself to the mast—twenty-first-century style.

The key is to devise these tactics *ahead of time* so that you're prepared to resist temptations when they arise. Because temptations will arise. Soon after Susan Bishop set forth clear rules for which clients she would *not* take, the siren song of lucrative client engagements beckoned. For two years, Coca-Cola had become a significant account, contributing 10 percent of Bishop's approximately $2 million in annual revenues. Now Coca-Cola wanted to offer her a new contract worth $250,000, her biggest single contract to date. Unfortunately, the searches weren't in media—and Bishop had just told all of her employees that they would only accept work in that segment. But could she really afford to turn down a contract this big?

For weeks Bishop anguished over the decision. But by proclaiming her rules to her employees, Bishop had tied herself to the mast. In the meeting with Coca-Cola, she clung to her rules, tying herself to the mast. "I said no, knees knocking and palms sweating," Bishop recalled. Unless they had media-related searches for her, she told the two stunned men in front of her, sorry, she couldn't help them. As she told us, there is no way she would have walked away like that had she not crafted the rules ahead of time. Bishop's "do less, then obsess" score climbed from the bottom 20 percent to the top 25 percent in our dataset. And her discipline paid off.

Bishop's business started to turn around, albeit slowly. When she landed a huge, high-level search contract for a media client in the United Kingdom, she could make the most of it, "because we weren't wasting our time working on low-paying searches out of our area of expertise." She could obsess to excel in a handful of key searches. After that, marquee media firms began to seek her out. The depth and accuracy of her executive searches improved. Her business began to thrive, with revenues and profits both rising.

We took the 20 percent of respondents in our study who most embraced the "do less" practice and asked them what key behaviors helped them focus and simplify. Many described making special arrangements that would let them work without interruption. Some went into the office an hour early or stayed late one evening. Others found a quiet conference room, put on headphones for a few hours, or left their smartphone behind.

Such methods are important in today's open office environments, where cubicles offer scant protection from interrupting office mates. They might even not go far enough. Employees at a beverage company who sought to concentrate on the tasks at hand installed fishing line across the openings to their cubicles. That way, they could deploy swimsuit cover-ups like curtains when they wanted time alone. Workers at a construction company developed a unique system to tell their peers to leave them alone: they wore orange armbands.[35]

There are many ways to tie yourself to the mast. Do it ahead of time, so that when you sit at your desk feeling the urge to distract yourself, you can't.

"It keeps me from looking at my phone every two seconds."

HOW TO SAY "NO" TO YOUR BOSS

A third tactic for doing less and obsessing is to manage your boss's expectations around your scope of work. A full 24 percent of people in our study blamed their inability to focus on their boss's lack of direction or a broader organizational complexity in their company. In general, it's far easier to embrace "do less, then obsess" if your boss is practicing it, too. Many top performers in our study reported having bosses who gave them clear direction, set specific goals, and had few priorities.

So what should you do if you work for a do-more boss? You aren't as powerless as you might think; it *is* possible to manage up and say "no."[36] James, a junior management consultant in our study, told me of one occasion when a partner asked him to help with a sales pitch.[37] "I was already working 100 percent on a really important merger project with an upcoming deadline," James said. He told this partner that he would be happy to help, but he couldn't cover both the sales pitch and the merger project. Which should he prioritize?

"Can't you do both?" the partner asked.

What Kind of Boss Do You Have?

Select the boxes that best describe your boss (or you). If you've checked all three to the right, you have a do-less boss (or you are one).

	Do-More Boss	Do-Less Boss
Goal and Strategy	Sets many goals, or goals are vague. *Example: "We accepted every client that called us and tried to make each one as happy as humanly possible." (Susan Bishop)*	Sets a clear goal and states what *not to* do. *Example: Only senior searches with minimum $50,000 fee; and with market rate salaries. (Susan Bishop)*
Priority List	Keeps a long list of priorities, and piles more on. *Example: "Her boss is making constant conflicting demands on her." (Study participant)*	Keeps a short priority list; doesn't add to it unless absolutely necessary. *Example: "My boss gives me clear expectations, deadlines and targets to allow for reasonable prioritization." (Study participant)*
Communication	Speaks and writes in long-winded, unclear, and muddled sentences. *Example: "We actually think that the industry is at a place where you can actually see line of sight to the subsidy equation just fundamentally changing in a very short period of time." (CEO, AT&T)* [1]	Speaks and writes in a simple, concrete, and clear way. *Example: "I made a mistake on Tesco. That was a huge mistake by me." (Warren Buffett)* [2]

Notes:
1. Lucy Kellaway, "And the Golden Flannel of the Year Award Goes to . . . ," *Financial Times*, January 4, 2015.
2. Warren Buffett, "Tesco Shares 'A Huge Mistake'," bbc.com, October 2, 2014, accessed June 6, 2017, http://www.bbc.com/news/business-29457053.

"Not if you want excellent work," James replied. "The merger project requires all my attention for the next three weeks, and there is no slack in the schedule. The key is to deliver the best quality, so we will need some more people on the merger project if you want me to help with the sales bid."

James expected a lashing from the partner, who was known for calling people "wimps." Instead the partner nodded. "I guess you're right." James suggested that the partner ask a colleague who was coming off another project.

Make clear to your boss that you're not trying to slack off. You're prioritizing because you want to dedicate all your effort to excelling in a few key areas. Ask if your boss would like you to reprioritize. Put the decision back on your boss's shoulders. You want to prevent your boss from forcing you into the "do more, then stress" category, since your performance will be much better in the "do less, then obsess" approach. Your boss will (or should) appreciate that.

It takes guts to do less, then obsess, when most of your colleagues are striving to work harder and undertake more activities. The good news is that you can start small. Apply Occam's razor to cut out a few needless, nonproductive parts of your work. Find a few techniques that enable you to "tie yourself to the mast," so that you aren't prevented from obsessing over key priorities. Ask your boss to prioritize some of your responsibilities so that you understand better where to focus.

The concept of "do less, then obsess" raises a critical question we haven't addressed yet: *What* should you concentrate on? Focusing and obsessing over the wrong tasks is a road to ruin. If Amundsen had gone all in on horses, he wouldn't have succeeded, no matter how much he obsessed, because horses were inferior out there on the polar ice. If Susan Bishop had focused on serving clients in the financial services industry, about which she knew little, instead of those in media, she would have continued to struggle. In the next chapter, we will explore the issue of *what* to focus on.

KEY INSIGHTS

DO LESS, THEN OBSESS

The "Work Harder" Convention

The conventional wisdom states that people who work harder and take on more responsibilities accomplish more and perform better. Countering this view, management experts recommend that people focus by *choosing* just a few areas of work.

The New "Work Smarter" Perspective

Doing more is usually a flawed strategy. The imperative to focus is also misunderstood. Focus isn't simply about *choosing* to concentrate on a few areas, as many people think. There is a second harsh requirement: You must also *obsess* in those areas to produce exceptional quality. The smart way to work is to first *do less, then obsess*.

Key Points

- People in our study who chose a few key priorities and then made huge efforts to do terrific work in those areas scored on average 25 percentage points higher in their performance than those who pursued many priorities. "Do less, then obsess" was the most powerful practice among the seven discussed in this book.
- "Doing more" creates two traps. In the *spread-too-thin trap*, people take on many tasks, but can't allocate enough attention to each. In the *complexity trap*, the energy required to manage the interrelationship between tasks leads people to waste time and execute poorly.
- This chapter highlights three ways you can implement the "do less, then obsess" principle:
  1. *Wield the razor:* Shave away unnecessary tasks, priorities, committees, steps, metrics, and procedures. Channel all your effort into excelling in the remaining activities. Ask: *How many tasks can I remove, given what I must do to excel?* Remember: *As few as you can, as many as you must.*
  2. *Tie yourself to the mast:* Set clear rules ahead of time to fend off temptation and distraction. Create a rule as trivial as not allowing yourself to check email for an hour.
  3. *Say "no" to your boss:* Explain to your boss that adding more to your to-do list will hurt your performance. The path to greatness isn't pleasing your boss all the time. It's saying "no" *so that you can apply intense effort to excel in a few chosen areas.*

THREE

REDESIGN YOUR WORK

Maybe if we reinvent whatever our lives give us we find poems.
—Naomi Shihab Nye[1]

It was a brisk spring day in 2010. As Greg Green steered his beat-up mini-van into the parking lot of Clintondale High School in suburban Detroit, he felt a sense of dread.[2] Green was Clintondale's principal, and in a few hours he would receive an email containing results from the school's most recent battery of student tests. If past performance were any indication, it wouldn't be pretty.

Student performance at Clintondale had been plummeting for several years, despite Green's best efforts, and because of some immense challenges. Although the state had raised graduation requirements, it had allowed the school's paltry budget to wither. Meanwhile, students' needs were far greater. Thanks to long-term demographic shifts and the 2008 collapse of the U.S. auto industry, about 80 percent of students were now poor enough to qualify for state-subsidized lunches. Local unemployment had surged to 14 percent and entire city blocks had been reduced to boarded-up ghost towns. With their families struggling, students weren't paying attention to homework, or passing exams. They had more pressing concerns, like taking care of their younger siblings while their parents scrounged for work.

Later that morning, the email came in. It was every bit as bad as Green feared. The school's dismal performance had dragged it into the bottom 5 percent of schools statewide. The federal government had passed an initiative, *Race to the Top*, awarding funding to states partly on the basis of their schools' performance on standardized tests. In an effort to improve performance, the state regulators in Michigan's capital, Lansing, had taken actions to replace administrators and had drawn up a list of schools to consider. So far Clintondale wasn't on it. With these new results, maybe it would be.

During the spring and summer, Green cast around for a solution that would reverse the school's fortunes. The district was running a $5 million deficit. It had no money to invest in new teachers or educational schemes. The teachers couldn't work much harder than they already were. They had tried all the traditional means to get the children engaged with their schoolwork: They had threatened to exclude students from sports if they didn't perform well in the classroom. They had held conferences with parents. They had sent home sternly worded letters. None of it had worked. Kids had only grown frustrated, and that in turn had fueled discipline problems. In one 20-week period, Clintondale suffered more than 700 disciplinary incidents. Teachers were burned out. "I felt like I didn't have control," Green told us in an interview during our visit to the school. "There were a lot of sleepless nights."

And then, on August 16, 2010, the situation got even worse. Green's boss, the district's superintendent, knocked on his door to tell him that Lansing had put Clintondale on the failure list. Drastic action was imminent. The state would close the school, transform it into a charter school, or—the likeliest scenario—fire the principal. *I'm a month away from losing my job*, Green thought.

But he didn't. Two years later, Green was still at the helm, and Clintondale High School was thriving. Students were graduating in record numbers. Green had become something of a national celebrity, interviewed on television and featured in the *New York Times*.

What had happened? Had a Washington bureaucrat descended from on high with aid? Had Harvard dispatched an emissary with the latest formula for educational success? No. In his despair, Greg Green had found inspiration in an unexpected place. Baseball.

A few years earlier, while coaching his son's Little League team, Green had discovered some instructional videos on YouTube that included annotated drawings illustrating the basics of the game. "You could actually see what each position did," he enthused in one of our interviews with him for our study. Green decided to show the YouTube video clips to his son's team and create some videos of his own. The boys studied the videos at home once a week and came to the baseball diamond prepared. "I realized that I didn't have to repeat myself over and over to each kid," Green recalled. "I also realized that the players could go back and review the videos periodically on their own."

Green, who had played baseball in college, ended up producing nearly 200 original titles, including *Defense: Fly Balls*, *Man on First and Third*; *Pitching: Throwing Arm Rotation*; and its sequel, *Pitching: Throwing Arm Rotation 2*. The boys loved them. Instead of standing around and listening to instructions from the coach during the few hours a week they had on the diamond, the players spent practice time *practicing*. The team went on a winning streak. Parents were ecstatic. Green wondered if he was on to something profound.

As soon as he learned that his school was on the list, Green gathered the teachers in a conference room. He jumped on the Internet and showed them his baseball videos. "Let's record our lectures and put the videos on the Internet to be accessed by students," he suggested. "How crazy would it be to try something like this at Clintondale?" Students would view the lessons at home and on the bus and then do "homework" in the classroom. The teacher would no longer be a lecturer, but rather a coach. They would *flip* the process: classroom at home, homework at school.

Staff members shook their heads. Had their principal lost his mind? To show that he hadn't, Green turned to data. Earlier that year, he had enlisted Andy Scheel, a tech-savvy former football coach who taught social studies, to experiment with a "flipped" curriculum. One of Scheel's classes was full of chronic failure. "Students really had one last chance for graduation," Green told us. Scheel's other social studies class, though, was performing well. "We weren't going to change the class that was doing well, but we could innovate with the class that was failing." The two classes were given identical material and assignments, but the struggling class used the flipped classroom model, watching videos at home and doing homework at school, with the aid of the teacher. As Green explained, "We had nothing to lose, so why not?"

A few months into Scheel's experiment, when Green sat down at his desk to check the students' first set of exam scores, he thought something had corrupted the data. Students in the flipped classroom were *outperforming* the traditional class. The lowest grade was now a C. Students who had been forced to repeat a grade were now thriving. Best of all, the failure rate had plummeted. To zero.

How was this result possible? Green suspected that Scheel's students had succeeded in the flipped model because they could receive help with their homework in the classroom. Once these students left school, it was hard for them to focus—their homes were too chaotic, their neighborhoods too dangerous, the demands of their after-school jobs and other obligations too heavy. These students usually had nowhere to turn for assistance if they had trouble with their homework, since the subject matter exceeded their parents' comprehension. Under the flipped model, students watched the lessons wherever they happened to be—on the bus, in their bedrooms, in the break room at the grocery store. During class time, when they dug into the work itself, a teacher or fellow student had helped them clear each academic hurdle.

Green's initial experiment had been encouraging, but it had only involved one class. Maybe the results had been a fluke. It would be risky to apply it to the entire school, as Green now proposed. Many teachers opposed the idea on principle. Not only did it contravene everything they had learned during their training—it overturned a 300-year-old model of education. As one administrator told us during our visit to Clintondale, many teachers also harbored doubts about Green's motives. They perceived "flipping" as a cash-strapped district's first step toward replacing teachers with technology.

Green told his teachers that it was time to try something radical. They had to rethink the work itself, *redesigning and transforming the way teaching was done.* "Why do we keep sending homework home when students aren't doing it?" Green asked the teachers. The old model wasn't working.

Despite Green's arguments, only a few teachers welcomed the shift at first. One administrator in the district was so skeptical of Green's overall approach that she told Green, "You'll never get off the list."

That did it. For a competitive former athlete like Green, it was game on. He would prove the doubters wrong—or go down trying. They would flip the school.

Green met with state regulators to explain his plan, and he received a two-year reprieve to implement the new model. He went to work. In the fall of 2010, as another experiment, they flipped four classes for ninth grade—math, reading, science, and social studies. Failure rates plummeted. "That's when the *aha* moment really came for me," Green said. "This could work."

As Green realized, the flipped model worked because it afforded much more teacher-to-student and student-to-student interactions, and because students could now progress at their own pace. Whereas before 80 percent of class time was devoted to lecturing and 20 percent to solving problems individually or in small groups, that ratio was now inverted to 20/80. Teachers regained evenings with their families because they no longer lugged home stacks of homework to grade. With more time available for students, they could spot and aid those who were struggling.

Other schools had experimented with flipping individual classes, but none had done what Green did next. In January 2011, Greg Green became the first principal in America to flip an entire school. Every grade. All 700 students. The following school year, he flipped the entire school for the entire year—fall and spring.

The results soared. Before the flip, 35 percent of the students failed one or more classes. After the flip, fewer than 10 percent did. After the flip, graduation rates climbed from a meager 80 percent to 94 percent in 2016 (see the chart). College attendance climbed from 63 percent for the class of 2011 to 81 percent for the class of 2014.

Results Soared Immediately After Greg Green's Flip

Student failure rates plummeted...

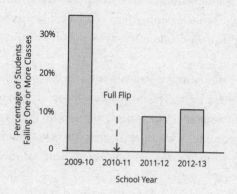

...and graduation rates improved.

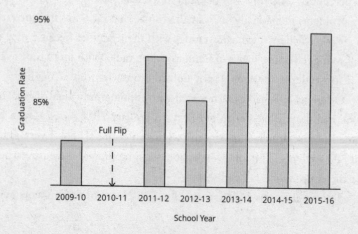

TO PERFORM BETTER,
REDESIGN WHAT YOU DO

Greg Green could have tried to turn the school around by compelling the teachers to put in longer hours. He could have disciplined students who shirked their homework. He could have introduced more testing of students and linked teacher pay to test scores, turning the school environment into a pressure cooker. With these options, Green would have pushed people to work harder within the existing model—to do more of the same. That's the traditional "work harder" paradigm. *Instead Green redesigned the work itself, changing the way teaching was done.* He found a way to achieve greater impact with the same effort—in other words, to work smarter.

As the Clintondale story illustrates, a smarter way to work often exists, provided we can craft clever redesigns of key tasks. Our study of 5,000 managers and employees demonstrates the benefits of that approach. We created a "redesign" scorecard comprising five statements, including, "Reinvented their job to add more value," "Created new opportunities in their work—new activities, new projects, new ways of doing things," and "Carved out an area of work where they are doing something really big and impactful." We found that people who placed highly on our redesign scorecard achieved much better results, on average, than those who didn't. If you want to perform at your best, you need to do what Greg Green and many others in our study did: break with convention and try new ways of working.

SQUEEZING THE ORANGE

Before we explore how you can work in new and different ways, let's first consider the alternative. How can you boost your performance if you don't redesign? The obvious alternative is to put in longer hours, working harder in the same way. Chances are you're already doing that. In a 2009 survey by Harvard Business School professor Leslie Perlow and research associate Jessica Porter, 94 percent of the 1,000 professionals surveyed reported working 50 hours or more a week, and a staggering 50 percent of them said they worked more than 65 hours a week.[3] The latter figure translates into 13 hours per day, five days a week. Ouch! In a study of high earners, management writers Sylvia Ann Hewlett and Carolyn Buck Luce found that a full 35 percent worked more than 60 hours a week, and 10 percent worked more than 80 hours a week.[4] A job with the traditional 40-hour workweek seems like a part-time gig.

Does working long hours increase performance? The prevailing "work harder" mindset presumes that it does, but the truth is more complicated. We analyzed the relationship between weekly hours worked and performance among the 5,000 managers and employees in our study.[5] As the "Squeezing the Orange" chart reveals, working longer hours enhances performance, but only to a point. If you work between 30 and 50 hours per week, adding more hours on the job lifts your performance. But once you're working between 50 and 65 hours per week, the benefit of adding additional hours drops off. And if you're working 65 hours or more, overall performance declines as you pile on the hours.[6]

Other research has documented the same inverted U. Studying factory workers at a weaponry plant in Britain in 1914, Stanford economist John Pencavel found that performance topped out at 64 to 67 hours per week, beyond which it began to fall.[7] Where the curve starts to flatten and where it plateaus may vary from job to job and industry to industry.

It's like squeezing juice from an orange. At first, you get a lot of liquid. But as you continue to squeeze and your knuckles turn white, you extract a drop or two. Eventually, you reach the point where you're squeezing as hard as you can, but producing no juice. You would have done better just to leave the well-squeezed orange alone. It's the same with hours worked. If you're already working 50 hours per week, resist the temptation to invest more hours at work. Instead, ask yourself: "Can I work *smarter*, rather than *more*?"

Squeezing the Orange
Less Performance Juice Per Hour Worked

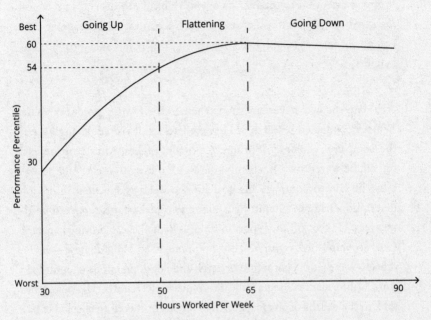

Note:
Based on regression analysis of 4,964 people. See Research Appendix for details.

REDESIGN FOR VALUE

Redesign isn't about working longer hours. It's about changing *how* you work. Yet, not all redesigns generate better results. One manager in our study reshuffled the organizational chart every twelve months, and *diminished* his organization's performance. A pharmaceutical saleswoman kept redesigning her sales pitch, and her revenues remained flat. So what distinguishes a great redesign from a not-so-great one?

Delving back into our data, we found that fruitful redesigns all shared one thing in common: *value*. A good redesign delivers more value for the same amount of work done. That begs the question: what is value, exactly?

As our study suggested, we should evaluate the value of our work by measuring how much *others* benefit from it. That's an *outside-in view*, because it directs attention to the *benefits* our work brings to others. The typical *inside-out view*, by contrast, measures work according to whether we have completed our tasks and goals, regardless of whether they produce any benefits.

Many people never question whether their work produces value. When I conducted research at Hewlett-Packard, I visited an engineer at the company's Colorado Springs, Colorado, offices. After I introduced myself, he waved me off, claiming he was too busy to meet. And he was busy: he had to complete his goal for the week as specified in his job description, namely, submitting a quarterly project status report to headquarters. He sent off the report in time, as he had every previous quarter. Goal accomplished, right? Yes, except for one issue. What I knew—and he didn't—was that the corporate research and development division in Palo Alto, California, no longer used those quarterly reports. His dispatches sank to the depths of an email box that no one bothered to check. He had met his goal according to his job description, but he had contributed zero value.

The advice "start with goals" when planning an effort, is wrong. We need to start with value, *then* proceed to goals. Ask yourself: what *benefits* do your various work activities produce, really?

You might wonder why so many people like our HP engineer focus on activities that yield marginal or no value. One answer: poor metrics. A customer order-handler in our study reported that his shipments reached corporate customers 99 percent of the time. That's pretty impressive—except for one thing. When his boss surveyed the customers, a full 35 percent complained that their shipments were arriving later than required. And why was that? The order handler was measuring whether the shipments left his warehouse according to his schedule (an inside-out view) rather than when the customer needed the equipment (an outside-in view).

Another problem is our perverse tendency to equate *volumes of activity* with accomplishments. Doctors have traditionally measured their performance according to the number of patient visits they handled rather than how often they arrived at the correct diagnosis. Lawyers bill clients based on how many hours they work, regardless of whether they're dispensing good counsel. Salespeople fixate on revenues, regardless of whether their products end up benefiting customers. Then we have people who rack up volumes of activities and run around bragging about how busy they are, as if busyness equals value. People mistake the number of meetings, task forces, committees, customer calls, customer visits, business trips, and miles flown for accomplishments, even if in reality all these activities may not add value. Being busy is not an accomplishment.

As our study revealed, a number of people *do* add value by taking an outside-in view and focusing on how they can benefit others (see the chart for how to pursue value, not goals). Terry, a production technician working at a New Orleans food packing plant, oversaw a machine that stuck labels on cans and packed cans in boxes.[8] His boss measured him on "throughput"—the number of boxes processed. But Terry didn't just concern himself with that narrow measure. When boxes streamed out of his machine, they headed to the warehouse, where workers stacked them onto pallets for shipment. "The other day," Terry told us, "I went over to the warehouse and asked, 'Is there something we can do better?' They said that the boxes weren't square coming out of my machine—they were closed, they were proper, but they weren't perfectly squared." As a result, it took extra time to assemble the pallets, and trucks filled with them were leaving the warehouse late.

DON'T PURSUE GOALS, BUT VALUE[9]

EXAMPLES OF HOW VALUE CREATION
DIFFERS FROM GOALS

Job	Goal-focused (internal metric)	Value-focused (benefits to others)
Human resources professional	Complete annual performance reviews for 70 percent of managers	Ensure 70 percent of managers receive helpful feedback for how to improve
Business logistics operator	85 percent of shipments must leave our warehouse according to our schedule	Deliver 85 percent of shipments to customers when they need them
Salesperson (retail clothing store)	"Up-sell" one additional garment to each buyer visiting the store	Only "up-sell" to buyers wanting an additional garment
Elementary school teacher	Complete three years of teaching math and obtain tenure at school	Help 90 percent of students become proficient in math
Medical doctor	See 160 patients in the office during January	Diagnose patients accurately 80 percent of the time and give proper treatment
Lawyer	Achieve 80 percent billable hours in first quarter of year	Help clients solve legal problem in 80 percent of cases in first quarter
College professor	Get twelve academic papers accepted for publication in prestige journals in five years	Publish three academic papers that advance the field substantially (and are much cited)
Social services consultant (government)	Administer 200 case files (clients) during 2017	Ensure 70 percent of clients get positive outcome (job, housing, etc.)
Call center service representative	Process ten customer calls every hour	Fix customer's problem in the first call 90 percent of time

Terry redesigned his packaging process so that the boxes emerged perfectly square. This change allowed the warehouse department to improve its throughput and the trucks to depart on time. Terry didn't have to take that initiative. He could have confined himself to an inside-out view, paying attention only to the number of boxes he processed.

Because he focused on adding value and not simply fulfilling his job specification, he scored as one of the best performers in our study (top 15 percent).

To gain a more precise understanding of value, it helps to contrast it with how people have traditionally thought about productivity. Here's a traditional productivity equation:[10]

$$\text{A person's work productivity} = \text{output of work} / \text{hours of input}$$

Charles can transcribe 60 words per minute from an audio file, while Beatrice can manage 120 words per minute. She's twice as productive. Now consider an equation that emphasizes value:

$$\text{The value of a person's work} = \text{Benefits to others} \times \text{quality} \times \text{efficiency}$$

The value equation hinges on three components. The first of these, as we've seen, has to do with how much your work benefits other people or your organization. It's no longer an issue of how many words of text you can transcribe, but rather how beneficial that transcription is to others. Maybe the transcript isn't necessary in the first place. If the benefit is zero, the value is zero (that's why there is a multiplication sign in the equation, because total value goes to zero if the benefit equals zero). It doesn't matter how fast you type out a document if nobody reads it.

The phrase "benefits to others" can mean contributing to your department, your office, a colleague, your company, your customers, your clients, or your suppliers (or even to the community or environment). The benefits themselves can take various forms, including enabling others to do their jobs better, helping create new products, or devising better methods for getting work done. Terry helped his colleagues in the warehouse stack and ship the boxes more expediently.

The second component of value is the quality of your work—the degree of accuracy, insight, novelty, and reliability of your work output. We want an error-free transcription, for instance. Greg Green wanted to create a higher-quality education.

The final component of value is how efficiently you work. In the transcription example, productivity was measured through speed—the number of words per minute. Speed matters in the value equation, too. After all, you're not adding much value if you're delivering an error-free transcript at ten words per minute.

Putting it all together, we get a more precise view of value: to produce great *value* at work is to create output that benefits others tremendously and that is done efficiently and with high quality.

With our value equation in place, we're now better equipped to address the question we raised at the end of the last chapter. If you want to perform at your best, you need to home in on a few key tasks and channel your efforts to perfect them—the "do less, then obsess" principle. But *which activities* warrant such focus? If you're going to focus on a tiny set of activities, they'd better be the right ones. The answer is to *redesign work so as to focus on activities that maximize value*, as defined in the above value equation. But how exactly do you do that?

HUNTING FOR VALUE

If you live in Europe, there's a decent chance that the Chinese-made smartphone or television you purchased passed through the Straits of Gibraltar, a narrow channel of water separating Spain from Morocco. The Straits are one of the world's busiest sea-lanes, and a hub for global trade. The shipping vessels that arrive there from faraway ports need terminals where they can dock and unload the millions of containers they carry. These containers are then placed onto other ships or trucks for transportation elsewhere. One such terminal, one of the more than fifty owned by a division of the Danish shipping giant Maersk, sits at the northern tip of Morocco in Tangier.[11]

For several years, a German national named Hartmut Goeritz managed the terminal. When he first arrived, the facility performed reasonably

APM Terminal, Tangier, Morocco[12]

well in financial terms. But having worked for three decades in other terminals in Angola, Portugal, France, and the Ivory Coast, Goeritz wasn't particularly impressed. The whole facility lacked, as Goeritz told me in an interview for our study, "the basic skeleton of operational processes that you would expect of a key terminal."[13]

To help the facility improve, Goeritz settled first on a "do less" approach, cutting activities that didn't generate much revenue. The Tangier terminal handled around 900,000 containers annually, loading and unloading containers from ships and trucks going in and out of the terminal.[14] To lift revenues, the previous team had sold additional "stripping" services, industry-speak for opening the arriving containers and offloading the content (say, spare car parts) onto trucks. They also weighed the trucks. Although the facility had hoped to augment the terminal's profits by providing these services for a fee, the impact proved small. Goeritz wielded Occam's razor and eliminated the stripping and weighing of trucks, deeming them a distraction. That change freed up the staff's time and energy to improve on the one activity that created the most value: moving containers on and off ships faster and more cheaply.

With this "do less" approach in place, Goeritz and his team now began "obsessing," scrutinizing how they worked. One day, as Goeritz strolled around the container yard, he noticed something odd: some of the terminal's trucks were driving around empty. "They picked up the container at the side of a ship," he recounted, "then drove to the back of the giant yard to set it down, then drove back to the ship empty-handed to pick up the next one." That's how it had been done for years. Goeritz thought it was a waste of capacity. What would happen, he wondered, if trucks heading out of the yard picked up and carried containers destined for nearby ships? They wouldn't drive back empty. The facility would run more efficiently, without added cost.

Goeritz asked the terminal's employees to try out the idea, with truckers heading back to the ships asking their colleagues if they could pick up any waiting containers. Soon team members began using walkie-talkies, radioing one another so that they could find more containers ready to ship out. They then modified their information technology system to identify containers waiting for pickup, much like taxi companies match taxi drivers and passengers. The motto became, *Never drive empty*. This simple redesign—called dual cycling—nearly doubled the truck drivers' efficiency.

Goeritz and his team proceeded to implement several other redesigns, changing the yard's layout as well as its use of giant cranes. But they still weren't finished. At terminals around the world, issues such as traffic, labor strikes, and stormy weather slowed down service. What if Goeritz's team could take these factors into account and route ships accordingly? He and his colleagues developed a process for planning ahead and sending container ships to harbors in the company's system best equipped to handle the cargo. If circumstances in Tangier threatened to slow a shipper's ability to unload some cargo, Goeritz could send ships steaming on to Algeciras's terminal instead. This networking saved customers an estimated $73 million in 2015. Did Maersk charge extra for this service? You bet they did. Meanwhile, the advance planning allowed Maersk to save money by storing containers in its yards more effectively, reducing the number of times it had to move containers so as to get to others stacked below them.

These redesigns paid off. From a merely decent facility, Tangier became a great one. Over a four-year period, the annual processing of containers in Tangier increased by 33 percent to 1.2 million containers, with the same resources and yard capacity. In 2014, the team received the coveted "container terminal of the year" award from top management. Goeritz himself was promoted to run the company's entire hub portfolio, which comprised container terminals in Malaysia, Oman, Egypt, the Netherlands, and Morocco.

Many people helped implement these redesigns, but Hartmut Goeritz launched the initiative to create value. As he explained, "I question how things are done, and I look for new ways to do things. I look for quantum change." Goeritz first focused on the one activity that he thought could create the greatest benefit as stated in the value equation: Moving the containers in and out of the Tangier yard. *That's choosing the right thing.* Then he determined how he and his team could redesign that one activity and do it better, faster, and cheaper. *That's doing the thing right* (see the chart "Five Ways to Create Value").[15]

Five Ways to Create Value

Main Question	Way to Improve Value	Example
Are You Working on the Right Things?	**1. Less Fluff:** Eliminate or reduce existing activities of little value.	HP Manager's report that no one read; APM Terminals' "stripping" and weighing trucks.
	2. More Right Stuff: Spend more time on existing activities of high value.	Hartmut Goeritz focusing on container throughput.
	3. More "Gee, Whiz": Create *new* activities of high value.	Goeritz's "routing service" for shipping companies and freight operators.
Are You Doing the Things Right?	**4. Five Star Rating:** Find new ways to improve the *quality* of your chosen activities.	Greg Green changing the quality of teaching and learning by flipping the classroom; Goeritz's routing service.
	5. Faster, Cheaper: Find new ways to do your chosen activities more efficiently.	Goeritz's "Never drive empty" solution.

THE ARCHIMEDES LEVER OF REDESIGN

Goeritz's improvements to the Tangier terminal represented major operational change. Yet effective redesigns don't have to be so far-reaching. For years, staff at Yale–New Haven Hospital administered patient blood tests in the middle of the night. They barged into patients' rooms, woke them up, and stuck needles into their arms. That way, doctors would have the results handy when they made their morning rounds.

Did patients like being woken up? Heck no. But few members of the hospital staff questioned how they operated. When Dr. Michael Bennick, the hospital's medical director for patient experience, reviewed results from a Medicare survey asking patients whether their rooms were quiet at night, the level of dissatisfaction surprised him. Aiming to remedy the situation, he told the resident doctors: "If you are waking patients at four in the morning for a blood test, there obviously is a clinical need. So I want to be woken, too, so I can find out what it is."[16] No one ever woke him. Instead, the staff moved the blood tests to times when patients were already awake. The hospital's score on that survey question jumped from the 16th to the 47th percentile nationally, without any hit to the quality of care. By taking the patient's perspective (outside-in), and not a "what's-convenient-for-the-doctor" view (inside-out), Dr. Bennick created more value for patients, who now got a good night's sleep. In this case, a tiny change produced a sizable jump in the "quiet in the room" score.

Dr. Bennick's intervention holds a profound insight: When people redesign, the key is not the *degree* of change they're undertaking. Instead, it's the *magnitude of the value* they can create.[17]

Throughout the workplace, small redesigns can have a big impact. Want shorter and more effective meetings? You could create better agendas or discipline people so that they don't ramble on. Or here's another idea: try removing all the chairs in the room, compelling people to stand up. Research has discovered that stand-up meetings are 34 percent shorter than sit-down meetings, and the decisions they produce are equally effective.[18]

Want to increase performance in a call center? You could invest in more training and schedule an additional battery of team-building off-sites. Or instead, simply have employees take their coffee breaks together (with another group covering for them), rather than one person at a time. The Massachusetts Institute of Technology's Sandy Pentland conceived of this small intervention, and a bank supervisor piloted it. By having employees at a call center take coffee breaks together, individual team members began to develop and nurture more productive relationships.[19] Employee engagement rose, and average call handling time fell by 8 percent overall and 20 percent in low-performing teams.

These examples of small but powerful redesigns recall a famous teaching from the Greek mathematician Archimedes. "Give me a place to stand," he said, "and a lever long enough, and I can move the earth." How do you move a huge rock in your backyard? Sure, you can ask five muscular neighbors to help and have them huff and puff trying to lift it together. Or you can get the same result for less effort by employing a lever and fulcrum. Clever redesign is about finding that proverbial lever and using it in a clever way. It's working smarter, not harder.

IS REDESIGN FOR EVERYONE?

Sure, you say, redesigning work sounds great. For bosses, maybe—those fortunate few who get to make their own rules. But what about the rest of us? I wondered if only senior people occupying a few types of positions could attempt redesigns, so I scoured our database for answers. To my surprise, we found widespread use of the practice. Our data showed that senior and junior people excelled at it in equal measure (see the chart below).

Likewise, I thought that people who had only been in their company a short period of time wouldn't have earned the autonomy to carry out redesign, but our data showed that people with a tenure of fewer than three years excelled at redesign as much as people with a tenure of ten years or more. I also believed that it would be harder to carry out redesign in larger companies, because those organizations tend to be more

Redesign Is Widespread

Percentage of People Who Excelled at Redesign, by Category

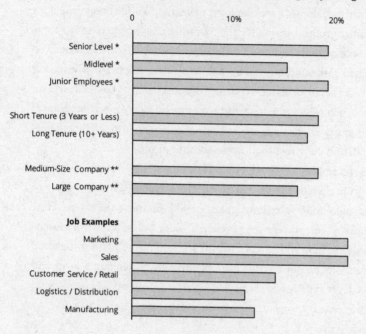

Notes:

These percentages capture the proportion of people who excelled by scoring a 7 (completely agree) on the survey statement, "he/she created new opportunities in work—new activities, new projects, new ways of doing things." Note that this is just one of five items to assess mastery of redesign in our measurement scale.

* Senior Level = CEO, president, SVP, VP, general manager, division manager. Midlevel = supervisor, office manager, administrator. Junior Employee = non-managerial jobs including tradesmen, technical specialists, customer support, factory workers, etc.

** Medium-size = 2,000-5,000 employees; Large = 10,000 or more employees.

bureaucratic and to have more job rules that impede redesign. But no: roughly the same proportions of people in medium-size and large companies excelled at redesign.

Finally, I considered that certain "creative" roles like marketing would see more people doing terrific redesigns. And yes, the proportion of people doing so is higher in marketing and sales jobs. But we also saw a reasonable proportion of people redesigning well in presumably less creative roles, like customer service, logistics, and manufacturing.

Overall, many people in lots of different work situations redesign. Of course, junior staff might attempt redesigns that are smaller in scope than those of their bosses. Janet was a twenty-nine-year-old corporate trainer in the hospitality industry. On her own initiative, she had launched the "flipped model" in three workshops she conducted to teach customer service to receptionists and restaurant hosts. Workshop attendees watched videotaped lectures before attending group discussions, while they worked on problem examples during the session. She attempted in her own, small way what Greg Green did for a whole school. She didn't need her boss's approval to modify how she delivered her content. She just did it. Janet scored a perfect 7 on redesign and placed as a top 20 percent performer.

Not all of us have the kind of autonomy that Janet had on her job, and not all job activities lend themselves to redesign. Most jobs have tasks you can't just eliminate (a math teacher has to cover a set curriculum, for instance). Still, most jobs and roles afford you some latitude to change parts of how you work and what you work on. Let's examine two practical tips for how to get started with a redesign where you work.

HUNT FOR PAIN POINTS

To identify opportunities for redesign, chase "pain points," thorny problems plaguing a set of people. Carmen, a forty-five-year-old business analyst, worked for a New Jersey–based life insurance company.[20] She processed payroll for the company's insurance agents scattered across the country. For years, she helped the agents handle so-called third-party sick pay (don't ask) as they stumbled through the bewildering throng of steps and tax filing implications. Carmen estimated that she received, on average, a phone call each day from an agent irate over the labyrinth of steps required to get through the paperwork. That's a pain point.

One day, Carmen decided she'd had enough. She reached out to the company's software coders and got them to help her streamline the enrollment procedure. "We took a very confusing industry complexity and turned it into a single-user interface screen . . . it's basically just a few clicks . . . everything is sorted out for them." Now, agents log on and within minutes, boom, they're done. As for Carmen, she scored a perfect

seven on the redesign scorecard and ranked in the top 15 percent of performers among the 5,000 people we studied.

As Carmen's story confirms, pain points are just that, painful. They
differ from "pleasure points" in the way "this sucks" differs from "I want."

In Silicon Valley, venture capitalists hunt for start-ups that aim to
cure pain points for the simple reason that customers crave those services.
Google's founders Sergey Brin and Larry Page sought to address consumers' deep frustration with inaccurate searches on the Internet. PayPal's
founders remedied the agonizing process of wiring money to a stranger
online. As the Silicon Valley saying goes, "It's easier to sell aspirin than
vitamins."[21]

What pain points can you spot in your workplace? What do people
complain about again and again and again? What gets people confused
and frustrated and saying "this sucks"? Where does work tend to get
bogged down?

Hunting for pain points is counterintuitive. When we hear people complain, we tend to dismiss them as whiners. Carmen might have grown to
resent all those angry insurance agents. Instead, she went beyond her job
specification and worked with software coders to create a better setup. As
annoying as complainers might sometimes seem, they do us all a service:
they identify the pain, for free!

You can create tremendous value in your job if you spot and help
colleagues, customers, and suppliers alleviate their most significant griev-
ances. The more acute the discomfort and the more people suffering from
it, the louder they yell—and the greater the prospect for a powerful remedy to create value.

ASK STUPID QUESTIONS

Sometimes we fail to imagine great new redesigns because we're trapped
inside webs of convention. We only see the current use of a practice,

process, or method, for instance. A hammer is used to punch a nail in the wall, and that's what a hammer is for. A classroom in a school is used for teaching, and a teacher in that classroom is used for lecturing in front of the room—and not as a coach helping individual students, as in the case of the flipped classroom. As Dan Pink has argued in his book *Drive*, we're entrapped by what academics call "functional fixedness"—our inability to solve problems due to our fixation on how work has always been done.[22]

Effective redesign requires that we loosen the shackles of the familiar and ask why things are the way they are, and whether there's a better way. To make these discoveries, I recommend that you start asking some "stupid" *why* questions:

> Why do hotels have a reception desk for check-in?
> Why do we make presentations filled with slides?
> Why do we call Monday morning staff meetings?
> Why do kids have two months of summer vacation from school?
> Why do we have to submit expense reports?
> Why do patients have to spend two days in a hospital bed after
>   surgery?
> Why do we conduct annual performance reviews?

Once you've gotten into the habit of asking such questions, ask some "what if" questions. What if kids only had one month of summer vacation, and another month of community service? What if instead of spending two days in a hospital bed after surgery you could go home and have health-care workers monitor you remotely? What if slide presentations were banned in meetings and replaced by questions to be discussed? The combination of asking a "stupid" question and crafting some "what-ifs" can help you discover a nifty redesign and lift your performance.

So much of how people work today is old, born at the dawn of the industrial revolution. The dreaded performance review dates from at least the 1940s and draws intellectually from Frederick Taylor's work on scientific management during the early twentieth century.[23] Ethical codes and other rules of professional conduct originated in the nineteenth century, when modern professions were first taking shape.[24]

Technology is now upending many of these conventions, and people are pushing beyond "business as usual" and questioning how work gets done. The way companies get ahead in such a volatile time is by innovating products and services. The way individuals get ahead is by innovating work.

Don't just see yourself as an employee—see yourself as an innovator of work. Hunt and cure pain points, ask stupid questions, and zoom in on how you can redesign and create value for others.

People who redesign their work strive to work on the right things and to do them right. Yet the best performers in our research also understood a fundamental insight about change: You can't just jump from one big redesign to another. Once you've made a major change, you have to stick with it and refine it little by little over time. Principal Greg Green understood that switching to the flipped model was just the beginning. Afterward, he and his team had to learn how to operate better within the flipped method, day in and day out. But how can you continuously learn and improve while also concentrating on performing your job? That's the topic to which we now turn.

KEY INSIGHTS

REDESIGN YOUR WORK

The "Work Harder" Convention

The more hours people work, the better they perform. Great performance is about delivering on existing goals, tasks, and metrics as defined in one's job description.

The New "Work Smarter" Perspective

If you already work at least fifty hours a week, piling on still more hours won't improve your performance much. It can even make it worse. To achieve great results, redesign work. Upend the status quo and craft new tasks, goals, and metrics that maximize the value of your work.

Key Points

- Our statistical analysis of 5,000 managers and employees demonstrates that those who redesigned their work performed significantly better than those who didn't.
- According to our statistical analysis, if you work up to 50 hours, performance improves as you add more hours. Beyond 50 hours, the benefit of adding more hours starts to wane. Beyond 65 hours, adding more hours causes performance to decline. Outworking others is not a clever strategy.
- Good redesigns create more *value*—the benefits work activities bring to others. That outside-in view is very different from traditional, inside-out ways of setting goals, tasks, and metrics. People can achieve their goals and be very productive, yet produce zero value.
- The value equation emphasizes three distinct components. To produce great value at work is to create output that *benefits others* tremendously and that is done *efficiently* and with *high quality*.
- Explore five ways to redesign work to create value:
  - *Less fluff*: eliminate existing activities of little value
  - *More right stuff*: increase existing activities of high value
  - *More "Gee, whiz"*: Create new activities of high value
  - *Five star rating*: improve quality of existing stuff
  - *Faster, cheaper*: do existing activities more efficiently.

- Where to start redesigning your work? You can hunt for and cure pain points, and you can dare to ask stupid questions.

FOUR

DON'T JUST LEARN, LOOP

The arrogance of success is to think that what you did yesterday will be sufficient for tomorrow.

—William Pollard[1]

On April 5, 2010, thirty-year old Dan McLaughlin of Portland, Oregon, quit his well-paying job as a commercial photographer to devote himself to becoming a professional golfer. He planned to practice the game full-time, and to subsist on funds he had saved over the past five years. There was just one problem. Dan had never played a full round of the sport, and had only been to the driving range a few times. He had never partici-pated in competitive sports, beyond a year of high school cross-country. Although "not exactly a couch potato," he was, in his estimation, "much closer to that than to [Olympic sprinter] Usain Bolt." Was Dan crazy?

Dan described his quest as an experiment, an attempt "to prove to himself and others that it's never too late to start a new pursuit in life." [2] Having read Malcolm Gladwell's bestseller *Outliers*, he had learned that people can master a field with 10,000 hours of practice. And so he crafted "the Dan Plan": To practice golf for about 30 hours per week for seven years to rack up the required hours.

Four years and 5,200 hours later, Dan was on track. He had achieved a handicap of 2.6, which, as any golfer will tell you, is superb (the smaller the number, the better).[3] By comparison, the average male golfer has a handicap of 14.3.[4] Dan's handicap put him in the top 5 percent of the nearly 24 million golf players in the United States.[5] Dan may never turn pro, but that doesn't matter one bit. He had already accomplished the extraordinary in four years.

How did he pull it off? Well, he assembled a team of people to support him, including a pro golf instructor, a strength trainer, a personal coach, and a chiropractor. And as you might expect, he also put in a *ton* of practice. He was out there day after day, month after month, in sweltering heat, pouring rain, and freezing cold, whacking at the ball again and again and again. As our parents and teachers have drilled into us, mastering a skill means repeating it endlessly. *Practice makes perfect*, right?

Wrong. The secret isn't repetition. The idea that it takes 10,000 hours of practice to master a skill is misleading. One year of practice repeated in the same way for ten years doesn't make perfect. Rather, a certain *kind* of practice makes perfect. Professor K. Anders Ericsson of Florida State University and his colleagues have studied how people achieve mastery in music, science, and sports. As Ericsson and Robert Pool discuss in their book *Peak*, two factors contribute to mastery: hours of repetition, yes, but more important, what Ericsson coined *deliberate practice*. Individuals who progress the most meticulously assess outcomes, solicit feedback based on known standards of excellence, and strive to correct tiny flaws that the feedback has uncovered.[6] This purposeful and informed way of practicing explains why some learn at a much faster rate than others.

Dan devoted himself to such deliberate practice. When he measured his golf swings and where the ball landed, he was meticulous. It wasn't just "a little to the left of the hole," but "11 feet to the left." He knew what percentage of his shots went down the fairway (40.9 percent), what percentage missed going left (31.0 percent), and what percentage missed going right (28.1 percent). He tracked his driving accuracy for each round of golf, and he graphed his recovery performance (41.5 percent "scrambling" and 23.5 percent "sand saves").[7] He used sophisticated 3-D technology at a facility outside Atlanta to capture a three-dimensional scan of his movements. Sharing this information with his coach, he obtained precise feedback and concrete suggestions for the next swing ("widen your stance by one inch," the coach might say). Dan also tracked his progress by monitoring one key performance metric: his handicap score.

As a result, Dan's practice sessions benefited him far more than they would have had he merely repeated his swing over and over and relied on vague metrics. As he told us in our interview for our study, Dan encountered many other golfers who practiced in this less thoughtful way, just hitting the ball over and over. They didn't concentrate so hard on what they were doing, and they didn't make much progress. Dan made every minute of practice time count. It was this *quality* of learning, and not the *quantity* of repetitions, that helped Dan achieve that 2.6 handicap in four short years.

Given the impressive feats that top performers in sports, music, chess, and spelling bees have achieved using deliberate practice, you would think that legions of employees in the working world would rely on this approach to master their job-specific skills. Yet most individuals don't. Companies have long deployed improvement techniques such as "six sigma," and a whole field called "organizational learning" has arisen to help businesses improve quality in manufacturing, logistics, customer ordering, and service.[8] Yet this approach has not expanded much outside such organizational processes, and it has not filtered down to *individual* employees. If you glance around the workplace, you'll find that few people strive to enhance their skills the way Dan enhanced his golf game. As a result, people conduct meetings or give presentations or make sales pitches just as they've always done. They become "good enough," but not great at work.

Employees who wish to practice skills at work face some challenges. Experts haven't articulated how people can use a continuous learning technique like deliberate practice in their daily work. And most organizations aren't geared to support such techniques. Take performance reviews. Deliberate practice requires that a manager or employee receives helpful feedback every day, yet most people only receive it during their annual review. Imagine the tennis great Roger Federer getting feedback on his serve once a year from his coach. "Hi, Roger, I have been observing your serve for a year now, and I think you should serve a tad more to the left next year." Absurd. Still, that's what we do at work.

Deliberate practice is also incompatible with the realities of today's hurried workplaces. The idea of "practice" in sports and the arts entails rehearsing exhaustively *before* the real performance (a concert or competition). But most employees struggle to set aside their regular work to rehearse skills—they're too busy. Athletes also have an easier time measuring outcomes than employees. Dan can track the exact movement of his golf swing and where the ball lands (eleven feet to the left). But how do you measure skills like prioritizing tasks, making a sales pitch, handling a customer complaint, writing an effective email, and listening in meetings?

For these reasons, some experts don't recommend deliberate practice for individuals at work. As Professor Ericsson notes, deliberate practice only helps in situations where a performer possesses a clear performance metric, and where he or she knows the skills required to perform well and can break them down into discrete steps. "What areas don't qualify?" he writes. "[M]any of the jobs in today's workplace—business manager, teacher, electrician, engineer, consultant, and so on."

I respectfully disagree. Deliberate practice translates far better to the workplace than we might think. But there's a crucial twist. As we discovered in our research, we can't just take deliberate practice and "copy and paste" it into the workplace. Instead, we must implement a different version—what I call *the learning loop*. Employees and managers who improve their skills at work follow several tactics that you don't find in traditional deliberate practice as deployed in the performing arts and sports. They discard isolated practice in favor of *learning as they work*, using actual work activities such as meetings or presentations as learning opportunities. They also spend just a *few minutes* each day learning, eschewing the three-to-four-hour practice sessions common among musicians and athletes. They also rely on informal, rapid feedback from peers, direct reports, and bosses, and not just coaches. And they take steps to measure the "softer" skills that permeate the workplace. As I will detail, people embracing the learning loop follow six highly effective tactics geared specifically to the workplace.

People in our 5,000-person study who adopted the learning loop performed much better than those who didn't.[9] We created a learning loop scorecard consisting of six items that included phrases such as: "makes changes in an effort to improve"; "tries out new approaches"; "learns from failures"; "is curious;" "doesn't believe he/she knows best"; and "experiments a lot" (see the research appendix for the complete wording of each item). We found a clear result: effective learners were likely to place *15 points higher* in our performance ranking than the less effective ones.[10] Say a salesperson is currently performing in the top 20 percent among all the salespeople in her company. By mastering the learning loop, she would climb to the top 5 percent, emerging as an outstanding sales rep.

The top learners in our study didn't master their skills by working crazy hard and repeating the same habits over and over again. They worked on average 48 hours per week, only one hour more than the ordinary learner. Instead, they worked smart by focusing on the *quality* of each of the loops when learning at work. To understand how they might have done so, let's look in detail at one individual in our study who sought to improve her job skills, constantly reviewed how she worked, learned from failures, and became a top 10 percent performer as a result.

LOOPING AT WORK

Brittany Gavin, a food and nutrition services supervisor at Scripps Memorial Hospital in La Jolla, California, had just finished a meeting when her phone rang. It was her boss, telling her that a patient was furious about the quality of his lunch. "Oh, no," Brittany said, "not another one." Her team served meals to patients, employees, family members, and visitors. Laboring over hot stoves and in back storerooms, her 22 frontline employees made sure that patients at the 432-bed facility got the nourishing food they needed. Yet in recent months, the team had underperformed. Patient satisfaction scores were disappointing, and employee engagement was average at best. Almost every week, Brittany had to trek over to a patient's room to apologize for the quality and taste of the food her team served.[11]

Brittany had worked in her supervisory job for about a year and a half. Given her department's poor performance, she was starting to question whether "management was something I could even do." She remained highly motivated, yet she felt at a disadvantage. Her undergraduate degree was in nutrition, not business management. She knew her way around an institutional kitchen but sensed she had considerable room to improve as a boss. One area of management in particular stymied her: fostering problem-solving skills among people on her team. Every day her team members plodded through the same routine, contenting themselves with maintaining the status quo rather than improving. "There wasn't much innovation or idea generation," she said. Yet Brittany didn't know how to prompt others to propose ideas for improvement. Like many managers, she felt more comfortable simply offering her own solutions to problems as they arose.

Brittany needed to learn a new skill—how to run idea sessions with her team, where she would ask questions to solicit opportunities for improvements (OFIs) from team members reluctant to speak up. When she first started to run such sessions, the conversations with staff went nowhere. At 10:45 a.m. staff meetings with her team (called "huddles"), Brittany asked questions like, "Do you have any concerns about your work?" Usually people just stared back at her or mumbled "no." Brittany couldn't fathom how to ask questions and spark a discussion so that people would open up and contribute.

She enrolled in a formal Scripps training program, and then set about applying the tactics she had learned. During a huddle with staff one morning in February 2015, Brittany tried a new approach to asking questions. Whereas before she had asked, "Do you have any ideas?" she now posed that question differently: "What ideas do you have to improve patient food service?" Her coaches Steve and Marlys had suggested that such a seemingly trivial change would invite people to suggest ideas. And sure enough, one staff member responded: "How about we start knocking on the door and introduce ourselves to patients, and saying we're from meal services?"

Okay, that was a measurably better outcome: An idea! Brittany responded: "Okay, great." And then the session went silent. Oops, not such a great outcome after all. In a debrief later that day, coach Steve asked how she could have done it differently, and Brittany said she struggled with the follow-up question. They came up with a modified plan to ask better second questions.

With this bumbling try at posing a question, Brittany had just completed her first learning loop. She tried a new approach to asking questions ("do"), gauged the outcome of soliciting an idea ("measure"), received analysis and suggestions from Steve to follow up ("feedback"), and altered her plan to ask a second question ("modify"). These basic steps feature in any behavioral learning model, but they differ in some fundamental ways from how Dan the golfer performed them. Brittany's desired skill was more abstract than Dan's (generating ideas in her team vs. swinging the club in observable movements). Her desired outcome was more difficult to measure (whether staff proposed good ideas vs. "ball landed eleven feet to the left of hole"). And constructive feedback was harder to come by (change the question vs. widen your stance by one inch when swinging the club).

Brittany's deviations from Dan's deliberate practice method underscore the challenges inherent in learning while working. She broke down

Basic Steps in a Learning Loop

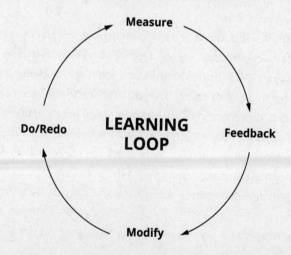

the abstract skill she sought into a specific behavior (asking a good question). She measured her behavior by zooming in on two metrics (number of ideas proposed and implemented). She received constructive feedback by working closely with a coach, while also receiving feedback from her team. And she only spent a few minutes each day focusing on learning.

The following week, Brittany held another huddle where again she asked the question, "What ideas do you have for improving patient service?" A staff member suggested, "How about asking patients before we leave what else we can help them with?" Brittany followed up with: "Okay, great, when can you start doing that?" Another staff member mumbled, "Whenever we can," and that was it. Oops, not such a good outcome, either. In the debrief, coach Marlys suggested that she needed to ask people explicitly to get involved. So again Brittany modified her plan, completing her second learning loop.

In a huddle a few weeks later, she again posed the question, "What ideas do you have for improving patient service?" Staff members were now more excited and proposed more ideas, including, "How about we plan better to avoid out-of-stock items?" Brittany responded: "That's interesting, let's get together this week in a smaller group to work on that, okay?" Which they did. In the debrief, coach Steve praised her improvements, and they planned the next modification. In this third loop, she finally mastered the art of soliciting ideas and ensuring a commitment from staff to follow through.

And so it went, with Brittany addressing many issues over a couple of dozen learning loops. Her boss, too, joined the huddles from time to time and provided feedback. Brittany learned to spend less valuable meeting time on announcements (implemented in a learning loop), to talk less about the data and more about how to solve problems (another learning loop), to ask employees how she as a manager might support them (another learning loop), to follow up on previously discussed ideas (another learning loop), and so on.

Brittany displayed humility during all of this learning, with her boss awarding her a top mark in our learning scorecard on the statement "doesn't believe she knows best." She also learned from her failures, which was an important part of her effort to improve. In our learning loop scorecard, her boss gave Brittany the top score ("completely agree") on the statement, "is excellent at learning well from failures to avoid repeating the same mistakes." Only 17 percent of people in our 5,000-person dataset scored this high. Almost half scored low or very low, suggesting that many people can benefit from becoming better at learning from their failures.

Observing Brittany's progress, we find that it's the *quality* of each of these loops that helped her improve and not their sheer number. Imagine what might have happened had she attempted an endless series of repetitions with no learning from failures, no feedback, and minimal modifications. She would have invested a great deal of hard work but progressed very little. Learning on the job is not about practicing for 10,000 hours; it's about making sure you perform each loop with high quality.

Brittany saw exceptional progress from her effort. We asked her boss to rate her performance before and after she embarked on the learning loop. Before the effort, her boss ranked her in the top 30 percent of her peer group. After eighteen months of looping, Brittany moved up to the top 10 percent in her peer group, receiving a rating of "outstanding."

Her team's performance also improved. Staff suggested 104 opportunities for improvements during a thirteen-month period, and they implemented 84. These improvements, posted on a public board every week in the department for all to see, included:

- Insert a barrier at the bottom of trash cans to reduce the volume of trash placed in it. (This prevented back injuries among staff.)
- Create a floor stocking process with times when each item would be stocked, thus ensuring that food items are in stock if patients require them between formal mealtimes.
- Revise the way milk is retrieved from the facility's walk-in cooler so that it remains cold as meals are assembled.

As Brittany noted, "the way I learned to ask questions made all the difference" in helping her team generate all these ideas. And the 84 ideas that were implemented affected critical outcomes. Patient satisfaction with food temperature, food quality, and the courtesy of staff members all rose. The number of products out of stock in the department plummeted from 22 per week to six. Employee back injury incidents fell from

Brittany Gavin's Learning Loop Led to Results

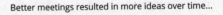

Better meetings resulted in more ideas over time...

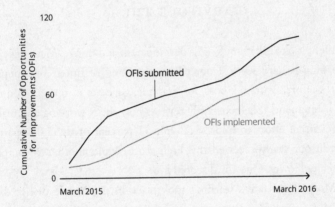

...which led to high quality of food served.

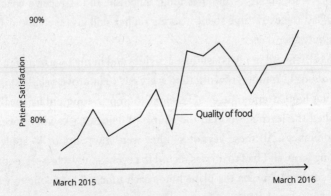

five to zero. Employee engagement scores rose from 63 to 98. Brittany no longer doubted whether she could become a good manager. She'd proven she could.

In improving her skills, Brittany enjoyed the support of her boss and her coaches. But what if you lack that? We've found that people can apply the learning loop even in situations where there is no official support. As Brittany's journey and other cases in our study revealed, people who learned well while working followed six "smart work" tactics.

LOOPING TACTIC #1

CARVE OUT THE 15

You might look at Brittany's skills development and think, "Man, this type of learning is hard work. I don't have that kind of time." Yes, looping requires effort. Brittany's boss, for example, gave her a top score on our survey statement, "She constantly reviews how she is working and makes changes in an effort to improve." Only 11 percent of the 5,000 participants in our study received this high score, while another 26 percent scored a tad lower. One-third scored low.

Most of Brittany's learning took place in the course of her daily work, not during formal training. Her *job* was to lead those huddles and implement ideas for improvements in her department. The coaching and looping required some additional time, but not much. Brittany's coaching sessions were about 30 minutes long. Since she didn't receive coaching every day, the extra time spent working on her skill averaged about 15 to 20 minutes per day.

As I've found in my consulting activities and in my own experience, it takes about 15 minutes of work time every day to improve a skill using the learning loop. Some time ago, I sought to improve my public speaking. I applied the learning loop in the course of delivering keynote speeches at conferences. All these keynotes—they were my real job. To apply the learning loop, all I had to do was record the event, study a few segments of the recording while on the plane home each time, ask someone to watch parts of it for 10 minutes, and then receive feedback about the one be-havior I tried to improve. In all, I invested 30 minutes of extra work on each keynote I delivered—15 minutes per day for a two-day trip. It is that constant yet brief effort that counts.

Can you really hammer out significant progress by devoting just fif-teen minutes a day? Yes, so long as you stick to the *Power of One: Pick one and only one skill at a time to develop*. It's hard to master a skill if you're also working on ten others. Just think of all the behaviors we cover in this book. Imagine an employee sauntering into work one morning and telling himself, "Today I am going to prioritize more, find a new task that deliv-ers more value, infuse my work with passion, inspire my coworkers, and foster debate in our morning meeting." He wouldn't have time to do them well. Ask yourself: Which skill would, if improved, lift your performance the most? Choose that one to work on first, and devote fifteen minutes a day—yes, just fifteen.

LOOPING TACTIC #2

CHUNK IT

To start improving a skill, effective learners in the workplace break it into manageable chunks, what I call micro-behaviors.

A *micro*-behavior is a small, concrete action you take on a daily basis to improve a skill. The action shouldn't take more than fifteen minutes to perform and review, and it should have a clear impact on skill develop-ment.

Brittany broke her overall skill area of "getting the team to generate ideas" into the micro-behaviors of "asking a question that gets people to propose an idea," "asking a follow-up question that generates more detail," and "securing follow-up commitment from team members," among others. I broke my "improving keynote speaking" skill into a few areas (opening, closing, stage movement, punch line on each slide), and used the "power of one" to work on each. For "stage movement," I worked on "start by planting your feet like cement on the floor (vs. moving restlessly like a caged tiger)," "move a few steps then stop again," "make eye contact with one person, then move to another," and "extend your arms outward to claim space." These actions might seem trivial, but I could go onstage and remember to do just one of them at a time. They were concrete and actionable.

In a leadership development program I have been running for the Scandinavian media company Schibsted, we tackled a tough but common challenge: getting managers to embrace and implement the company's leadership competencies on a daily basis. Many companies articulate such competencies, yet people often fail to embrace them. Schibsted adopted twelve leadership competencies, including "cultivate speed and flexibility," "execute and follow through to results, no excuses," and "insist on fact-based decisions." Although managers understood these formulations, they needed to translate these into daily, concrete actions. To help them do so, we crafted ten micro-behaviors for each competence. Managers completed 360-assessments to identify their specific areas of development. They then used the "power of one" to pick one and only one competence at a time. To help them, we developed a smartphone "app" that each week sent them two micro-behaviors they could use while working.

For example, Bård Viken, a thirty-one-year-old manager in charge of online subscriptions in Norway, elected to work on "executing and following through to results, no excuses." On Monday at 8 a.m., as Bård was walking into the office, his phone lit up with a notification, and a micro-behavior appeared on his smartphone: "Today, approach one employee where you think there may be an issue with prioritization, and have a brief conversation to make sure that the most important tasks are the first priority." Bård blocked off ten minutes in the afternoon to talk with two of his direct reports about the need to prioritize. During this brief conversation, Bård reminded his reports that their top priority at the moment was to get quick results on a pressing issue: how to prevent online customers from leaving.

Over five weeks, Bård received nine more micro-behaviors on this competence, including "make it a habit to complete one task before moving on to another—look at your list of tasks and pick one that you will definitely finish soon before starting new ones" and "make sure that you're not slowing others down—check your messages right now for a pending question from a colleague who needs your response and answer it." By practicing these micro-behaviors, Bård could translate the abstract principle of "executing and following through to results" into specific, daily actions. His skills improved in turn.

LOOPING TACTIC #3

MEASURE THE "SOFT"

When you're on a diet, you can monitor what you eat and hop on the scale every morning. K. Anders Ericsson's studies on deliberate practice likewise focused on measurable activities. In their book *Peak*, Robert Pool and Ericsson describe a man who used deliberate practice to memorize a string of 82 random digits. I can hardly remember a ten-digit phone number—imagine memorizing 82! As impressive as that was, this memory whiz had it easy in one respect: measuring the outcome of each attempt was straightforward. When trying to repeat back 82 numbers in the right order, he knew immediately whether he got it right or wrong. It is much more difficult to measure "soft" professional skills, such as listening in meetings or prioritizing a list of responsibilities.

To solve this problem, you can measure micro-behaviors associated with softer skills, as well as the result of those micro-behaviors. Brittany couldn't easily measure the overall quality of the daily discussions she was leading. But she could measure whether she was implementing the micro-behavior of asking specific questions such as "What ideas do you have?" rather than less effective questions such as "Do you have any ideas?" She could also track the outcome of this micro-behavior, noting how many ideas employees proposed and whether they agreed to a follow-up.

In our era of "big data," measuring "soft" behaviors has become easier. We flock to Internet sites like Yelp to rate our doctors, plumbers, electricians, and lawyers. If you're a dermatologist looking to improve your patient-oriented behaviors, you might already have access to a trove of data (of course, some of that might be biased). Ours is also the era of the "quantified self." We enjoy access to a raft of tools designed not merely to help us track fitness goals but to help us home in on what we do well or poorly at work. The downside is that it's easy to become overwhelmed with all this data. The "work harder" paradigm would have you amass reams of data on all kinds of work activities. That's wrong. Ask yourself: Which one or two metrics will, if tracked, make a big difference in my efforts to improve my work performance? Brittany, for example, zoomed in on opportunities for improvements (OFIs) submitted and implemented and tracked those over time.

LOOPING TACTIC #4

GET NIMBLE FEEDBACK, FAST

Measurement and feedback often go together. But be careful: The *quality* of feedback matters. It's easy enough to assign a restaurant four stars on Yelp and type in a comment recommending the General Tso's chicken. Useful feedback, however, requires more than a simple rating. It includes information about how well a person did and suggestions for how to modify behaviors. As *Financial Times* columnist Lucy Kellaway wrote: "'Great post!' and 'Spot on!' do not help me write better, any more than 'I can't believe you get paid to write this drivel.'"[12] Likewise, "the meeting sucked" is not going to help you run better meetings. But a comment like, "the debate in the meeting was superficial. Ask more specific questions next time" delivers both an assessment (it didn't go so well) and a helpful tip.

For best results, experts—a coach, boss, or mentor—might scrutinize an employee's behavior and provide immediate feedback with suggestions for improvement. However, relying on experts is much harder in workplace settings than it is out on the athletic field or in a music conservatory. In companies, most formal feedback is sporadic (mainly annual), and coaches are rarely available. What can you do if, unlike Brittany at Scripps, you don't have access to a coach?

You can turn to technology. The "app" we developed for Bård Viken at Schibsted allowed him to request nimble, "140 character" feedback from peers. At the end of the week, having approached his employees and reminded them to prioritize the online customer migration problem, Bård clicked on the app to request feedback from them and two other employees. "I'm working on setting clearer expectations," he wrote. "I worked on clearly communicating priorities. Did it help? One thing I can do better?" The first brief feedback he received within a day was, "Communication was clear, but it is important that you walk the talk" (68 characters). Another one: "Clear improvement, but take the time needed with your team to define what should be done and measured" (104 characters). His team used the app to give him rapid, honest, and constructive feedback. Each team member needed only a minute to share his or her opinions and advice (no coach needed). Assessing their feedback, Bård realized that he himself often failed to follow through on the most important initiatives. This feedback prompted him to prioritize time to help his team on this important issue. In lieu of such an app, you can use email or texting. You could even go old school, sticking your head into a colleague's office and asking for thirty seconds of feedback on how the meeting went.

LOOPING TACTIC #5

DIG THE DIP

Fertility doctors have a choice when patients visit their office. They can screen for and refuse the most difficult cases. Those patients include women who are more than thirty-five years old, who have a low egg count, and who have already tried in-vitro fertilization without success. Excluding these high-risk cases boosts the doctor's success rate (the proportion of patients who ultimately give birth), which in turn burnishes the doctor's reputation. Refuse the tricky patients, and you can perform better. Yet there's a snag. If you never take on challenging cases, you won't learn anything new, and you won't improve.

Professors Mihaela Stan of University College London and Freek Vermeulen at the London Business School gathered data from 116 British clinics whose doctors had treated 300,000 women from 1991 to 2006.[13] They distinguished between clinics and doctors that had treated only easy cases and those that had also accepted difficult cases. Sure enough, clinics and doctors that mainly treated easy patients boasted a 10 percent higher success rate, enough to steer more patients toward their practices.

Ah, but wait. What happened over time? If you treat difficult patients, your performance dips in the short term, because it is harder to help those patients. But you can also expand your knowledge. As one doctor in their study remarked, "When you get a difficult case, with complex pathology . . . you change the practice, you start tinkering with the parameters, adding new things, adjusting doses and sequences so that it fits." Moreover, you can use wisdom gained from the complicated cases to treat more straightforward cases with greater insight. Said the doctor: "You start tinkering with the procedure for the easy case as well; you take what you've learned from that difficult case to the easy case."

That's indeed what happened. Over time, doctors who treated tough cases went on to excel. For a clinic's first 100 cases, doctors who stuck with less complicated patients enjoyed a higher success rate. *After* 100 cases, doctors who had treated more difficult patients all along snuck into the lead, because benefits from their learning kicked in. At 400 cases, their success rates surpassed those of the "easy case" doctors by 3.3 percent, and their learning continued. Their looping had made them the top performers.

"Quality management" techniques in companies urge employees to eliminate the defects and waste that cause performance to vary. These techniques seek to drive out variation and failure. That's a grave mistake. Variation—trying new ideas—is essential to learning. And tackling difficult problems can provide rich learning opportunities. People who pursue the learning loop typically see their performance dip over the short term as they introduce challenges and experiment with ways to solve them. But they realize gains over time. The challenge, then, is to learn to tolerate failure in the short term.

A number of people in our study possessed healthy attitudes toward failure. Christy, a financial analyst at a Dallas insurance company, told us that the more mistakes she makes, the more "I actually learn about what's technically going on, and all the aspects involved in the accounting that I do."[14] When she encounters a new problem, "I have better ideas of where to start and how to face that problem." If you expect perfection each time, you won't take a chance on risky patients. Or on a new and challenging client. Or on a different way to make a sales pitch. You'll think, "What if it goes wrong?" You'll stymie your own growth.

Our 5,000-person study revealed a yawning gap in people's inclination to experiment. A full 32 percent scored low on the question, "I often try out new approaches to see if they work." Only 11 percent scored high on that metric.[15]

The people in our study who dared to risk a short-term performance dip reaped performance benefits. Statistically, we found a strong positive association between experimentation and excellent performance.

Now, there is a smart and a dumb way to experiment. When trying out an idea, you don't want to take big risks. If you do, you won't just see a dip—you'll fall off a cliff. As we saw in the previous chapter, Principal Greg Green started small when trying to "flip" the education method at Clintondale High School. Rather than flipping the whole school, he piloted his new approach in one social studies class. He retained the old method for the other class and then compared the results. That's called A-B testing: You test your new idea on group A, and then compare it to the control group (B). If the flipped social studies class had fared poorly, Green could have just dropped the flipping idea. Once Green understood the new model's power thanks to a few more experiments, he went "all in" and flipped the whole school. By first experimenting, Green took a smaller risk and gathered evidence that would support a subsequent, more ambitious redesign.

CONFRONT THE STALL POINT

Magnus Carlsen is no ordinary chess player. Born and mainly raised in a small Norwegian town, he started playing seriously at age eight. By thirteen, he had become the second-youngest grandmaster ever, and by nineteen the youngest chess player in history to rank number one in the world. Two years later, he hit a peak rating of 2,882 points—the highest ever achieved, surpassing the great Russian champion Garry Kasparov. In 2013, at age twenty-three, he won the world championship in chess. He defended it the following year and again in 2016.

Carlsen is Exhibit A for inborn talent. He has a gift for the game and has been held up as a counterpoint to those who believe that anyone with enough practice can achieve greatness. His fellow grandmasters proclaim him a genius. You and I will never reach Carlsen's level in chess, even if we practice 100,000 hours, let alone 10,000. Playing chess taps into his natural strengths.

But there's more to Carlsen than merely his chess genius. We can't just compare him to ordinary people and say that he has a supertalent they lack. We must also compare him to other chess masters and ask why Carlsen outperforms *them*. After all, they, too, are prodigies. When we delve deeper into Carlsen's career, we find that he outplays his peers in part because he brings a unique learning attitude. After becoming world champion in 2013, he said, "I am still far away from really knowing chess, really. There is still much I can learn, and there is much I still don't understand. And this makes me motivated to keep going, to understand more and more and develop myself."[16] Really? You're the best chess player on earth, yet you say you don't really know chess? That's one humble learner. Carlsen clearly subscribes to Stanford Professor Carol Dweck's growth mindset theory, even though he may not know about her work. In Dweck's theory, those who believe that you either have talent or not (a fixed mindset) don't bother to improve much, while those who believe that talent is malleable (a growth mindset) put in extra effort, even when they excel at something.[17]

Carlsen's mindset to keep pushing and improving regardless of his past achievements prevented him from falling into a common trap: *the stall point*. As people develop expertise and skill in an activity, they can become very good, even excellent. But then something happens. They plateau. A large-scale study in North Carolina, for example, showed that teachers improved from zero to two years of teaching experience, but then stalled.[18] Teachers with twenty-seven years of experience (that's more than 40,000 hours of practice[19]) were not much more effective than those with two years in improving students' achievement, as measured by their proficiency in English and Math. So much for the 10,000-hour rule! People seek out new improvements, but only until they reach a certain level of satisfaction. Then they stop, judging themselves "good enough." The Nobel laureate in economics Herbert Simon termed this "satisficing" (a play on words that combined "satisfying" and "sufficing"[20]).

Push Beyond the Stall Point

The Learning Loop Leads to Better Outcomes Than Mindless Repetition, but You Must Push Through the Stall Point

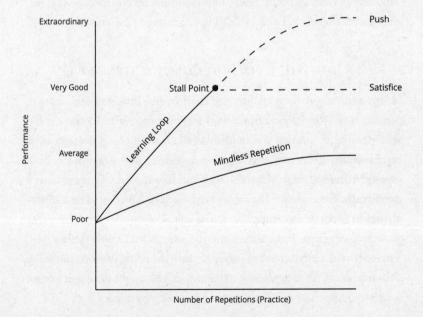

Why do so many people stall upon becoming "good enough"? Researchers have found that many of us *automate* our skills.[21] At first, we might struggle to develop a sales pitch. Now we can do it in our sleep. So we do. We let skills that once required fierce effort lapse into habits. Sometimes that is a good thing. We couldn't function if we had to contemplate every last action during our workday. But the moment a behavior becomes automatic, our learning stalls. Unless, that is, you take a tip from Magnus Carlsen and constantly push the boundaries, even when you're on top.

The top performers in our study followed Carlsen's dictum. A whopping 74 percent of the top performers in our dataset constantly reviewed their work in an effort to learn and improve. That compares with only 17 percent of people in the underperforming category.[22]

Top performers don't rest. They keep learning. Remember Jiro, the sushi chef from chapter two? At age eighty-five, he was still pushing himself. "All I want to do is make better sushi," he said in the film. "I do the same things over and over again, improving bit by bit. Even at my age, after decades of work, I don't think I have achieved perfection."

HOW DO YOU AVOID BECOMING OBSOLETE?

In this and the previous chapter, we've discussed how you can improve performance by redesigning your work and how you learn. Yet there is another reason to redesign and implement the learning loop. *You also adapt better to changes in the workplace.* In many industries, new technologies have ushered in innovative working methods and automation.[23] Graphic design has disrupted the work of newspaper typesetters. Voice mail and smartphones have eliminated many secretarial jobs. Online travel sites have displaced travel agents. Robots have gnawed away at traditional factory jobs. These are punctuated changes—they rupture the fabric of work and make skills irrelevant. As such disruption continues, you might need to innovate the way you work so as to stay relevant and keep your job.

Sidebar: What Hurdles at Work Prevent You from Looping?

Hurdle at Work	Tactical Looping Solution at Work
I am too busy with work to deal with training and practice.	**#1.** Carve out just 15 minutes per day of your time, and focus on one key skill at a time (the power of one).
I don't know where to start—it's too difficult to improve a broad skill, like "prioritize better."	**#2.** Chunk it, breaking your desired skill into small, concrete, daily micro-behaviors.
I don't know how to measure the outcome of what I am doing. For instance, how do I know I am listening better in a meeting?	**#3.** Focus on tracking micro-behaviors. If you're working on listening better, did you make eye contact with the person who was speaking (yes/no)?
Our annual performance review doesn't give me feedback when I need it. It's too sporadic.	**#4.** Solicit nimble feedback: brief, informal, instant comments—from peers. No bloated surveys!
I am afraid to try new ways of working that may fail. I am doing just fine with my current setup.	**#5.** Conduct small experiments to limit any downside, and then implement those that work.
I've gotten comfortable in my routines and am no longer making much progress.	**#6.** Push beyond "stall points" by de-automating your routines.

The best performers adapt successfully to disruptions by combining redesign and the learning loop. In their seminal study, Professors Amy Edmondson, Richard Bohmer, and Gary Pisano at the Harvard Business School chronicled how a few surgery teams managed to adapt to a new technology that disrupted their profession: They shifted from open-heart surgery to a new method, minimally invasive cardiac surgery (MICS), while others struggled to do so.[24] The successful adopters first embraced the redesign because they understood minimally invasive surgery for what it was: a radical departure from traditional surgery. By contrast, unsuccessful teams that couldn't cross over to the new surgical method regarded it as simply an extension of existing methods. Second, the successful teams looped their learning. They held trials and incorporated feedback from team members. Unsuccessful teams did so sparingly or not at all and didn't meet to solicit feedback.

High performers in our study embraced a similar two-part approach. They scored very high on both the redesign *and* the learning loop practices. Those who mastered both redesign *and* looping placed in the top

83rd performance percentile, compared to only the 23rd percentile for those who did neither.[25]

To position yourself to succeed in a changing work environment, start by confronting the facts. Don't ignore reality and write off the new technology or emerging trend as a minor fad. If you're a teacher, accept that online education will disrupt your profession and embrace corresponding changes in your daily work. Then apply the learning loop to keep on making yourself better little by little. Redesign *and* loop.

Of course, that kind of intense, sustained effort to redesign work and learn requires a terrific degree of motivation. How do the greatest performers stay energized and enthusiastic? What drives them to keep on changing and improving, day after day, year after year? That's the topic to which we now turn.

KEY INSIGHTS

THE LEARNING LOOP

The "Work Harder" Convention

We need 10,000 hours of practice to master a job skill. Practice—repetition—makes perfect.

The New "Work Smarter" Perspective

It isn't how many hours you practice. It's *how* you learn. And that "how" differs in the workplace from the deliberate practice pursued by athletes and musicians. The best performers at work implement the learning loop, in which the quality—and not the quantity—of each iteration matters most.

Key Points

- Statistical analysis of our 5,000-person dataset showed that people who applied the learning loop perform much better than those who didn't.

- To learn well at work, we must overcome important challenges that people don't face when trying to master skills in sports, music, chess, and memory tests (the areas where most research on deliberate practice has been conducted).

- The Learning Loop is an approach to learning while you perform your daily work: you try out a new approach in a small way (e.g., how you ask a question in a meeting), then measure the outcome, then get quick feedback, then tweak your approach based on that feedback (e.g., ask the question differently).

- You can deploy six tactics to implement the learning loop in your job:
  1. *Carve out just 15*
  2. *Chunk it*
  3. *Measure the "soft"*
  4. *Get nimble feedback, fast*
  5. *Dig the dip*
  6. *Confront the stall point.*

- Effective learners break an overarching skill into *micro*-behaviors: they are small, concrete actions you take on a daily basis to improve a skill. The action shouldn't take more than fifteen minutes to perform and review, and it should have a clear impact on skill development.

- How do you thrive in your career even when technological and other disruptions threaten to render traditional job skills obsolete? Combine the learning loop with redesign (chapter three).

FIVE

P-SQUARED (PASSION *AND* PURPOSE)

What counts in life is not the mere fact that we have lived. It is what difference we have made to the lives of others that will determine the significance of the life we lead.

—Nelson Mandela[1]

In 2008, on a brilliantly sunny day in Palo Alto, California, Oprah Winfrey delivered a soaring commencement address to Stanford's graduating class. Recounting her own rise to wealth and stardom, she lauded the role of emotion and listening to your gut—the importance of making sure you feel passionate about your job choices. "When you're doing the work you're meant to do," she said to the 25,000 people assembled in the stadium, "it feels right and every day is a bonus, regardless of what you're getting paid." And then she delivered the punch line: "So, I say to you, forget about the fast lane. If you really want to fly, just harness your power to your passion. Honor your calling. Everybody has one. Trust your heart and success will come to you!"[2]

Motivational speakers, self-help gurus, successful entrepreneurs, human resource executives, and branding experts have all talked up passion, so much that you might believe loving what you do is the *only* requirement to perform at your best. Think of Southwest Airlines and its slogan "the airline that love built."[3] Or Richard Branson's remark, "Since 80 percent of your life is spent working, you should start your business around something that is a passion."[4] A *Huffington Post* blog summed up what has become a mantra for our age: "The Key to Success: Loving What You Do."[5]

But is passion *really* "the key to success"? As many a failed actor in Los Angeles will tell you, following your passion can lead to unemployment. Success stories like Oprah's are nice, but they're also misleading. Stanford doesn't invite unsuccessful people or struggling alumni up on the podium. Only the supersuccessful, like Oprah Winfrey, get to tell swooning crowds that they have followed their passion. As the well-known venture capitalist Marc Andreessen tweeted: "The problem is that we do NOT hear from people who have failed to become successful by doing what they love."[6] It's possible that passion played a role in making Oprah successful. But it also may have played a role in preventing countless others from reaching their full potential.

Had freelancer David Sobel been in the audience for Oprah's Stanford address, he might have held his applause. As Sobel recounted in a *Salon* article, he labored for years at a "respected social policy research organization," formatting reports from his perch in a "windowless office." Then at age forty-two, having seen economics professor Larry Smith deliver a popular TED talk about "following one's passion," he decided to make his move. He quit his job and threw himself into a new career, one he thought he'd love: "I was determined to rebrand myself as a digital copywriter."

Rather than finding a successful, enriching career, Sobel suffered through months of unemployment. No matter what he did, he couldn't find work. To pay for health care, he cashed in his retirement savings and begged money from his parents. He found and then lost a job working at a doggie day care. Eventually he landed in a mental hospital, where he "sat in group therapy sessions with addicts." "I never should have followed my dreams," Sobel concludes.[7]

The advice to follow your passion—in other words, letting your passion *dictate* what you do—can be dangerous. But what's the alternative?

Ignoring your passion isn't so great, either. It leads people to plod along, doing dull, empty work to earn a paycheck. In a commencement address delivered at Maharishi University of Management, comedian Jim Carrey recounted that his father might have been a talented comedian, but he had feared failure. He chose the "safe" route—accounting—only to lose his job when Carrey was twelve, leaving his family in dire straits. "I learned many great lessons from my father," Carrey reflected, "not the least of which was that you can fail at what you don't want, so you might as well take a chance on doing what you love! [applause]."[8] Sadness crossed Carrey's face as he recalled how his father achieved neither financial stability nor passion.

We've been thinking about passion in our careers all wrong. Some of us believe we should follow our passion, regardless of our chances of success. Others among us assume we must pursue a career and earn safe money irrespective of whether it taps into our passion. Neither of these options is very attractive, and as a result, many of us bounce between the two, unsure of what to do, groping for the best way forward.

Is there a solution to this tradeoff between "following" or "ignoring" passion? Yes. Our research uncovered a third option: "matching." Some people pursue passion in navigating their careers, but they also manage to connect this passion with a clear sense of purpose on the job—they contribute, serve others, make a difference. *They have matched passion with purpose.*

Let's be clear what we mean by passion and purpose. To be passionate about work is to feel energized by it, to experience a sense of excitement and enthusiasm. For some, passion is a quiet, inner sense of satisfaction and contentment. For others, it's a louder, "*Let's go!*" kind of thrill.[9] As for purpose, scholars and self-help gurus have advised that we organize our lives around contributing to the well-being of society. Yet that's an overly narrow view of purpose. It can also mean creating value for an organization, as defined in chapter three. Just because you're not saving kids in Africa or helping homeless people on the streets of Chicago doesn't mean your job lacks purpose. Our study led us to define purpose more broadly: *You have a sense of purpose when you make valuable contributions to*

others (individuals or organizations) or to society that you find personally mean-
ingful and that don't harm anyone.

Purpose and passion are not the same. Passion is "do what you love," while purpose is "do what contributes." Purpose asks, "What can I give the world?" Passion asks, "What can the world give me?"[10]

It's possible to experience a strong sense of purpose in a job and *not* feel deeply passionate about it—and vice versa. Theresa, a forty-year-old biomedical engineer in our study, had worked for a large orthopedic medical device company in Boston, Massachusetts, for ten years.[11] Her job was to test products to get data that could then be used for Food and Drug Administration clearance. While Theresa reported a strong degree of purpose (scoring a 6 out of the maximum 7 on "making societal contributions"), she didn't report feeling very excited about her job (she scored only a 2 for passion). Theresa contributed, but didn't love what she was doing. By contrast, Marianne, a "Lean Six Sigma Black Belt" program manager, loved her work doing continuous improvement projects at a consumer electronics company. Yet she derived no larger meaning from what she was doing. She was deeply passionate (scoring a 6) but felt no strong sense of purpose (scoring only a 1).

Theresa and Marianne both would have benefited from *matching* passion and purpose. Our statistical analysis of 5,000 people shows that people who match passion with purpose perform much better, on average, than those who lack either purpose or passion or both. Of the seven factors in this book that predict performance, high levels of both passion and purpose—"P-squared," as I call it—was the second most important one, predicting a boost in a person's percentile rank of 18 points compared with a similar person who had neither passion nor purpose.[12] People who had just one of the two—passion but no purpose, or purpose but no passion—scored lower on performance. The key therefore is to infuse your work with both passion and purpose, to aim for P-squared.

P-SQUARED AND PERFORMANCE

Why is matching passion and purpose so effective? I initially believed that it enhanced performance simply by spurring people to work longer hours. After all, if you love what you're doing and find it purposeful, wouldn't you hit the office earlier and leave later than anyone else? Our data squashed that explanation. Among our 5,000 participants, we found that people who scored high on passion and purpose worked an average 50 hours per week compared to 43 hours for those who scored low. Seven hours more isn't trivial, but it isn't that much, either. Passion and purpose didn't compel people to pour 70 or 80 hours into their jobs.[13] Our analysis also revealed that those additional seven hours of work didn't enhance performance much, only 1.5 percent.[14]

We had stumbled upon a mystery: Why did passion and purpose correlate with performance? To resolve it, we dug deeper into our case studies.

Genevieve Guay, a study participant, is a concierge at Auberge Saint Antoine, a luxury hotel in Quebec City in Canada. Most of the time, Genevieve fields routine requests from well-heeled guests: Restaurant recommendations, theater tickets, insider shopping tips. But on one wintry morning in 2010, a documentary photographer called. She was staying at the hotel, and she wanted to photograph a couple of dozen, hard-to-find objects that represented the region's unique people and culture. Could Genevieve help?

Most concierges would have brushed off the request, directing the photographer to a souvenir store to snag snow globes, key chains, and "Trust me, I'm Canadian" T-shirts. Not Genevieve. During the several days of the photographer's stay, Genevieve took field trips around Quebec City hunting for objects. She came back with a stuffed snowy owl, brown bear claws (right and left), a gramophone horn, an old mirror, a wooden fish, and a little wooden house. She even hunted down a specimen of the local cecropia butterfly, with its distinctive bands of vibrant orange and red. To obtain a cecropia, she had to make a few phone calls, eventually chasing down a researcher at nearby Laval University who lent a few specimens and hand-delivered them.

Hunting down stuffed owls went well beyond Genevieve's job specification. So what drove her to mount such an intense effort? Genevieve told me that she becomes enthusiastic and engaged when interacting with guests. It isn't just another job to her: "I love to improve the lives of others with my personal touch. This job gives me a chance to meet a lot of people from everywhere around the world without having to move from my desk. And I have direct impact. I can see directly what I gave, even with simple things like a restaurant that worked for them." When I asked Genevieve what her profession meant to her, she described it as "a great love story." She mentioned the word "care" time and again: "I care about my guests. Caring comes with energy, and the energy you project, you get back from guests."

Many hotel staffers drift between postings, using their jobs to fund their educations. Not Genevieve. Helping guests is her calling. By the time we spoke, she had worked as a concierge for nine years. Her boss had promoted her to Chef Concierge at the hotel and rated her as a top performer in our study. She had also become recognized in her profession, having gained admittance to Les Clefs d'Or (the Golden Keys), an international association of concierges dedicated "to make the impossible possible."[15] Earning a spot in Les Clefs d'Or is some accomplishment. Genevieve had to pass a slew of tests, among them a special trial in which she had to impress six "mystery guests" sent to judge her.

Genevieve's passion ("I love interacting with people") served a purpose (helping and caring for hotel guests). Unlike so many of us, she found magic in her career, landing in that special place where passion and purpose overlap. As a result, Genevieve brought a higher level of *intensity* to her work. She charged out of bed each morning, eager to get to her hotel. Once there, she greeted guests warmly and did everything she could to make their stay memorable, even when she was tired and cold on a dark January morning in icy Quebec. Yes, she tapped into her natural talents, and yes, she worked long hours—both contributed to her success. But it was the *energy* she brought to her work—born from her sense of passion and purpose—that allowed her to excel.

What's the real magic of P-squared? It provides people with more *energy* that they channel into their work. Not more hours as in the "work harder" paradigm, but *more energy per hour of work*. That's working smart.

Analyzing our data, we discovered a strong association between intensity of effort and having both passion and purpose. We performed an additional analysis called "structural equation modeling" where we disentangled two types of effort—the number of hours worked per week, and effort during those hours. The analysis showed that passion and purpose strongly predict *effort during working hours*, and not the number of hours worked per week (see section 3.2.5 in the Research Appendix for details).

Other studies confirm this finding. A study of 509 employees in an insurance company showed that those who were passionate about their job channeled more energy to their working hours: they were more absorbed in job tasks ("when I am working, I am completely engrossed in my work")

Matching Passion and Purpose

When People Achieve P-Squared, They Bring More
Focused Energy to Their Job and Perform Better

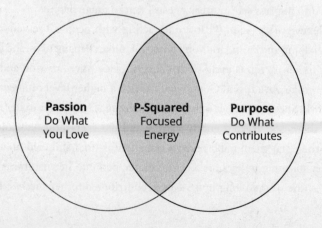

Passion
Do What
You Love

P-Squared
Focused
Energy

Purpose
Do What
Contributes

and paid much higher attention to their tasks.[16] Being absorbed and paying attention in turn improved employees' performance.[17]

If you love what you do, you'll show up with a certain amount of vigor. And if you also feel that you're helping other people—that they need you and depend on your contributions—your motivation to excel becomes that much greater. You're targeting your efforts toward making contributions to your purpose. As our study shows, you activate positive emotions such as joy, excitement, pride, inspiration, and hope, all of which gives you more energy. You're paying extra attention at meetings. You're engaging with colleagues and customers. You're noticing the details. You're jumping in with new ideas. You're doing *everything* better.

(NEARLY) EVERYONE CAN MATCH

Sadly, many people feel stuck in boring and meaningless jobs, experiencing nothing of Genevieve's enthusiasm and excitement. So is she one of the fortunate few? Where can *you* get a job that provides passion and purpose? To answer these questions, we returned to our data to locate those special workplaces where people report high levels of passion and purpose. Guess what? There were no truly "special" workplaces. We found that nearly *every* industry or occupation boasted at least some people who reported lots of passion and purpose. The idea that only certain industries and jobs allow for passion and purpose is a myth.

Consider passion. The chart below shows the distribution of passionate people by job function in our data. Sure, we can spot some major differences—health-care workers were more excited about their jobs than construction workers, for instance, and salespeople tended to love their jobs more than strategic planners. Yet we found passionate people *in all kinds of jobs and industries*, with no industry or job type coming in below 10 percent. You don't hear much about passionate truck drivers or store clerks or call center employees, but as our data indicate, they're out there.

Likewise, many people think that employees who work at large, bureaucratic companies struggle more to find passion in their jobs than those who work at smaller companies, and that passion wanes the longer they stay in a job. Wrong! Neither company size nor the number of years on the job had much bearing on how much people loved their work.

Our preconceptions about purposeful jobs are inaccurate, too. We think that more mundane or menial jobs can't contain purpose, and

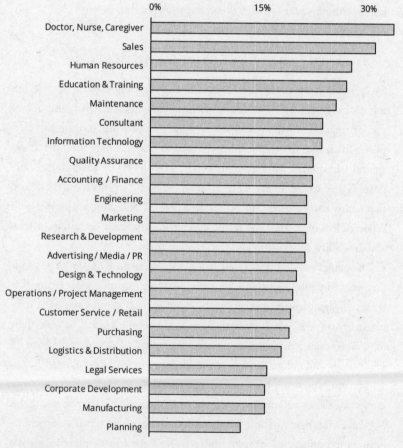

Many Passionate People Across Jobs

Percentage of People Who Scored
"Extremely Passionate About Work"

Note:
Survey sample of 4,964 people, see Research Appendix.

indeed some research has shown that many people don't find low-paying service jobs meaningful.[18] But other research has revealed the opposite— that some people can and *do* derive a sense of purpose from even the most menial, low-status tasks. As Yale School of Management professor Amy Wrzesniewski discovered in her study of hospital janitors, some found their jobs highly meaningful. In their eyes, they weren't simply cleaning floors. They were caring for patients and helping their families during their times of need.[19]

Our study found a big spread across industries in the percentage of people who felt they were contributing to society—about 40 percent of those working in health care did, for instance, as opposed to only 3 percent of those working in industrial products or services. Yet many people in our dataset who didn't work in the more "obviously meaningful" sectors felt a strong sense of purpose. Twenty-eight percent of people working in

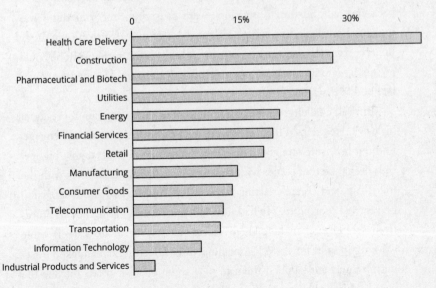

Purpose at Work

Percentage of People Who Scored High on "Contributing to Society"

Note:
Survey sample of 4,964 people, see Research Appendix.

the construction industry completely agreed with the statement: "I feel that my work makes contributions to society beyond just making money." Some of them built homes for families. Others built hospitals, schools, or other buildings with a public benefit.

All of this data adds up to some pretty good news. If people have found passion and purpose in nearly every corner of the economy, then chances are you can find it in your job, too. You don't have to quit your job or leave your company in a risky quest to search for passion and purpose. In fact, as our case studies show, there are three steps in particular you can take to find and grow your passion and purpose while staying in your organization.

HUNT FOR A NEW ROLE

Between 2001 and 2011, Steven Birdsall rose rapidly within SAP, the $22 billion-in-sales German software giant.[20] By the summer of 2011, however, he was feeling restless. He had served in multiple chief operating officer (COO) roles and was now SAP's corporate COO for sales. These back-end, administrative positions were satisfying, but something was missing. For a year, he pondered his next career move. Sure, he could stay in his current job and work to improve it bit by bit. Alternatively, he could go into a regional executive role and sell SAP software. He knew he would be good at that, too.

Birdsall challenged himself to pinpoint what excited him most about his work. He realized that he longed to sit down with customers, engage, find out how software could help them, negotiate, bond, laugh a bit, feel the adrenaline that comes with closing a deal, delight customers with the follow-up, and create a lasting relationship. And he had another passion he yearned to explore. He had long thrived on developing new ventures from scratch and making them successful. Earlier in his career, while working in sales for the ATM manufacturer Diebold, he had taken existing products and applied them in new commercial markets outside the core banking markets. As Birdsall recalled, the entrepreneurial nature of the job felt electrifying. His current job had not tapped this passion—nor would traditional sales leadership roles.

As his year of introspection at SAP dragged on, Birdsall felt stuck. He was not going to find a job at his company that would let him harness both his sales *and* entrepreneurial passions. But quitting SAP and going to a start-up would mean taking a huge risk—like pursuing Oprah's mantra of "follow your passion" without any realistic possibility of success. If he stayed at his current job, he would be ignoring his passion. Neither option appealed to him.

Day after day, week after week, Birdsall turned this dilemma over in his head. He thought through his options again and again. There had to be some solution. Finally, an epiphany came to him: What if he stayed at SAP and developed a new business?

At the time, SAP's customers were craving software systems that wouldn't cost tens of millions of dollars and take years to bring online. SAP had an answer, a simplified off-the-shelf product it had developed called "rapid deployment solutions" (RDS). Demand for this product existed, but the sales department hadn't yet championed it. The person who could build this business would make a substantial contribution, and Birdsall thought he was just the one. He did wonder whether it was worth the risk to leave his global COO role, but after further reflection, he decided it was. "Quite frankly," he told me in one of our interviews, "it's what I'm passionate about. I really enjoy building new businesses from scratch, taking product to market. It's been like that from the time I was in high school."

After so many months of anguish, Birdsall had decided. He presented a plan to SAP's board about what to do with the RDS business. The board endorsed it. Birdsall's boss, the president of SAP, asked him to take ownership of RDS. Ditching his COO responsibilities, Birdsall refocused all his energy on a single goal: making RDS a success. He hired a new team of experienced risk takers and traveled to meet with hundreds of customers in countries all over the world, racking up hundreds of thousands of air miles along the way. His "all-in" efforts paid off. Within two and

Striving for P-Squared

Steven Birdsall's Matches. In the last column,
assess yourself in your current job.

	Steven Birdsall's Alternatives				Your Assessment
	Current Role (COO)	Traditional Sales	Startup	Rapid Business	Current Job (or Alternative)
Purpose: Create Value and Contribute?	Yes	Yes	Uncertain	Yes	*Purpose?*
Passion: Customer Interactions? Entrepreneurship?	No No	Yes No	Yes Yes	Yes Yes	*Passion?*
Match Passion and Purpose?	No	Somewhat	No	Excellent match	*Match?*

a half years, RDS mushroomed beyond anyone's expectations, achieving $1.3 billion in annual revenue.

Like Birdsall, you can seek opportunities within your existing company to merge your passion with a strong sense of purpose. But be prepared: It takes work. Even though Birdsall's career move may seem straightforward in hindsight, it emerged out of months of contemplation on his part. He explored dozens of options before finding a good fit. He refused to settle until he found his match.

Many people assume that finding the "right" role—as Birdsall did—is the only way to find passion or purpose or both on the job. In one study, 70 percent of working adults reported that they thought they could only find passion at work if their job "fit" them perfectly from the outset. They neglected the possibility that they could *develop* their passion *in their current job*.[21] Let's examine how you can better match passion and purpose within the job you already have.

GROW YOUR CIRCLE OF PASSION

Here's a short quiz. On a scale of 1 to 7, use the scale below to rate the following statement:

"I am passionate about my job because I very much enjoy doing my tasks every day."

Completely agree (a score of 7)

Strongly agree (6)

Somewhat agree (5)

Neither agree nor disagree (4)

Somewhat disagree (3)

Strongly disagree (2)

Completely disagree (1)

How did you do? As we found in our research, some people equated passion with the specific tasks they perform on the job—helping a patient, selling a product, designing a strategy. How well they did at the task didn't matter. It was the pleasure of the task itself that counted. Such people feel what academics call "intrinsic motivation." Unfortunately, intrinsic motivation is uncommon. When we analyzed our data, we found that fewer than 15 percent of people in our data set completely agreed with the statement: "I feel that the actual work I do is rewarding in and of itself." For most of us, the actual work may be somewhat rewarding, but not *that* rewarding.

So are most of us doomed to plod through our current jobs, unhappy and uninspired? Not at all. Our research turned up other sources of passion besides the specific work tasks we do. Break out that 1 to 7 scale again and rate the following:

"I am passionate about my job because I relish the experience of achieving results and success."
(achievement passion)

> *"I am passionate about my job because I am energized*
> *around the creative aspect of my work."*
> (creative passion)

> *"I am passionate about my job because I adore*
> *working and socializing with my colleagues."*
> (people passion)

> *"I am passionate about my job because it affords me the*
> *opportunity to learn and grow professionally and personally."*
> (learning passion)

> *"I am passionate about my work because it gives me*
> *the opportunity to do what I do best every day."*
> (competence passion)

For some of us, the exhilaration that comes with achieving success matters a lot. In our study, just shy of 20 percent of people completely agreed with the statement: "I feel good about my job because it allows me to experience success." Not surprisingly, people in traditionally competitive fields such as sales took more pleasure in achievement-based passion.

The ability to create something also excited some people in our study. Forty-six-year-old Karen, leader of a team that provides HR software solutions for companies, reported feeling deeply passionate about her job's opportunity to be innovative: "If you've ever built anything completely from scratch, it's an amazing experience, because all the things that you take for granted as being there . . . are no longer there. You have to build it piece-by-piece. And along with that building comes this huge flexibility . . . for being, you know, artistic and creative with what you're doing."

A different source of passion at work is what we might call "people passion." We relish the deeper relationships we form at work, the sense of being cared for.[22] Sophia, a thirty-year-old financial analyst in our study, reported how "really kind and generous" the colleagues in her office were: "I just had a major life event happen, and everyone was beyond supportive of me; people would come over and just check in and see how I'm doing on a daily basis. And that just provides a sense of care."[23]

Another dimension of passion we encountered in our study involved the passion that can come from learning and developing professionally. A full 56 percent of people were enthusiastic about their job because it gave them a chance to learn and grow.

Finally, we have what we can call competence-based passion—you love your work because it taps into your strengths. (You might recognize the last statement above as the one used in the "StrengthsFinder" approach to matching your strengths with your job.[24]) Such passion may emerge: you become very good at a job, and that in turn fuels your passion. The stove turns from cold to hot.[25]

Passion at work is an expanding circle that encompasses all six areas: joy doing the tasks, excitement at succeeding, the thrill from unleashing one's creative energy, enthusiasm from being with people at work, delight from learning and growing, and elation from doing one's job well.

A work activity can tap into one or more of these sources of passion. For two years as we worked on our book *Great by Choice*, my coauthor Jim Collins and I held weekly phone calls that we called "Chimposiums," after the monkey character Curious George. I thoroughly enjoyed those calls, and reflecting on it now, I know it was because they tapped into four sources of passion: intrinsic (I enjoyed the task of discussing and brainstorming the topics); creative (I felt happy to be creating new insights); developmental (I was learning); and social (I enjoyed doing it with my good friend Jim).

Go back and review your answers to the above statements. Consider how you might bolster your feelings of passion across each of the six dimensions. Look for a task that requires creative problem solving. Seek out a customer-facing activity to experience the thrill of success. Attend a training seminar to learn a new skill. Make sure you get invited to brainstorming meetings. Sign on to competitive projects, like a sales pitch against a competitor (or if not that, join that department's softball team). Ask your boss to assign you a stretch goal to challenge yourself. Seek ways to spend more time working with people you like and admire. Avoid colleagues who sap your energy. Identify the most passion-sapping task you have and find a way to get out of it. Seek to become really excellent in one job activity. If you tap more passions and go deeper into each one, you will become more motivated and inject more energy into every hour of work. That in turn will improve your performance and make it easier for you to find a passion-purpose match.

CLIMB THE PURPOSE PYRAMID

Another way to maximize your passion-purpose match is to infuse your present job with more purposeful activities. Let's remember the key difference between passion and purpose. Passion is doing what you love; purpose is doing what contributes. So how can you increase your contributions to others? My research uncovered three distinct ways of approaching purpose at work. I depict them as a pyramid—the "Purpose Pyramid"—to indicate a logic of increasing order. The premise of the pyramid is that you should fulfill the first level before moving upward. The higher you climb, the stronger your sense of purpose at work.

CONTRIBUTE VALUE (WHILE DOING NO HARM)

Value creation forms the foundation of the Purpose Pyramid. As you'll recall from chapter three, redesigning work is about creating value in your job by making contributions to others, such as your company, colleagues, suppliers, and customers. If you produce little or no value, you're not doing purposeful work. Period. Think of that engineer at Hewlett-Packard who produced a quarterly report and submitted it on time every time, even though corporate headquarters stopped reading the reports long ago. Although he may have felt passionate about the work, he created zero value and thus served no purpose.

The Purpose Pyramid

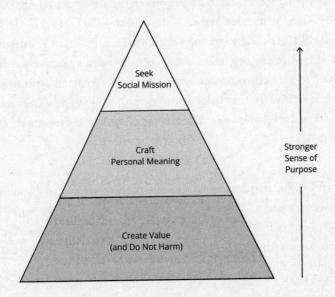

Many people conceive of purpose as social contributions alone and not as "value added," but they should reconsider. When you create value for your organization, you contribute, and your work has purpose. Recall Hartmut Goeritz from chapter three, the manager who turned around the container terminal in Tangier, Morocco. His actions contributed to the operational efficiency and quality of the terminal and to the profits of the company. He created value. Purpose it is.

Yet you have to be careful about *how* you add value. If your work harms other people, that harm cancels out the value you add, draining your work of purpose.

Consider the car company General Motors. In 2003, GM's car engineers put the finishing touches to a new model, the Cobalt. It turned out that a little piece of metal—the ignition switch—malfunctioned while the car was driving. The air bags would not deploy in a crash because the car's system considered the engine to be "off." Engineers detected this problem as early as 2004 but took no remedial action. The results were devastating. On July 29, 2005, *the year after engineers knew about the malfunction*, sixteen-year-old Amber Marie Rose died when the red Cobalt she was driving smashed into a tree without the airbag deploying.[26] Only in 2014—nine years after Amber Marie's death—did GM recall the Cobalts. By 2015, the faulty ignition switch had been linked to 124 deaths.[27]

Did GM employees and managers contribute in a positive way back in 2004? In a strictly economic sense, yes. By forgoing an expensive recall for several years, they helped produce profits by keeping costs down. They created economic value. Yet this "value" came at the expense of drivers of the cars.

If we only define purpose as giving to others, we miss a crucial distinction: You can contribute to one group, yet damage another. Contribute to General Motors, yet harm young Amber Marie Rose. A strong sense of purpose only arises when you don't harm anyone—customers, suppliers, your boss, your organization, employees, the community, the environment.[28]

To achieve more purposeful work, avoid associating yourself with products, services, and practices that harm others. Better yet, work hard to change products and practices that are causing harm, even on a small scale. If you're a physician, take extra care before ordering a potentially harmful test. If you're in sales, don't push products on people who don't need them. If you're a boss, stop berating your staff, recognizing the damage it can do to their emotional health.

Even small changes can help others, while also enabling you to find more purpose on the job. Consider one person we interviewed in our study. Ofer Kolton runs a one-person business, cleaning carpets in the homes of San Francisco. Some years ago, he switched to nontoxic and eco-friendly cleaning products to make sure that his service didn't also damage the environment. It was a small step to reduce harm. He served his customers by cleaning their carpets and helping to keep their homes nontoxic and their environment healthy. His job became more purposeful.

CRAFT PERSONAL MEANING

Many people stop at the first step in the purpose pyramid. Among the managers and employees we surveyed, 36 percent contributed value in their job but didn't climb further. That's too bad. If you're already adding significant value, and you're not causing harm to the wider world, then you can continue ascending up to higher levels of purpose. Enhance your purpose-passion match by taking the next step—crafting personal meaning.

The meaning we attach to our jobs varies considerably. Two individuals can have the same job, with only one feeling that it is of any consequence. In a 2009 study of zookeepers, researchers found that some saw cleaning cages and feeding animals as a filthy, meritless job, while others saw it as a moral duty to protect and provide proper care for the animals. Same job, different feelings of purpose.[29]

Or take car rental clerks. Samantha, a forty-three-year-old participant in our study, works at a car rental branch in Green Bay, Wisconsin.[30] She gave her job a 7 (completely agree) on the statement "I feel that my work makes contributions to society beyond just making money." That sounds strange—she rents out cars and feels her job benefits society? Come on. Well, she sees it differently. As she told us, her job held purpose for *her* because she could help people who had gotten into accidents and whose cars were in for repair. When they rent a car, "they're not stranded," she says, "they have a vehicle to drive. I feel good about providing that service." Countless other car-rental employees plod along, seeing their work as drudgery and wishing for their shift to end. Again, same job, different feelings of purpose.

What matters, as far as purpose on the job is concerned, is how each individual *feels about his or her own work.* As long as people are contributing value in their job, it's up to each individual to determine whether they see their work as purposeful.

To progress up the Purpose Pyramid, take steps to feel that what you're contributing is meaningful. You can do this in your current job by *reframing its meaning*. The hospital janitors in Wrzesniewski's study identified meaningful moments on the job.[31] A janitor named Jason took it upon himself to start talking to patients to brighten their mood. "Usually every morning I have to knock on the door. I'll just say, 'Housekeeping, is it okay if I clean your room?' . . . and if they can talk they say 'Yes' and I'll just talk to some of them that want to talk. Just somebody to talk to. . . . Every now and then one might say, 'Well I'm glad to see your smiling face.'" As Jason cleaned, he livened up patients' moods. This in turn conferred a sense that he was contributing. It gave him purpose.

SEEK A STRONG SOCIAL MISSION

There are few more horrible deaths than that wrought by cystic fibrosis (CF). The disease is incurable. It kills its mainly young victims slowly by saturating their lungs with thick mucus. Eventually, those stricken with the disease suffocate. For the longest time, a diagnosis of CF meant a rapid death sentence. But over the last several decades, doctors have pioneered therapies that can lengthen a patient's life for decades.

In a 2004 *New Yorker* article titled "The Bell Curve," Atul Gawande described the work of Warren Warwick, a doctor of pediatric pulmonology at the University of Minnesota who became one of cystic fibrosis's greatest adversaries. During the 1960s, Warwick realized that he could lengthen the life of a child diagnosed with CF by finding ways to clear the kid's lungs. But Warwick wasn't interested in merely doing the best possible job with the technologies available at the time. He was determined to try every possible angle—and he did. In ensuing decades, he developed a new toolkit of therapies: new stethoscopes with special bells attached to track the symptoms; a chest-thumping vest used to break up the mucus in the lungs (so that it could be coughed up); and even a new technique for coughing that allowed more mucus to make its way out of a patient's lungs.

What Warwick found, over time, was that making small changes on the margins could improve each patient's lung capacity. At a glance, improving a patient's lung capacity from 99.5 percent to 99.95 percent didn't appear so significant. But in reality, it made a huge difference. Over the course of a year, it dropped a patient's odds of getting sick from 83 percent to 16 percent. For a kid living with CF, those reduced odds could increase his or her life expectancy. As Warwick's methods spread to others in his field, his contributions helped lift the life expectancy of this dreadful disease from about 10 years in the 1960s to nearly 40 years by 2013.[32]

Warwick maintained a strong sense of social mission—the highest level in the Purpose Pyramid—throughout his career. To assess whether you have climbed to the highest level of the purpose pyramid, consider how strongly you agree with this statement: "My work makes a strong contribution to society, beyond making money." Very few of the 2,000 self-report employees in our survey—17 percent—said they "completely agreed" with that statement. Those who did, however, performed better than those who didn't. They channeled their energy toward a greater social mission and labored more intensely, allowing them to achieve more every day they were on the job.

Whenever possible, seek out assignments and tasks that contribute socially, even just a little. Help your bosses understand ways to make a difference that they may have missed. And if you're a manager, find opportunities for your team to give back. In 2005, when Hurricane Katrina struck the Gulf Coast, a number of health organizations sent teams to help desperate storm victims. One of them was California-based Scripps Health, which mobilized a Medical Response Team it had created for the first time. As CEO Chris Van Gorder recounted, the effort galvanized the entire organization and created a new sense of pride in working at Scripps. Even employees at this large and formerly embattled health-care company who previously might not have felt a strong sense of purpose in their jobs wrote that they did now. One executive assistant described having shed "tears of pride and gratefulness for the courageous and selfless efforts of all the Scripps disaster relief team."[33] Scripps's managers helped their employees climb to the top of the Purpose Pyramid.

Many people experience a sense of emptiness because their job doesn't seem to serve a clear social purpose. But as the pyramid suggests, purpose at work isn't just about reaching the top level of contributing to society. It also includes adding value and finding personal meaning. If you lack a clear social mission at work, you can still discover purpose in your job by looking further down the pyramid. Try to craft activities that add more value and that also carry personal meaning.

INSPIRE YOURSELF—AND OTHERS

Achieving a match between passion and purpose—P-squared—is a smart way to work. Feeling passionately about what you do and making valuable contributions boosts your motivation. It charges you up to make the most of every hour you work. That extra energy translates into better performance.

You can infuse your job activities with both passion *and* purpose by using the three techniques I've described—selecting a new role, enlarging your circle of passion, and climbing the Purpose Pyramid. As you craft more passion and purpose into work, try shifting the metric in your mind from hours worked per week to energy per hour. Count the number of hours in a day in which you had high energy. Watch that number rise as you feel more passion and purpose.

Watch your output per hour increase as well, especially if you follow the other practices we discussed in chapters two, three, and four. As you infuse your work with passion and purpose, try channeling that energy into a few focus areas (do less, then obsess) that provide value (redesign for value) and that you keep on improving (learning loop).

P-squared is the "fuel"—the energy—that makes all this intense effort and concentration possible. It's how you can inspire yourself to become great at work. And once you have inspired yourself, you can inspire *other people* so that they will support your plans and goals. It is to this topic that we now turn.

P-SQUARED

The "Work Harder" Convention

Follow your passion at all costs and no matter how hard you work. If you do what you love, success will come. Conversely, if you *ignore passion*, you're setting yourself up for a career that is bleak, unsatisfying, and filled with drudgery.

The New "Work Smarter" Perspective

Passion is key, but doing *only* what you love is bad advice—it can lead to failure and ruin. The best course is to strive to *match passion with a strong sense of purpose*—to aim for P-squared. People who do so unleash a tremendous amount of energy that they apply to every hour on their job. They don't work the most hours. They work smart by aiming for the most effort per hour of work.

Key Points

- Many people either follow their passion, or they ignore their passion. But as our research shows, the issue of achieving passion at work is not a matter of "following" or "ignoring," but rather of "matching."
- In our study, managers and employees who matched passion and purpose performed far better than those who didn't. They were likely to place 18 percentile points higher than those who didn't in our 5,000-person dataset.
- People with a strong sense of both passion and purpose are more energized, getting more done in *each hour of work* (and they don't work many extra hours).

- There are three ways to expand your passions and sense of purpose:
    - *Discover a new role.* You can likely find that match right where you are; you don't have to leap to another profession. Seek a new role within your existing organization that better taps your passions and gives you a stronger sense of purpose.
    - *Expand the circle of passion.* Feeling passionate about work isn't just about taking pleasure in the work itself. Passion can also come from: success, creativity, social interactions, learning, and competence. Expand your circle of passion by tapping into these dimensions.
    - *Climb the Purpose Pyramid.* Find ways to add more *value* (from chapter three), taking care that your contributions don't cause harm. Second, pursue activities that are *personally meaningful*, no matter what others think. It helps to *reframe* one's job to experience the significance it might just hold for you. Third, pursue activities that have a clear *social mission*.

PART II

MASTERING WORKING WITH OTHERS

SIX

FORCEFUL CHAMPIONS

I've learned that people will forget what you said, people will forget what you did, but people will never forget how you made them feel.

—Maya Angelou[1]

You know those flashes of insight that come to you out of nowhere, like when you're standing in line or showering? Back in 1999, during the height of the dot-com boom, a young sales manager at Dow Chemical named Ian Telford had one such epiphany. Other salespeople at the time dreamed of hawking clothing, concert tickets, or hotel rooms online, but not Telford. He wanted to sell an industrial substance called epoxy online. Dow had long sold epoxy by the ton to large companies, but new online marketplaces were cropping up that would allow customers to find cheap epoxy providers—think Amazon.com for business transactions. Telford thought that Dow could create such a site called e-epoxy.com, sell its epoxy there at lower prices with no "frills," and appeal to a new market segment of smaller customers.

From another angle, this strategy seemed foolhardy, even crazy. If the same epoxy was available online at lower prices, what would stop Dow's existing customers from buying it cheaper there? Telford thought he knew. As he told me in interviews for our study, and as he related in an IMD business school case by professor Bala Chakravarthy, larger customers liked Dow's existing, high-touch sales process.[2] If they needed technical support or changes to existing orders, all they had to do was call their dedicated salesperson. By contrast, the new online business wouldn't offer any frills and have strict business rules and order penalties. Dow could pursue two different models for two different kinds of customers—one first class, the other economy.

Telford brought his idea to his leadership team. His argument was solid, he thought. Yet the leadership team hated it. Nine out of twelve members voted "no." "The leaders didn't think that our big customers would pay more for high-touch service," Telford explained. "They'd take the lower price offered online." Telford saw his bosses' rejection as typical of the company's risk-averse culture. "They didn't want to change what was already working. Why should they? There's a quote that people used to say: 'Dow is a company where everyone can say no and no one can say yes.'"

Accomplished in karate and extreme rock climbing, Telford didn't buckle under a challenge. He asked his manager for a second chance and was granted three months to draft a better plan. Reflecting on his bosses' reaction, Telford thought about his proposal from the leaders' perspective. They worried about pricing—and maybe they had a point. If a buyer at a large customer saw a lower price online, he or she would feel cheated. Imagine how a frequent flyer would react upon discovering that he'd paid twice the price for his airplane ticket than the first-time passenger seated next to him.

Pondering this problem, Telford dreamt up a nifty solution: What if the prices Dow showed online were higher than those available to their existing key customers? In that case, large customers wouldn't complain. They would say, "Well, those Internet customers are paying a lot for their epoxy, but *I'm* getting first-class service." Telford also proposed that e-epoxy.com offer a promo code for the new, smaller customers to enter online, allowing them to access a lower price or take part in special offers. Everyone would be happy.

Telford had cracked the pricing problem that had doomed his first proposal. Still, he was under no illusions. No matter how he presented his new idea, his bosses wouldn't "get it." They were the old guard, sitting in their comfortable offices in Zürich, Switzerland, or Midland, Michigan, far from Silicon Valley, the epicenter of the digital revolution. Someone had to rattle their traditional way of thinking. Telford had built a reputation inside Dow for doing just that.

In the weeks leading up to his big presentation about the new pricing scheme, Telford devised a bold (some might say reckless) plan for convincing his bosses. He drafted a fake email that would alert leaders at his company to an impending competitive announcement. As the rumor went, a major chemical distributor, two chemical competitors, and a large Internet company were joining forces to create a new online site called Epoxies-R-Us.com. When his bosses saw this correspondence, Telford reasoned, they would perceive the new online site as a major threat to Dow and agree to fund his epoxy idea. It didn't matter that the emails were fake. Telford would have made his point.

The email went out. To lend it credibility, Telford had a spoof television segment created where a journalist, an analyst, and a distributor (all acquaintances of Telford's who were in on the spoof) commented on the news and announced that Dow's stock price had tumbled 10 percent in response. Telford let it be known that through his contacts, he could rush a copy of the upcoming television interview to headquarters for the leadership team to preview.

On the day the video arrived, Telford holed himself up in a conference room and watched from a distance as the drama played out. Most people on the leadership team watched the video all the way through, oblivious to the ruse. The big boss, however, watched for thirty seconds before he shouted, "Telford!" and ran out the door. His boss's boss was angry and didn't talk to him for a month, but he acknowledged that the stunt "did serve as a wake-up call." Having aroused leaders' fears about the prospect of losing in the marketplace, Telford got $1 million in seed money to develop the e-epoxy.com venture. The pricing solution wasn't ideal, he thought, but he had made a workable concession with the promo code.

Then came an organizational earthquake. A new president, Bob Wood, took over the division after a reorganization. Wood put Telford's project on hold pending review (read: the death knell). If Telford had any hope of succeeding, he had to muster support for his project all over again—and fast. Unbowed, he got to work. He presented his idea to Wood's senior managers, convincing them to rank e-epoxy.com as the most critical project for the division to pursue. Then he cajoled his boss to set up an urgent meeting with Wood. In that session, Telford extolled the merits of his venture in the strongest possible terms. "The key was Ian's enthusiasm," Wood enthused. "I was betting on the entrepreneur. I had to look him in the eye and see if he had fire in his belly."[3] Wood approved the project.

Now Telford was in business, again. With a handpicked and terrific three-person team in place, he moved fast. But he faced one more obstacle. Dow's IT department sought to stifle his venture. They didn't want some lowly epoxy person like Telford building his own online system. "Our big fear was fragmentation and incompatibility," said one manager.[4] To neutralize their threat to shut him down, Telford resolved to become a model internal "customer." He labored to meet all of IT's requirements, including those for standardization, every time and on schedule. When the new online epoxy business clocked its first customer order, he picked up the phone and called to congratulate his IT colleagues, telling them, "This is as much your success as it is mine." Thanks to his outreach, IT came to see themselves as playing an important part in the project.

Fourteen months after its debut, the online e-epoxy.com business was operating in the United States and Europe. The site was built on time and under budget, and it became Dow's most successful e-business, creating a positive cash flow in less than a year. Telford was promoted, becoming one of Dow's top 200 leaders worldwide before leaving the company in 2008 for another endeavor.

CONVINCING OTHER PEOPLE

As Telford's story demonstrates, getting our work done hinges on our ability to gain support from others, including bosses, subordinates, peers, colleagues in other departments, and partners. These individuals control resources we need—information, expertise, money, staff, and political cover. Yet they may not wish to lend a hand, and they may even block our efforts. Telford would have gotten nowhere if he hadn't understood how to surmount obstacles without alienating the senior leaders and IT staff who opposed his project. His awareness of others' concerns coupled with his ability to convince enabled him to have substantial impact.

The ability to advocate for one's goals and gain the required support is only one of a broader set of people interaction skills required in modern workplaces. An IBM study of 1,709 CEOs concluded that "CEOs are changing the nature of work by adding a powerful dose of openness, transparency and employee empowerment to the command-and-control ethos."[5] Organizations are "flatter" and less hierarchical. As a result, employees and managers must interact more across departments and work more in teams, including teams composed of members from different departments.

That changes the skills you need to succeed in your job. In the IBM study, two-thirds of CEOs regarded collaboration and communication as "key drivers of employee success to operate in a more complex, interconnected environment." We found in our study that such complexity has made certain skills more important. As respondents told us, employees and managers now have to become more adept at working with people from many different departments, over whom they have no formal authority. A full 69 percent strongly or completely agreed with the statement that in their job it was "important to work with people from different areas of the company."

Analyzing our data, we found that top performers mastered working with others in three areas: advocacy, teamwork, and collaboration. The next chapter focuses on how to perform by working in teams, while chapter eight discusses how to collaborate effectively across boundaries. In this chapter, we explore the vital task of advocating for your goals so as to win other people's support.

CHAMPION FORCEFULLY

Many of us believe that we need to appeal to people's rational minds to gain their support for our projects and goals. Just *explain* the merits of the case using logic and data, and others will rise up in support. And so we present rational arguments in lengthy emails and PowerPoint presentations in an effort to convince. And if we can't snare people's attention with one email, well, we just send another one, and another one. If they don't "get it," we hammer our argument even harder. We fall once again into the "do-more" paradigm of work, drowning people in an all-too-familiar avalanche of emails, slides, texts, reports, and data. Communicating more of the same when people aren't listening or accepting our message doesn't seem like a smart way to work.

When we analyzed our case studies, I was struck by how the best performers went beyond rational arguments and adopted various tactics to advocate for their projects. I discovered that the best advocates—what I call *forceful champions*—effectively pursued their goals at work by mastering two skills to gain the support of other people. They inspired others by evoking emotions, and they circumvented resistance by deploying "smart grit."

First, the forceful champions in our study *inspired* people, appealing to their emotions as well as their rational minds to garner support. As Maya Angelou reminds us, people never forget how you make them *feel*. Her point is echoed by academic theories that show how leaders gain support by making others feel excited about their vision, goals, and plans.[6] While leadership theory often emphasizes the role of personal charisma in eliciting such emotions, you don't need to be charismatic to inspire others.[7] The forceful champions in our study used a number of practical techniques to stir emotions that everyone can adopt regardless of their job titles.

The second skill that the forceful champions in our study used, smart grit, entails persevering in the face of difficulty and deploying tailored tactics to overcome opposition to their effort.

Psychologists such as University of Pennsylvania professor Angela Duckworth have demonstrated that grit—which she defines as perseverance and passion for long-term goals—distinguishes successful people from others.[8] In pursuing their goals, forceful champions in our study applied such grit to overcome opposition. But rather than simply plod forward, mustering endless amounts of energy and verbiage to overcome obstacles, they also deployed smart tactics to address their colleagues' specific concerns. Like Ian Telford, they identified and "read" their opponents' intentions and took steps, such as compromising or co-opting, to convince them to support their cause.

As our study found, inspiring others and applying smart grit is a highly effective way to advocate for one's goals. The most forceful champions in our 5,000-person study were likely to be ranked 15 percentage points higher in their performance ranking than those who didn't practice these skills.[9] Ian Telford scored high in both areas: his inspirational score was 6.3 (out of a potential top score of 7), while his smart grit score was 6.8. His total forceful champion score placed him in the 97th percentile in our 5,000-person dataset, and he performed exceptionally well as we saw with the epoxy business. Like Telford, managers and employees in our study who scored high on both inspiration and smart grit performed much better than those who could manage either inspiration or smart grit, but not both.

Interestingly, the impact of being a more forceful champion was much larger for men than for women. Our data didn't explain why, although I can offer a few speculations. It may be that men deploy these tactics more effectively because they feel more confident trying to influence others, having done so more often over the years and perceiving it as "normal." Or perhaps gender stereotypes play a role, leading people to celebrate forceful tactics in men and disparage them in women. As studies have shown, people commonly perceive women in the workplace as either competent or liked, but not both.[10] Research shows that when competent women assert themselves, as forceful champions do, they risk being sanctioned and downgraded.[11] One study, for example, found that in a sample of seventy-six supervisory-employee relationships in a law enforcement agency in the southwestern United States, female employees who asserted themselves by using tactics such as "deal forcefully with others when they

Forceful Champions Perform Better

The More People Adopted the Forceful Champion Principle,
the Better They Performed (and Men More So Than Women)

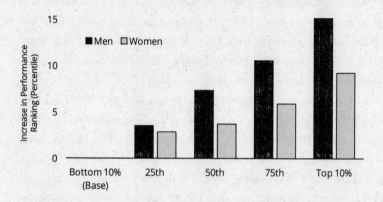

Note:
The chart shows the effect of becoming a more forceful champion on performance. For
example, a man who goes from not being forceful (bottom 10%) to very forceful (top 10%) is
likely to move up 15 percentiles in the performance ranking (e.g., from 70th to 85th percentile).

hamper their ability to get their job done" received *lower* performance
ratings than women who didn't use such tactics. Male colleagues, in contrast, received *higher* ratings when displaying the same behaviors.[12] So
when a boss evaluates a man who uses forceful champion tactics, the boss
may think, "Wow, smart guy." When a competent woman does the same,
he may think, "Really aggressive woman" and downgrade his perception
of her performance. Our finding in part may be shaped by such a gender
stereotype: People regard female forceful champions as performing more
poorly than their male counterparts, when in reality they are not.

Despite the gender difference, everyone in our study benefited from
becoming forceful champions. Let's examine the forceful champion tactics in more detail, considering first the task of appealing to others' emotions so that they *want* to support our efforts.

MAKE THEM UPSET . . . AND EXCITED

A great way to inspire others is to foster both negative and positive emotions—getting people upset about the present and excited about the future. Ian Telford got it all wrong at first. In proposing his idea for an online business, he aroused negative emotions among the managers. They worried that the future online business would cannibalize their existing business. And they felt happy about the present state—meaty profits from that existing business.

Telford's spoof reversed those emotions, rendering his bosses *fearful* about the current state (falling behind the competition) and *joyful* about the prospect of keeping existing customers and adding revenues from new online customers. Now their emotions lined up in Telford's favor, and they supported his proposal. Of course, the prank was borderline unethical, and as such it sparked an additional emotion that risked getting out of hand: anger—at him.

Telford's strategy points to an important insight about emotions: When your goal is to convince, not all emotions are equal. In a study reported in his book *Contagious*, Wharton Business School professor Jonah Berger scrutinized online messages, and specifically the importance of "high arousal" emotions. These emotions prompt a "state of activation and readiness for action. The heart beats faster and blood pressure rises."[13] Excitement and joy are high arousal emotions, as are anxiety and anger. Contentment and sadness aren't. In his analysis of *New York Times* articles published over a three-month period, Berger and coauthor Katherine Milkman found that articles producing high-arousal emotions were 24 to 38 percent more likely to make the "most e-mailed" list than those that evoked other types of emotions.[14] People acted on those high-arousal emotions. "Make people mad, not sad," Berger concludes.

To inspire people and gain their support, line up high-arousal emotions on your side—make them mad and fearful about the present, and joyful and excited about your proposed future goal. The chart "Lining Up Emotions in the Right Ways" lists high-arousal emotions that you will want to provoke when persuading others to follow your lead.

Lining Up Emotions in the Right Ways

Arouse Negative Emotions About the Status Quo	Evoke Positive Emotions About the Future State (i.e., Your Goal)
Fear	Excitement
Anger	Joy
Frustration	Passion
Resentment	Thrill
Disgust	Ecstasy
Anxiety	Delight

Many of us stumble by lining up "high arousal" emotions incorrectly. Mike Lunden, a forty-five-year-old manager in our study, had a nifty cost-cutting idea for the sales office he was managing: no more free coffee in the office.[15] The policy backfired, leading to minuscule cost savings and disgruntled employees. Why? Because the change sparked fury among his office workers about the future state (no free coffee) and nostalgia about the status quo (that delightful aroma of fresh-brewed dark roast in the morning). Lunden could have taken a different approach. He could have angered his team members by pointing to the paltry bonuses they'd received the past year, and he could have fired up his team by showing them how much bigger the bonus pool would be if they could reduce operational costs. He could have made team members upset about today and excited for tomorrow—as opposed to the other way around.

SHOW IT (DON'T JUST TELL)

In 2009, celebrity chef Jamie Oliver faced an arduous task: convincing residents of Huntington, West Virginia, America's most unhealthy town, to eat more healthily.[16] Arriving at an elementary school, he prepared a delicious and healthy meal of chicken and vegetables and asked the kids: "Chicken or pizza?"

"Pizza!" they yelled.

Oliver could have reasoned with parents, convincing them to change the behavior of their little pizza lovers. He could have recited the brutal facts: 32 percent of the town was obese, and three in five kids were overweight.[17] Yet rational arguments probably wouldn't work, not least because many locals were skeptical of Oliver. West Virginia had long been the butt of jokes among residents of wealthier parts of the United States. Having a British chef come to teach them how to cook—well, that was too much.[18]

Oliver dispensed with rational arguments. He convened a meeting of parents and kids in a parking lot. They arrived to find Oliver directing a giant truck into the lot, microphone in hand. Backing up toward the parents and kids, the truck dumped a massive load of pure animal fat into a huge open dumpster right in front of them. A big, white, disgusting mountain of fat. Giant, jiggling blobs of it.

"This is the fat consumed by the entire school for one year!" Oliver yelled. He jumped on top of the mound, grabbed a chunk, held it up, and cried, "Come feel it!"

"Nooo!" the kids screamed back in disgust.

The parents were aghast.

Oliver lifted a hunk of fat into the air and addressed the parents. "Are you fine with this?"

"Nooooo!" they shouted.

Oliver surveyed the crowd. "You need to know I am on your side," he said. And then came the pitch: "Parents, will you support me?"

"Yes!" they howled.

Oliver knew he needed to arouse emotions, but he also knew that words—even rich, vibrant ones—wouldn't garner the impact he desired. So he endeavored to *show not tell* what kids were eating at school. The mountain of fat looked ugly, and it *was* ugly. The sight of it hit parents in their gut and generated feelings of anger and disgust (and, I am sure, guilt). Oliver aroused negative feelings about the status quo and then led the charge with a passion for healthier eating.

Like Oliver, a number of people in our study used photos, artifacts, videos, and demonstrations to dramatize their arguments and stir up emotions. Remember Anne from Skyline Hospital, as discussed in chapter two? To convince the cardiologists to cut out their step in the treatment of heart attack patients, she didn't just argue with numbers. No, she took them on a road trip and *showed* them another hospital that had accomplished the feat. They could literally stand there and watch the "demonstration" unfold as the staff at that other hospital went through the steps without the cardiologist.

Yet "showing, not telling" is by no means a common tactic. Only 18 percent of people in our 5,000-person dataset scored high on the statement, "frequently taps into people's emotions to get them excited about their work." That's too bad. As our study also revealed, arousing emotional responses gets results, including for junior people. In fact, about 19 percent of people in either a senior job position (division manager) or a junior one (technical specialist) scored very high on their ability to stir emotions.

Consider Elise, a thirty-three-year-old junior purchasing employee at a large global manufacturer. She was spearheading a project converting paper forms to electronic ones.[19] Although she was convinced that they could save money this way, it was difficult to excite people over such a mundane initiative. Hearing that the firm's CEO was visiting her Swiss subsidiary, Elise dumped a pile of paper and dozens of thick binders full of regulations and paperwork onto a table in a large conference room. Imagine—thousands of pages rising two to three feet high. When the CEO arrived, Elise escorted him into the room and explained what he was looking at. "Holy cow!" the CEO burst out, stupefied and frustrated. "Why do we use so much paper?" From then on, Elise and her project received support.

MAKE THEM *FEEL* PURPOSE

Our study revealed a third technique that forceful champions use to inspire people: connecting daily work to a broader purpose. Many companies have "purpose" or "mission" statements: one of the best known is Disney's purpose "to make people happy."[20] But purpose isn't just something for companies and CEOs. It's for all of us. As we saw in chapter five, individuals perform better if they have a strong sense of purpose in their work. You can also use purpose to inspire *other people* so that they will commit to your projects and goals.

In 2015, I delivered a keynote address to senior leaders at the life science, high-tech firm Agilent Technologies.[21] Before my presentation, I stood at the back of the auditorium as the speaker preceding me, an Agilent executive named Jacob Thaysen, presented his division's strategy. His business develops instruments used by scientists in the course of developing new drug treatments and diagnosing diseases. His presentation was dense with numbers and facts to outline and support the strategy. Some in the audience slouched in their chairs and strained to follow his impressive command of the numbers and logic.

In the course of wrapping up, Thaysen said, "I would like to highlight how our instruments have an impact." I was expecting still more slides, but instead he played a video clip from the Forbes Healthcare Summit.[22] It showed an athletic, twenty-two-year-old woman named Corey Wood who was stricken by lung cancer. She related how advanced instrumentation and DNA sequencing had allowed her doctors to understand her disease on a molecular level. Determining that her normally fatal cancer stemmed from a specific genetic abnormality, her doctors administered a targeted drug treatment that cured her of the disease. She was alive and healthy, she said, tears welling in her eyes as she thanked everyone who had helped save her young life.

As Corey Wood spoke, audience members sat up straight and ignored their smartphones, captivated by the young woman's story. After the video, Thaysen made the connection: "Her treatment would not have been possible without the instruments and reagents we develop." Silence. You could almost see a giant speech bubble hovering over the room: *Now that's why we come to work.*

In the single, masterful moment that Thaysen orchestrated, work became connected with deeper purpose. Six months later, when I had lunch with Agilent CEO Mike McMullen and human resources vice president Dominique Grau, they told me that people were still talking about that moment.

While Thaysen inspired a crowd with a lofty purpose, people in our study managed to connect an overarching purpose to even the most tedious of tasks.[23] Fernando Lopez was a thirty-seven-year-old supply chain specialist working for a New Jersey medical device company.[24] Managing all the manufacturing done by external suppliers for the company's dialysis product, he felt a direct connection between his daily tasks and the compelling purpose of helping dialysis patients. But the people working in the outsourced manufacturing plants didn't feel that at all: "They do a piece of the pie for us, and they don't understand necessarily what the pie is," Lopez said. As a result, they weren't working as intensely as they might have when manufacturing and shipping the company's product.

To inspire the plant workers, Lopez traveled to their site to meet with them. "I gave them a lot of background and understanding on what they're actually doing, what they're doing for us and why it's valuable. I showed them that what they were doing was actually helping patients with kidney failures. And it resonated with everyone; I got a lot of feedback . . . about how that had inspired them to put a little bit of extra effort into what they were doing, because they realized it had a big impact." The manufacturing team did a better job supporting Lopez's scheduling and quality goals, increasing Lopez's own performance. He scored in the top 15 percent on the forceful champion behaviors and landed in the top 20 percent in our performance ranking.

Research confirms the power of connecting daily work to purpose. Wharton professor Adam Grant and colleagues conducted a study of people working at a call center to raise university alumni donations for scholarships.[25] Hour after hour, the callers worked on the phone, struggling through frequent rejections and never witnessing what happened with the money they raised. To change this, their manager showed the callers letters written by thankful students who'd received scholarships funded through their efforts. He then arranged a meeting with a scholarship student who explained to the callers face-to-face how their efforts had transformed his life. "Remember this when you're on the phone— this is someone you're supporting," the manager remarked at the end of this meeting. A month later, their weekly average fundraising increased from $185.94 to $503.22. If you make people *feel* the purpose, they will try that much harder to help you achieve your goals.

The tactics of lining up emotions properly, showing (and not just telling), and making people feel purpose enable you to inspire people so that they will support your efforts. Everyone can use these tactics; you don't have to have a charismatic personality to inspire colleagues at work.

Yet sometimes these inspirational tactics alone are not enough to overcome opposition to your plans and goals. Forceful champions, we learned in our study, also persevere against a constant stream of obstacles to reach their goals.

SMART GRIT

In 1998, Arunachalam Muruganantham, a resident of the rural village of Coimbatore in the Indian state of Tamil Nadu, caught his young bride Shanthi hiding something from him. She was collecting filthy rags, and when he inquired, she admitted that she used them to absorb blood during menstruation. "I would not even use it to clean my scooter," he confessed. He asked why she didn't use sanitary pads. She replied that if she bought pads she'd have to "cut our family milk budget."

Muruganantham decided to do something about it. He set out to develop his own cheap pad that his wife and others could use. He first designed a prototype sanitary pad made of local cotton and asked his wife to try it. It didn't work and his wife soon returned to using a rag. He realized that it would take years to develop a marketable product if he could only test it on his wife once a month. So he tried to conscript her sister, but she refused. Then he approached female medical students in the area, who rejected him as well. In this traditional society, no one seemed eager to help a lowly, uneducated villager (Muruganantham had dropped out of school at age fourteen to support his family).

Muruganantham eventually convinced twenty medical students to try his homemade pad and complete a survey. One day, however, he caught three girls filling out their surveys with fake data, sinking his "study."[26] With no one to test his experimental pad, he had crashed.

Then an idea occurred to him: Maybe he could test it on himself. He filled the bladder of a soccer ball with goat's blood that he obtained from a butcher friend. He strapped the bladder under his garment, donned a sanitary pad, and clambered about, squeezing it as if it were his uterus to see if his invention would absorb the squirts. Unfortunately, the goat blood started to stink in the heat. Some of the villagers suspected that he had gone mad.

It got worse. After months of this eccentric behavior, his wife couldn't stand the social censure and moved out. That should have been the end of it, but Muruganantham kept going. Determined to study used sanitary pads, he approached the medical students again and gave them pads, which he later collected. One Sunday, his mother caught him studying rows of bloody pads lined up in the backyard and started to cry. She, too, moved out.

The villagers were convinced that he was possessed by evil spirits and threatened to chain him upside down to a tree to be cleansed by the local soothsayer. Muruganantham escaped only by agreeing to leave the village. "I was left all alone in life," Muruganantham said. Yet he soldiered on.

Noting that cotton releases liquid under pressure, he wondered what material multinationals like Procter & Gamble and Johnson & Johnson used in their pads that allowed them to retain liquid. Only when Muruganantham got his hands on samples of the raw material did he realize what he was up against. The big companies employed expensive machines to process tree bark into cellulose, which doesn't release absorbed liquid when squeezed. Time to give up?

Muruganantham kept going. He figured that he needed to build his own mini cellulose plant. He started from scratch, breaking the task into four parts: defibration, packing, wrapping and finishing, and disinfection. He fabricated simple devices for each, powering them wherever possible by humans pedaling.

Four and a half years later, he had his machines. They were simple and cheap, and they looked scrappy, but they converted cellulose into sanitary pads at low cost. He had his pad, finally.

Muruganantham distributed free sanitary pads to the villagers who had banished him. The next day, he spotted kids playing with them in the streets and men using them to buff their scooter headlights. But women weren't using them. He had built it, but no one came. As we discussed in chapter three, he fulfilled his objective (building the machine) but created zero value for its intended beneficiaries (women benefiting from using the pads).

By any measure of grit, Muruganantham was off the charts. He spent *seven years* pressing ahead against severe obstacles. Although such perseverance is extreme, it is not uncommon. About a quarter of managers and employees (27 percent) in our study scored very high on the statement, "He/she relentlessly pursues objectives, no matter the obstacles he/she faces." Ian Telford at Dow Chemical scored a 7 (highest) on this statement: as we saw, he kept pursuing his venture, even though it met with resistance at first and almost died when a new boss arrived. Telford and the other such gritty people in our study performed better than those who didn't show grit, confirming the general hypothesis that sheer grit helps people reach goals and perform. Yet as Muruganantham's case suggests, such traditional grit has its limits. Muruganantham persevered in pursuing his goal, and it got him nowhere.

To vanquish opposition in the workplace, you must do more than persevere. *You also need to tailor your tactics to neutralize opposition from people.* Although Muruganantham had made the pads available and affordable, he had alienated the very people he was trying to help—his wife, mother, sister, and the poor villagers. As a result, they weren't using and spreading the word about his pads. His relentless pursuit—his grit—prompted him to adjust elements of his production or operational strategy (where to get the pads, how to test his idea, how to build the machine), but his approach to people remained rigid. He didn't listen to their concerns and instead barreled ahead. His sheer grit frightened them away.

Grit at work is not about putting your head down and bulldozing through successive walls of resistance. *Smart* grit involves not only persevering but also taking into account the perspective of people you're trying to influence and devising tactics that will win them over.

EMPATHIZE WITH YOUR OPPONENTS

Warm sunlight filtered in through the windows at Volpi Foods, a small St. Louis company selling Italian cured meat like salami and prosciutto.[27] Lorenza Pasetti, who would take over the family business from her father, was away at a foods show. It was a perfect time for staff back in the office to catch up on some admin. Then the office fax machine spat out a terse message from one of Volpi's biggest customers, the giant retailer Costco. Pasetti was chatting with a customer when she received a frantic call from the office. The fax was a copy of a threatening letter sent to Costco from the U.S. attorney of the powerful Consorzio del Prosciutto di Parma, one of Italy's global enforcers of food trademarks. "The letter denounced our prosciutto product and charged Volpi with infringement of U.S. label law," Pasetti explained in an interview for our study. "This situation was nothing short of a crisis—and it attacked Volpi's reputation, one we had built over a century."

It was the first volley in a surprise assault. The Consorzio charged Volpi with violating the law through its use of words like "Italian," "traditional," and "prosciutto" on its label, claiming that the company did not use traditional Italian methods for curing the meat. The charge would trigger a U.S. Department of Agriculture (USDA) investigation. Fearing a Consorzio lawsuit for carrying Volpi products, clients like Costco might pull their products from the shelves.

Pasetti jumped on the phone with the USDA to see where she stood. The regulators made it worse. Although they had approved Volpi's product labeling, they now claimed to have erred. They ordered Volpi to remove the word "Italian" from the labels. Their entire brand identity was based on being Italian, and now they couldn't use the word Italian?

Pasetti wasn't sure what to do. She could go on the offensive, but few in her company had the heart for a long legal battle. Her father, who had run the business for forty-five years, saw no way out. As Pasetti related, her dad "comes from a generation that believes in attorneys and trusts what they say. That generation wouldn't think of going against what attorneys told you. My brother-in-law, who was in the family business at that time, also thought we should give in."

Instead of countering right away, Pasetti spent time reflecting on the situation. She tried to see the issue from the Consorzio's point of view. Why were they after Volpi? Researching it, she realized that they weren't out to grab market share in the United States for domestic Italian producers. No, the Consorzio seemed obsessed with protecting the Italian heritage in production methods. Making sure "Italian" meant "Italian"—that was what the fight was about.

Based on this insight, Pasetti crafted a strategy. Forget about the American lawyer. Forget about the USDA. Pasetti would take the fight to the homeland. As a first-generation Italian American, she spoke fluent Italian and had visited the old country hundreds of times for work and pleasure. "I buy a lot of equipment from Italy," she explained, "and most of the manufacturers are located around the northern Italian city of Parma. . . . I asked one of the oldest and most respected equipment manufacturers to organize a meeting between the consortium and me. I thought that if they met me and I explained who we are and how we keep their traditions alive, they would agree to talk to their U.S. attorney. And by talking to the attorney, I meant tell him to back off."

On a sweltering day in August, Pasetti showed up in Parma and strode into the meeting room of her friend's equipment manufacturing headquarters. Facing her from across the massive 300-year-old table were two Italian businessmen nearly twice her age. She told them the Volpi story—how the family company had maintained a painstaking commitment to the Italian curing method, handed down from one generation to the next. She implored the Consorzio leaders to have some mercy on a company with a rich Italian heritage. "It was a little bit of theater, but it worked," Pasetti said, smiling. The old men were convinced. The Consorzio relented.

Pasetti's story illustrates how we can deploy smart grit in professional settings. Her first step in overcoming the opposition was to understand *why* the men in Italy were threatening her business. When she saw the situation from their point of view, she realized it had to do with Italian heritage. That was the crucial insight. Psychologists call her approach "cognitive empathy," which we can define as the capacity to understand another's perspective or mental state.[28] In his book *Power*, Stanford

Business School professor Jeffrey Pfeffer states that "putting yourself in the other's place is one of the best ways to advance your own agenda."[29] He notes, however, that our obsession with our own concerns and objectives prevents us from doing so. We assume that opponents just don't "get it," and thus we pummel them with more facts and arguments in an effort to *make* them get it. That's working hard, not smart.

Why might colleagues oppose you? Maybe they have conflicting agendas and their priorities clash with yours. A colleague might want to obtain resources for his marketing project, but your project will make that more difficult, so he will oppose your goals. People in organizations also play favorites (and you might not be among them). Alternatively, colleagues may perceive your department as an enemy and thus seek to undermine your efforts, even though they have nothing against you personally. In other situations, people may feel threatened by change, and they may perceive your proposal as too risky. That's how Dow's leadership reacted to Ian Telford's idea. Other times, people simply lack time or budget to lend you their support. Maybe their budgets just got cut, and your project drops to the bottom of their priority list.

Often, people's objections are reasonable, if you only take the time to see the issue from their point of view. Figure out what their considerations are, and you can take steps to surmount them.

CONFRONT . . . OR MAKE CONCESSIONS

Smart grit isn't just about empathizing. Action matters. Once Pasetti understood her opponents' position, she decided to confront the Consorzio in person. The tactic worked for her, yet confrontation can prove risky. Another option, making concessions, carries far less risk. Ian Telford conceded certain parts of his plan so as to overcome opposition to his e-epoxy .com business. After his first failed attempt, he empathized with the leadership team members and understood their anxiety about showing the prices on the Internet. To appease the opposing members, he offered to publicize a very high price on the Internet and then use the "promo code" to give customers the real price. Without this concession, his venture never would have gone forward, as the senior leaders would have voted it down yet again. A promo code wasn't ideal, but he could tolerate it. The pricing accommodation wasn't "do or die" for Telford, as the labeling was for Pasetti at Volpi Foods. He could find a middle ground. Whenever you can, give in a little bit to silence the naysayers.

INVITE THE OPPOSITION INTO YOUR TENT

When you can't bring yourself to concede anything, try turning your adversaries into allies, or as academics call it, co-opting them. Ian Telford deployed such tactics with the corporate information technology department that sought to torpedo his venture. He first strove to understand their concern (their desire to standardize IT systems across the company). Then he labored to alleviate those concerns and become a model internal customer. To grasp complicated IT issues, he spent hours talking to external IT firms like Accenture. He learned IT-specific terms to speak their "language." Understanding their constraints prevented him from making unreasonable demands, as so many Dow managers did. When the new online epoxy business clocked its first customer order, he even picked up the phone and called IT to congratulate them. "That gesture made a big difference," Telford said. "It made the IT folks feel like co-owners of the project. And the more they felt that way, the easier it was to get them and keep them on my side."

Our tendency when confronted by opponents is to pull out our swords and charge into battle. Yet sometimes it serves our own interests to make people part of our project, if possible. President Lyndon B. Johnson is supposed to have quipped about an opponent: "it's probably better to have him inside the tent pissing out, than outside pissing in."[30] Whenever you can, work smart and invite the opposition into your tent.

MOBILIZE PEOPLE (DON'T GO IT ALONE)

There is one more act to the story about Muruganantham, the "menstrual man," as he is sometimes called.[31] Once he had built the machine and produced the pads that women didn't use, his project had stalled. Seven years of hard work had yielded zero value for the women he aimed to help. But rather than give up, he realized his mistake and tried to fix it. He had barreled ahead without involving impoverished women, the very group he had tried to help. So now he turned his strategy around. He began to enlist women's help *in convincing other women* to use the sanitary pads.

With some aid money, Muruganantham placed machines in several villages and trained local women to use, produce, and sell the pads. Now women rallied to set up machines and start businesses. They began educating other women and selling pads to them. Not only were they helping improve health and hygiene; they were seizing the opportunity to become entrepreneurs and earn a living selling pads. By mobilizing women to convince yet more women, Muruganantham built an ever-growing coalition of influencers.

Impact, at last. Muruganantham's own wife and mother returned, and the villagers took him back. This smart grit tactic, and not grit alone, made him succeed.

Too many people try to get others to change by doing all the convincing themselves. They become lone crusaders for their efforts—and they exhaust themselves in the process.

It's better to enlist even just a few people to help convince others. In our study, some managers and employees rallied emissaries; 29 percent scored high on the statement, "She/he is very effective in mobilizing people to make change happen." Ian Telford scored a 7 (highest) on this statement. As you'll remember, he mobilized his boss to get an urgent meeting with the new top brass, Bob Wood, to plead for his venture. He didn't advocate alone. As our data showed, those like Telford who mobilized people performed better (the correlation between the mobilization aspect and performance was a high 0.66).

BETTER WORKPLACES, TOO

Ian Telford, Lorenza Pasetti, Jamie Oliver, Arunachalam Muruganantham—each channeled considerable energy and wisdom to gain other people's support. These individuals didn't wield formal authority over the people whom they sought to convince. Nor did they rely on personal charisma to dazzle their colleagues and others into submission. Rather, they mustered inspirational tactics and deployed smart grit to overcome opposition. Their tactics were behaviors, not personality traits. You, too, can learn to use these tactics effectively. The benefits are considerable. Forceful champions increase their performance, and they also build positive relationships with colleagues, customers, bosses, and others. Deploying forceful champion techniques allows us to amass this vital social capital, making it easier for us to galvanize support in the future.

Forceful champion techniques also enable us to change the tenor of our workplaces. By inspiring others and deploying smart grit, we can render work more engaging and exciting for everyone. Adversaries become neutral or even friendly, and the workplace becomes a more enjoyable setting. That is not to say that the workplace becomes conflict-free, or even that it should be. When your team faces a difficult problem and needs to make a decision, you *want* a certain amount of conflict between colleagues. As we'll see in the next chapter, conflict is part of performing in teams—and a key part of becoming great at work.

KEY INSIGHTS

FORCEFUL CHAMPIONS

The "Work Harder" Conventions

We often think that all we have to do is explain time and again the wonderful merits of our case, and bosses, peers, and employees will rise in support. We also believe that sheer grit—perseverance and passion for long-term goals—will allow us to overcome opposition to our work efforts. These conventions lead us to work harder—to communicate and then communicate some more, and to apply massive effort over time to overcome obstacles.

The New "Work Smarter" Perspective

The best performers don't just argue rationally for their ideas. They compel others to support them by deploying a two-punch maneuver. First, they *inspire* by evoking emotions in individuals whose support they need. Second, they apply *smart grit*, tailoring and adjusting their tactics in the face of opposition. Forceful champions—those who inspire others and apply smart grit—are more likely to persevere and achieve their goals at work.

Key Points

- In our 5,000-person dataset, forceful champions overall were likely to score a substantial 15 percentage points higher in their performance ranking than those who didn't inspire or use smart grit.
- Forceful champions use a variety of behaviors to arouse emotions and *inspire* coworkers to support their efforts:
  - They make people angry about today and excited for tomorrow.
  - They *show and don't just tell*, using striking photos and demos to evoke intense emotions.
  - They make people *feel* purpose, connecting daily tedious work to a grander purpose.

- Forceful champions display *smart grit* to break down opposition and garner support for their projects:
  - They consider the perspective of opponents ("standing in their shoes"), tailoring their tactics to address opponents' specific concerns and agendas.
  - They confront opponents, when needed.

- They make concessions they can live with to appease opponents.
- They co-opt opponents, so that they, too, feel a sense of ownership.
- They exert pressure by mobilizing people to advocate on their behalf.

SEVEN

FIGHT AND UNITE

Diversity in Counsel, Unity in Command

—Cyrus the Great[1]

Ulises Carbo was going to make history.[2] He and 1,400 other Cuban exiles were part of a planned invasion that would liberate Cuba in 1961 from Fidel Castro's communist regime. Air, naval, and ground forces had all been trained and mobilized. The strategy was to land on the beach, push aside the small defensive force, and inspire Cubans by the tens of thousands to rise up and march on Castro's army.

Carbo was on board the freighter *Houston*. One of the four transport freighters, it left first with its cargo of men, fuel, and ammunition to rendezvous with the landing craft at the Bay of Pigs the night of April 16. Battle plans started to go sideways when the promised landing craft failed to show on time. Outboard motorboats meant for shore patrol were pressed into service. The noise from the steam davits—cranelike devices used to lower the motorboats over the side of the ship—alerted the Cuban defensive forces to the invaders' approach.

The delayed craft was supposed to have landed everybody in an hour and a half. Instead, by sunrise, only half of the troops were ashore. By dawn, the *Houston* and the other ships came under attack by T-33 fighters and aging Hawker Sea Fury fighters. At about 8:00 a.m., the Castro army fired two rockets that ripped giant holes amidships. Captain Luis Morse, seeing that repair was hopeless, drove the *Houston* toward land to beach it. It sank, with only a few feet of superstructure above the water, half a mile from shore. The oil oozing from its wounds made evacuation difficult. Non-swimmers were packed into two thirty-man lifeboats, while Carbo and the others struggled to swim ashore. Carbo managed to stay afloat by shedding his pants and boots. He ended up standing on the beach in his underwear.

Carbo and his fellow invaders still succeeded in pressing past the meager defense forces on the beach. But over the next three days, Castro's 20,000 soldiers wrested control. The invaders were captured or killed. The uprising never materialized. Castro later traded the survivors to the United States for food and medicine. It was not the kind of history Carbo and his fellow men had hoped to make.

So who planned and implemented this fiasco? It must have been the B team, right? Actually it was "the best and the brightest," a group of exceptionally qualified men in President John F. Kennedy's administration.[3]

Arthur Schlesinger, a Harvard historian who had been appointed special advisor to Kennedy, participated in the meetings where leaders

MIGUEL VINAS / AFP

Bay of Pigs: Cuban Exile Soldiers Captured by Castro's Army

discussed whether to launch the covert military force into an area known as the Bay of Pigs. As Schlesinger recounted, "an intimidating group sat around the table—the Secretary of State, the Secretary of Defense, the director of the Central Intelligence Agency, three Joint Chiefs resplendent in uniforms and decorations."[4] Allen Dulles, head of the CIA, and Richard M. Bissell, deputy, were the masterminds behind the Bay of Pigs scheme, with Bissell showing maps and pitching to the group in the White House. According to Schlesinger, Bissell's mind "was swift and penetrating, and he had an unsurpassed talent for lucid analysis and fluent exposition."[5] Other talented participants included Robert McNamara, Secretary of Defense and former president of the Ford Motor Company; and McGeorge Bundy, National Security Advisor, who at age thirty-four became the youngest-ever dean of the Faculty of Arts and Science at Harvard University.

The problem with these group meetings wasn't lack of intelligence in the room. It was lack of critical thinking and thorough debate about the plan, its assumptions, and its weaknesses. You know those stilted meetings at work when everyone nods their heads and nobody has the courage to raise a dissenting view? That's what happened here. Before making the decision, President Kennedy asked for the opinion of his advisors, including Undersecretary of State Thomas Mann, who earlier had opposed the plan privately with his boss. "As everybody present expressed support," Mann said, "I did the same."[6] Recalled Secretary of Defense McNamara: "I don't think Secretary of State Dean Rusk and I were enthusiastic, but we did not say no, don't do it."[7] McGeorge Bundy, the national security advisor, abdicated responsibility: "It was not my job to be in visible dis-agreement with the President; once he leaned in favor, I supported him." Schlesinger offered his doubts at the outset, sending several memos to President Kennedy outlining the hazards. But in the crucial days leading up to the decision, he, too, censored his objections, and he lived to regret it. "I bitterly reproached myself for having kept so silent during those crucial discussions in the Cabinet Room."[8]

The Bay of Pigs disaster stands as a monument to a horrible team decision-making process. As the leader of the group, President Kennedy failed to foster a rigorous debate. The individual participants failed, too, in their responsibilities to voice dissent and articulate the downsides of the proposed plan. The best and the brightest failed.

MEETINGS, MEETINGS, AND MORE MEETINGS

As this fiasco demonstrates, how leaders and participants behave in teams can affect their individual performance a great deal. People achieve not just alone, but also by working in teams. In our 5,000-person study, a full 80 percent of people reported that leading teams well was "really important" in their jobs. Teamwork involves dividing up work among individuals, coordinating that work, debating in meetings, deciding, and implementing what's been decided.

Much of a team's work occurs in group meetings. It follows, then, that a team's performance and your own individual performance hinge on the quality of team meetings—how well people debate issues, and how fully they commit to implementing decisions.

While team meetings are a crucial part of teamwork, many of them aren't effective. And there are lots of them. One source that summarized a range of studies calculated that 36 to 56 million meetings occur every day in the United States.[9] And yet, in a worldwide Microsoft survey of 38,000 people, 69 percent said their meetings weren't productive.[10] A Harris poll of 2,066 employees even found that almost half of respondents would "prefer to do almost anything else instead of sitting in a status meeting." Would they rather watch paint dry? A full 17 percent said yes. Root canal? Eight percent nodded their heads.[11]

What do you do if your team has a poor meeting where you didn't resolve the issues? Meet again! One participant in our 5,000-person study who works in the finance department of a midsize manufacturing plant scolded Karen, his forty-two-year-old manager: "My boss plans too many unnecessary meetings that rarely have final results. The meeting result is another planned meeting."[12] *One perverse consequence of all those ineffective team meetings is that they lead to even more meetings.* We end up with volumes of activity—a "work harder" approach—because we didn't have a rigorous discussion in the first place.

We don't need teams to conduct a vast number of meetings to get their work done. Rather, we need *smarter* team meetings where people debate rigorously and commit to decisions. But how do we accomplish that?

HAVING ONE HECK OF A FIGHT

In 2009, my quest to understand the secret behind superior team performance took me to Slough, an industrial area near London's Heathrow Airport. As part of a study unrelated to this book, my colleagues Herminia Ibarra, Urs Peyer, and I had decided to create a ranking of the best-performing CEOs of major public companies (this study was published in the *Harvard Business Review* in 2010 and 2013).[13] We pulled data on 2,000 CEOs and companies from across the world for every year since 1995. Stitching together reams of data across numerous spreadsheets, we ranked the CEOs from 1 to 2,000 based on stock market performance.

When I received the final spreadsheet one morning sitting at my desk, I opened it, rubbed my hands in anticipation, and began scanning it from the top on down. The top-performing CEO was no surprise: Steve Jobs of Apple. The next few names were familiar, too—leaders like Amazon's Jeff Bezos and others from fast-growing high-tech and energy companies. Numbers five, six, seven, eight were all pretty interesting, but not surprising. Nine, ten, eleven, twelve, thirteen, fourteen, fifteen—I yawned and looked out the window.

Then I got to number sixteen. I put down my coffee mug. What was this? A CEO named Bart Becht, who ran a company called Reckitt Benckiser in England. I'd never heard of them. I looked up Reckitt Benckiser on the Internet. I assumed it must be some cool high-tech company or an energy firm exploiting a growing market. As the company's page loaded, I almost fell off my chair. They sell soap. For dishwashers.

The dishwasher soap industry is not exactly a high-growth business.

So how can you sell soap and be a *top 1 percent* performer among 2,000 companies? Okay, Reckitt Benckiser sells more than just soap, but still.

I had to find out, so I called Bart Becht and asked if we could perform an analysis of them as part of our study.[14] He agreed, and my research associates and I flew to company headquarters in Slough. We entered a small room lined with shelves holding the company's cleaning products. The place was little more than a closet—no fancy boardroom, no floor-to-ceiling windows, no portraits of the board of directors. There we interviewed Becht and later seven other executives. As we discovered, the company's superior performance had *a lot* to do with how their teams ran meetings.

Two team meeting principles stood out among the rest. The first was something most of us don't feel good about: fighting.

When teams have a good *fight* in their meetings, team members debate the issues, consider alternatives, challenge one another, listen to minority views, scrutinize assumptions, and enable every participant to speak up without fear of retribution.

As Becht told us, he didn't like bland meetings in which everyone just went along with others and helped them feel good. No, he liked charged meetings in which people disagreed, argued, and yes, even fought. "We actually encourage 'constructive conflict'!" he said. "When there is a group of people who feel passionately about a set of ideas, I want to ensure those ideas are allowed to flourish. They should not be silenced by the majority consensus. And if they come armed with facts and are prepared to argue their point of view, they will be encouraged to keep working away. . . . Of course, this can lead to some lively meetings."[15]

I'll say so. When executive Freddy Caspers first walked into a meeting upon joining the company in 2001, he was stunned to find a room full of people jumping up and down and arguing. "It's not like a physical fight," he said, "but you could say it's a mental fight." On another occasion, a midlevel marketer fought for a product called Air Wick Freshmatic, a battery-operated dispenser that sprays air freshener at regular intervals. Over the previous five years, the company had only sold this product for use in South Korean office spaces. This marketer thought the company should sell it in other countries—not just in offices, but in homes as well. His colleagues considered this idea "completely nuts," and said so, according to an article in *Bloomberg Businessweek*.[16] That would have ended it in most companies. But, after a strenuous debate, his minority view prevailed. Air Wick Freshmatic launched in sixty-nine countries.

Based on our interviews, I tried to discern the unspoken rules—social scientists call them "implicit norms"—for having a good fight at Reckitt Benckiser. I came up with the following list:

- Show up to every meeting 100 percent prepared.
- Craft an opinion and deliver it with conviction (and data).
- Stay open to others' ideas, not just your own.
- Let the best argument win, even if it isn't yours (and often it isn't).
- Feel free to stand up and shout, but never make the argument personal.
- Always listen—really listen—to minority views.
- Never pursue consensus for its own sake.

At Reckitt Benckiser, team members didn't take any decisions until they had turned over the options, exploring the pros and cons. Yes, meetings sometimes grew heated. But in the end, this rough-and-tumble way of interacting produced high-quality, considered decisions. And as everyone we interviewed agreed, this way of working in teams led to much better performance.

UNITE

And yet, these norms, by themselves, also posed a danger. They could lead to endless debate. That's why at Reckitt Benckiser another set of norms arose around a second principle, *fostering unity*. The company expected managers in a meeting to decide quickly and commit to a decision. Becht recalled a meeting in Amsterdam between managers from the recently merged companies, Benckiser of the Netherlands (where Becht was CEO) and Reckitt & Colman in England. The managers had labored through a difficult session and time was running out. After lunch, one of the Reckitt & Colman managers announced that the team needed to wrap the meeting up in order for his group to catch their flight back to London on time. But the two sides had yet to agree. This made the Benckiser people very nervous. They had grown accustomed to never leaving a meeting without a clear agreement and an abiding sense of team unity.

"So what happened?" I asked Becht. "Did the Benckiser guys lock the door to the conference room?"

Becht chuckled. "That's exactly what happened. They said, 'Nobody is leaving until we take a decision.'"

Once teams discussed issues, they achieved closure and moved quickly. If a Reckitt Benckiser team couldn't decide within a reasonable period of time, the senior person in the room, usually the chair, made the final call. Every meeting ended with a judgment that was acted upon—fast. "You're through and out the other side at the speed of light—and then on to the next one," one executive said of meetings at the company.

Everyone also committed to *implementing* the decision. No second-guessing or political maneuvering would transpire in the hallways to undermine a path already chosen. "I think it [politics] is poison," Becht said about the tendency to undermine decisions.

Reckitt Benckiser performed so well in part because so many of its managers and employees not only fought but also united.

In teams that *unite*, team members commit to the decision taken (even if they disagree), and all work hard to implement the decision without second-guessing or undermining it.

We find similar teamwork cultures at other high-performance companies. At Amazon, the company expects managers and employees to "challenge decisions when they disagree, even when doing so is uncomfortable or exhausting" and "once a decision is determined, they commit wholly."[17] Silicon Valley investor Marc Andreessen described how his company's investment team debates when a partner proposes a deal. "It's the responsibility of everybody else in the room to stress test the thinking," Andreessen says. "Whenever [partner Ben Horowitz] brings in a deal, I just beat the s—- out of him. And I might think it's the best idea I've ever heard, and I'll just, like, trash the crap out of it. And I'll get everybody else to pile on." If the partner prevails, they will stop arguing. "We'll say 'OK, we're all in, we're all behind you.'"[18]

We don't see too many examples like these. And they characterize company cultures, not individual behaviors throughout the company. I wondered if managers and employees in the trenches who pursued the pattern of fighting and then uniting would perform better than those who didn't. Our statistical analysis of 5,000 managers and employees found that those who mastered both fighting and uniting in their teams did perform better overall than those who didn't fight and unite.

Persistent gender stereotypes hold that men are naturally better at the "tough" task of fighting in team meetings, while women are better at the interpersonal job of forging unity. Our quantitative study refutes these perceptions. In our sample, just under 30 percent of men scored high for their ability to fight in discussions, as compared with 32 percent of women. Women were slightly better at uniting, with about 38 percent scoring highly as opposed to about 34 percent of men. But these are small differences.

Our research also showed that more education doesn't make someone better at fighting and uniting teams—yet another blow to the "best and brightest" team strategy. Nor are senior leaders any better at it than more junior staff. This last finding might seem surprising. I would have expected that people in positions of authority would have enforced unity better. But unity is not something that you "enforce." You need true commitment, not mere obedience.

So how can you get better at fighting and uniting? Let's first review some tactics for showing up at a meeting and having one heck of a productive fight.

SEEK DIVERSITY, NOT JUST TALENT

A team can't fight well unless it encompasses diverse viewpoints. Decades of research in the social sciences confirm that diverse groups are more creative and debate better. Columbia Business School professor Katherine Phillips has concluded that diversity "encourages the search for novel information and perspectives, leading to better decision-making and problem solving."[19] Likewise, University of Michigan professor Scott Page has demonstrated that the key to a fruitful debate is "cognitive diversity," the presence of dissimilar perspectives on an issue.[20] He argues that diversity based on demographics and expertise helps insofar as it makes people see the world from different vantages and with different information.

Most people don't assemble teams or show up at meetings with diversity in mind. We tend to mingle with people like ourselves—what sociologists call "homophily." When we seek out the best and the brightest, we don't look far but instead tend to gather teams with people whose backgrounds resemble our own. President Kennedy's national security team may have been exceptionally bright, but it comprised an amazingly homogeneous group that sat around the conference table: white males in their forties and fifties, hailing from the same elite universities.

Further, none of the "best and the brightest" in President Kennedy's team sought to bring external, dissenting viewpoints into the debate. When planning the operation, the CIA, according to Arthur Schlesinger, estimated that "the Brigade, once established on the island, could expect the active support of, at the very least, a quarter of the Cuban people."[21] Why else would President Kennedy have agreed to send 1,400 men to fight Castro's army of more than 20,000? The plan rested on the crucial assumption that the Cuban people would rise up in revolt. But no one reached out to the Cuba desk at the Department of State, which had information indicating that Castro was still widely admired and that an uprising would not likely follow. Had one person on the team—Mann, Schlesinger, McNamara, Rusk—sought and provided that different perspective, the team would have had a more exacting debate about this crucial assumption.

To fight better, try to bring in people with more diverse backgrounds and viewpoints. Bart Becht of Reckitt Benckiser told us, "It doesn't matter whether I have a Pakistani, a Chinese person, a Brit or a Turk, man or woman, sitting in the same room, whether I have people who have done sales or something else—so long as I have people with different experiences. Because the chance for new ideas is much greater when you have people with different backgrounds."[22]

If you're a participant, you don't necessarily get to pick who's on your team or who gets invited into the conference room. Still, you can inject diversity by seeking out viewpoints and information from different places. Go consult peers who are not part of the team. Find that new market report that no one has bothered to consult. Seek out the "crazy" engineer who always has a contrarian thought. Then bring these different viewpoints to the next team meeting, either by inviting those people or presenting their views.

Some people in our study did just that. Gunther, a thirty-eight-year-old engineer at a South Carolina electric utility, suspected that a contractor working on one of the company's power plants was implementing a wrong solution.[23] Gunther organized a meeting with the team, the contractor, his boss, and two other engineers from his company who had not been involved and who would bring new perspectives. During the meeting, one of the engineers whom Gunther had invited proposed a very different but seemingly superior solution to the contractor's. "The contractor wasn't listening to him," Gunther said, "but my boss was very good about advocating for [the engineer] in the meeting, so that his voice was heard." Even though Gunther was junior, he orchestrated the meeting and enhanced the intellectual diversity in the room. He scored in the 98th percentile on the fight-and-unite principle and in the top 6 percent in performance in our study.

MAKE IT SAFE

In 2009, Heineken brought its young talent, lanky thirty-six-year-old Dutchman Dolf van den Brink, into its regional headquarters in White Plains, New York, to turn around its sagging U.S. operation. Van den Brink had worked in the Congo, Africa, where he had doubled the local business's market share in a few short years. When I spoke to him, he recalled that when he started, there was "a lot of fear" at the headquarters, and "nobody was speaking their mind."[24]

To provoke discussion, he couldn't just yell, "Speak up, people!" No. He had to set clear expectations. Van den Brink hit upon the idea of using props to establish new rules for meetings. When his team members filed into the room one morning, they noticed several 2x3 inch cards on the table. The red card read: *Challenge, Have Another Solution.* Another, a green card, declared: *All in—Ask Me Why!* The last card was gray with a warning: *Shiny Object Alerts, Get Back on Track.* Every team member could grab and hold up one of the cards to disagree (red), support a point of view (green), or refocus a colleague who was going off in the wrong direction (gray). There was also a toy horse, which people could toss at a speaker who was blathering on for too long—as in "beating a dead horse."

Was this silly? You bet! But on purpose. As van den Brink explained, "There was so much fear that everybody was looking to me or whoever

The Heineken Meeting Cards[25]

was most senior in the room. What the presence of [the red card] meant was that anybody could legitimately raise a challenge. Putting those cards there, in kind of a funny way, sent a signal—'Guys, we want you to challenge us, we want to hear you.'" By setting expectations and inviting people to speak, van den Brink cultivated an atmosphere of psychological safety, as Harvard professor Amy Edmondson calls it, a "climate in which people feel free to express work-relevant thoughts and feelings."[26] In our study, about a fifth of participants (19 percent) were adept at creating such climates, scoring very high on the statement "he/she is extremely good at making people feel it is safe to speak up in meetings." As the data showed, those who scored high performed better (the correlation was a high 0.63).

At Heineken, van den Brink's tactic worked. Over time, people on his team started to speak up. Soon the cards were no longer needed, and they disappeared from the room. Alejandra de Obeso, who was working in strategic planning at the time, noticed how the new expectations had enabled quiet people to participate vibrantly in the discussions. "There was one person with an introverted nature who significantly changed," she remarked. "This person always had a very nuanced point of view of what was going on in meetings but was anxious about sharing it." Over time, urged on by a sense of inclusiveness and clear rules for debate, this person began to speak up, becoming "a reconciling force and taking the conversation a level further."

Van den Brink believes that the shift to vigorous debate enabled his team to introduce more new products. As he reflected in 2015: "Our innovation rate was essentially flat four years ago; now six percent of our revenues are generated by the products we have launched the last three years. The more you can improve the quality of the debate, the better the quality of the outcomes."[27] More innovation benefited the company, and van den Brink, too. He received another promotion—a coveted position in Mexico running Heineken's largest local operating company.

PROD THE QUIET TO SPEAK

Even with clear expectations in place, many shy and quiet people will still refrain from speaking up. In her book *Quiet*, Susan Cain describes how introverted people (those who prefer their own "inner" mental life and solitary activities) find it hard to participate in buzzing, heated meetings where loud people wave their arms and contest the point.[28] They often feel left out of the discussion.

Tammy, a forty-nine-year-old lawyer in a data analysis company, prods quiet colleagues to contribute. "Sometimes I'll talk to folks in advance of a meeting, saying 'Hey we're going to have this meeting, I know you have a particular viewpoint, I think it's very important that it gets heard, I'd like to make sure you share it with the group.'" Tammy ranked in the top 10 percent among our 5,000 study participants in stimulating debate, and in the top 20 percent in performance.

Donald, a forty-four-year-old engineer who designs components for nuclear power plants, gets quiet colleagues to speak up by provoking a reaction.[29] "I sometimes throw out a ridiculous answer; I find people will speak up and say 'That doesn't make any sense whatsoever.'" He'll then ask them what *they* think. "I poke and prod the folks who are sitting there quietly, looking out the window, to get the entire team involved in the answer." Donald scored in the top 20 percent on fostering debate and in the top 14 percent in performance overall in our study.

SPEAK UP (CORRECTLY)

If you're a team participant, you can also model participation by speaking up yourself. Beware, though, not all forms of participation are equally helpful. Of the following four mindsets you might have during a team discussion, only one advances debate. Can you identify which?

1. "I am here just to listen"
2. "I want to sell people hard on my idea"
3. "I am completely impartial in meetings"
4. "I advocate my ideas"

If you answered (4), then you're in good company among high performers. You're not in meetings to "just listen." You're there to contribute.

Good performers also don't show up behaving like an impartial academic ("on one hand I think . . . on the other hand I think . . ."). You're also not there to sell your ideas. What matters isn't whether your suggestions get accepted. It's whether the team can generate the best possible solution, which may or may not involve your solution.

CIA deputy Richard Bissell didn't understand this point when discussing the Bay of Pigs invasion. He thought that his job was to get *his* plan approved, when in reality it was to help the group get to the *best* decision. Bissell later confessed, "So emotionally involved was I that I may have let my desire to proceed override my good judgment on several matters."[30] Those emotions led him to speak less candidly with the president about the risks of the operation, so that his plan would go ahead. "It is possible that we in the Agency were not as frank with the President about deficiencies as we could have been." He didn't grasp that good advocacy involves not only recommending a solution but also articulating the assumptions underlying it and its weaknesses. The failure to advocate properly cost Bissell. He was pushed out of the CIA after the fiasco.

The best performers advocate properly: They craft an opinion, argue their case with vigor, outline its weaknesses and assumptions, listen to other points of view, debate the issues, and change their mind if warranted. (See the sidebar for tips for debating and listening drawn from my conversations with hundreds of managers and employees.)

ASK NONLEADING QUESTIONS

On February 1, 2003, NASA's space shuttle *Columbia* broke apart upon re-entry to earth, killing all seven astronauts on board. Earlier in the mission, while *Columbia* was traveling in space, mission manager Linda Ham had scheduled a team meeting to go over a number of items. These included an assessment of foam that had broken off from the shuttle's external tank and struck the left wing during takeoff. Was the foam a mere maintenance issue or a safety concern? Ham hoped it was a maintenance issue. If it were a safety concern, the team would have to take drastic action with the shuttle now in orbit.

TIPS FOR DEBATING WELL

- Present new data: "I pulled some market data from Atlanta that is interesting . . ."
- Jot down three questions beforehand (and especially around key assumptions): "Does your number assume that customers will buy additional products?"
- Jump into a dissenting role: "For the sake of argument, let me state an alternative point of view . . ."
- Build on other viewpoints. ("If we expand your idea to a larger market . . .")
- Change your mind from time to time. Fight for the best idea, not for yours.

TIPS FOR LISTENING WELL

(so that you can build on what others say)

- Don't interrupt. Let others finish their thoughts (except for that long-winded colleague).
- Don't listen just to prepare your own answer. First listen to *understand* (a golden nugget from Stephen Covey's 7 *Habits*).
- Paraphrase what someone else said and check it for accuracy ("Did I get that right?")
- Make eye contact with whoever is speaking.
- Don't snooze. Or doodle. Or cross arms. Even if you *are* listening, your body language may suggest that you are not.
- Ask nonleading questions. Look for the truth, not for confirmation of your views.
- Put away that smartphone (multitasking doesn't work).

In the meeting, Ham asked an engineer whether the foam had caused severe damage by burning through the shield.[31] "No burn-through means no catastrophic damage, and localized heating damage would mean a tile replacement?"

The engineer responded that it didn't seem to be a safety-of-flight issue, which was just what she'd wanted to hear.

Ham followed up: "No safety-of-flight and no issue for this mission, nothing we're going to do different, there may be a turnaround [issue]?"

The engineer came back with more of an equivocal explanation this time.

Ham again: "Would be a turnaround issue only?"

Ham asked again and again, seeking confirmation of the answer she desired—that the foam damage was a maintenance issue only.

Like Ham, people often have a *confirmation bias*, asking for information that supports what they want to hear.[32] Ham got her answer, even though the engineers remained uncertain about the state of the foam damage (which, as it turned out, was the cause of the disaster). In the hearings following the accident, she came under heavy criticism for her inability to probe the issue:[33]

"As a manager, how do you seek out dissenting opinions?"

"Well, when I hear about them . . ."

"But Linda, by their very nature you may not hear about them."

"Well, when somebody comes forward and tells me about them."

"But Linda, what techniques do you use to get them?"

She did not reply.

People who crave to learn the truth about an issue don't ask leading questions. They ask *open-ended questions*—inquiries that do not convey an opinion or bias. Ham would have been better off putting her query this way: "What's your view on the foam damage?" Or she could have asked, "Does someone have a different point of view?" Or: "Can someone argue the opposite point of view?"

MAKE IT FAIR, THEN COMMIT

After you fight, you must unite. That means people on a team have to commit to a decision—to agree to it and exert effort to implement it. So why wouldn't people commit? Research on the topic of fair processes in groups has shown that employees have trouble committing to a decision when they perceive the process as unfair. In a meta-analysis of 148 field studies covering 56,531 employees, Professors Yochi Cohen-Charash and Paul E. Spector conclude that employees viewed a process as *unfair* if they could not voice their opinions before a decision was made. That perception in turn led people to harbor negative attitudes and engage in counterproductive behaviors (including spreading rumors, doing work incorrectly, and even stealing and destroying equipment!).[34] The first requirement to get people to commit, then, is to make sure everyone on the team has a chance to express their opinions and that people consider and discuss them. Then people will be more likely to commit to a decision, even if they disagree with it.

Employees in our study recounted instances when they committed to decisions, even when they objected. Christine worked for a pharmaceutical company selling skin treatment products to dermatologists.[35] She described how she once clashed with her team's decision to add a new product—I'll call it "Fungi"—that treats nail fungus. In Christine's view, the sales force didn't have enough expertise to educate doctors about Fungi. In a heated discussion, her boss asked for opinions around the table. Christine voiced her strong dissent, which led to a lively discussion. But she lost the argument. Fungi became part of the lineup.

But Christine didn't mope, in part because she felt the team had listened to her dissent. She threw herself at the challenge. She devoured product information, was the first to attend a training course, and called the company's experts to learn all she could about Fungi. She shot emails to her clients to alert them to their new offering and suggested that she pay them a visit to showcase the product. She evangelized to her colleagues. In short, she rallied behind the decision and did all she could to make it a success.

STOP PLAYING POLITICS

Office politics can undermine unity: People scuttle team decisions if those decisions conflict with their own selfish agendas. But as our study found, participants who scored high on "she/he goes to great lengths to eliminate politics that would prevent a decision from being implemented" performed much better (the correlation was 0.61). To stop playing politics and forge unity, try the following:

- Don't second-guess team decisions that go against your personal interests (avoid that hallway chatter, "I'm not sure we should be doing that . . .").
- Don't appeal a team decision that conflicts with your personal agenda to higher-ups. Accept it and move on.
- Clarify with your boss any conflict that may exist between your individual goals and a team goal ("I can't spend 100 percent of my time selling insurance when the new team goal requires me to help sell mortgages, too . . .")
- Send an email declaring your support to the team. "I am on board."
- Do one thing—fast—that shows you're implementing the decision, even if it goes against your interests ("I've already set up the meeting with the supplier . . .")
- Confront a colleague who's playing politics: "We made the decision, stop second-guessing . . . let's go and do it!"

CONFRONT THE PRIMA DONNA

It was the Eastern Conference semifinals in 1994 between the Chicago Bulls and the New York Knicks. The two basketball teams were tied at 102, with 1.8 seconds left in the game. The Bulls had lost the first two games of the best-of-seven series. They needed to win this game to keep their hopes alive.

With the Bulls in possession of the ball, they called a timeout and huddled courtside with their coach Phil Jackson. A meager 1.8 seconds was just enough for one final shot and a chance to win. Up to this point, Bulls superstar Scottie Pippen had propelled Chicago to 55 wins, only two fewer than legend Michael Jordan had during the team's previous season. Since Jordan's retirement, Pippen had emerged as the team's star. At the break, Pippen expected the coach to let him take the final shot and become the game's hero. Instead, Jackson drew up a play for rookie Toni Kukoč to take the shot. After the huddle, Pippen sulked at the far end of the bench. "Are you in or out?" Jackson asked.

"I'm out."

After the game, a terse Jackson confirmed of Pippen: "He asked out of the play. I left him off the floor."[36] That's right: At the moment that mattered the most, the star of the team didn't want to play because the coach didn't let him have the ball. It was man over team, an egotistical outburst that earned Pippen a spot in a ranking of "the 50 most unsportsmanlike acts in sports history."[37] But Pippen didn't get away with his bad behavior. Back in the locker room after the game, teammate Bill Cartwright, with tears in his eyes, laid into Pippen, "Look, Scottie, that was bullshit. After all we've been through on this team. This is our chance to do it on our own, without Michael, and you blow it with your selfishness. I've never been so disappointed in my whole life."[38] The team looked on in silence. Pippen apologized for letting his team down. It was a stunning and unforgettable moment of loss. Yet Kukoč had made that final shot, winning the game, 104–102.

Sometimes people on a team act in their own interest, like Pippen, without regard for what's best for the team. If these prima donnas don't get their way, they stop contributing, or they keep on challenging a decision, even though it has been made and everyone else is working hard to implement it.

Such selfish behaviors make it impossible for teams to unite. The answer is to do what Cartwright did: call out the prima donnas on the team.

Peer pressure can often serve to discipline even the most selfish individual star.

Cynthia, a thirty-eight-year-old "Lean Six Sigma Black Belt" manager in our 5,000-person dataset, used peer pressure when her team didn't reach consensus.[39] Her team had set clear ground rules early on in the project: Once a decision was reached, team members should commit to it 100 percent, even if they disagreed. "We have people on the team saying, 'I don't want to do it this way,' but the bottom line is, if the direction of the team is that way, everyone has to support it." On one occasion, a few strong-willed team members broke the rules and pursued their own agenda. Cynthia confronted them one-on-one: "I let them know that their action wasn't supportive of the decision and undermined it." She demanded they "commit 100 percent." The wavering teammates agreed. Cynthia scored a nearly top score (6 of 7) on the statement, "Makes sure everyone buys into decisions, once they are made," and she placed in the top 16 percent in the performance ranking.

In some cases, the leader must take firm action, getting rid of a selfish star. One CEO I interviewed for our study recalled a dreadful moment when he did just that. He had launched a turnaround plan for a crisis-ridden steel mill in Pittsburgh.[40] The plan involved huge cost reductions and layoffs. His whole team signed on to this plan, except the chief financial officer, who thought the cost reductions too drastic. Every time the team met to discuss *how* to implement the cost-cutting, he disrupted the meeting by revisiting *whether* they should cut costs that much. The leader took the CFO aside and warned him about his insubordination, but it persisted. After five months, the CEO sat down with the CFO and said, "You know, this is not working out, we need to part ways." Furious, the troublemaker stormed out. "It was the best—and most difficult—decision I made for that turnaround," the CEO told me.

Don't let a single disruptive person prevent the entire team from implementing a decision that has been well argued. Many people fail to intervene in such situations. Conversely, if you confront, like Pippen's teammate Bill Cartwright, Cynthia, and the steel mill CEO did, you'll increase your team's—and your own—performance.

SHARPEN THE TEAM GOAL

In many teams, personal goals and infighting prevail because the team lacks a compelling, common goal. Team members retreat into their own individual interests, and before too long, team unity dissolves. You can unite a team by sharpening the team goal.

In a business school case I wrote with famed mountaineer and filmmaker David Breashears and INSEAD professor Ludo Van der Heyden, we described how David led a team up Mount Everest in May 1996 to make a movie using an IMAX camera.[41] Three team members were trying to scale the mountain for the first time. Any climber in this situation yearns to reach the summit—that's a selfish goal, not a team objective. The IMAX team, however, had a clear and compelling collective goal: get that ninety-pound heavy camera—which they affectionately called "the pig"—on top of the mountain so that they could capture the shot from the summit. Keep in mind, every ounce counts on a journey up Everest. Climbers will cut a *toothbrush* in half to save weight on the exhausting trip into thin air. So hauling the pig up the mountain was a colossal affair.

The team goal—get the pig to the top—drove every decision and united the team. Individual goals such as summiting were secondary. *Pig over person.* In one instance, Breashears ordered Sumiyo, a Japanese climber on the team, to stay behind on summit day because she was climbing a bit slower than the rest. The team could not afford to slow down, even though she was a strong individual climber.

In the end, the team made it. Team members filmed their movie on top of Everest. They triumphed in part because of their sharp, unifying goal. Think about how you can sharpen your team's goal and make it the most important priority for everyone on the team. That way, team members will downplay their own selfish agendas and commit to the team's decisions.

DO *YOU* FIGHT AND UNITE?

Do you argue your points of view forcefully, yet let the best arguments win? Do you eventually set the fighting aside, let the issue go, and unite behind decisions? When you lead teams, do you make it possible for others to join in rigorous debates and then forge unity? To gauge your skill level at fighting and uniting, take the assessment on the facing page. If you're a participant, your position on the chart indicates what kind of behaviors you bring to the team. For example, if you land in the "groupthink" area, you strive for unity but don't challenge others in debate. You go along just to get along. If you land in the anarchy area, you're that annoying colleague who never offers constructive solutions to problems, but who at the same time never supports the solutions that others come up with.

If you're a team leader, your position on the chart indicates the kind of behavior likely taking place among people on your team. If you land in the "fight and *undermine*" area, your team excels at debating, but you're having trouble forging unity around the final decision. This situation can lead to difficulties with implementation. If you're in the groupthink domain, your team affords a very nice environment (everyone is going along to get along), yet you're not challenging one another enough to produce the best decisions.

To improve, pinpoint your position in the chart. Then select relevant tactics from among those described in this chapter to move yourself into the "Fight & Unite" corner. Becoming a better fighter and uniter in teams will lift your own individual performance. The teams you're on will do better, and those results will reflect positively on you.

To fight and then unite allows you to tap into the group's collective wisdom and harness the power of a team. But beware: Great teams can fall into a trap. They become so good at working together that they shut out the rest of the world. They forget that excellent work requires collaboration *among many teams*, not just work within a single, insulated team. In the next chapter, we'll explore how to improve your own performance by collaborating more effectively across team boundaries.

You as Team Participant

To what extent do these two statements describe you in a team setting?
Give yourself a score from 1 to 7.

Completely Agree 7	Strongly Agree 6	Somewhat Agree 5	Neither Agree Nor Disagree 4	Somewhat Disagree 3	Strongly Disagree 2	Completely Disagree 1

1. *I always make excellent contributions to debates and say what I truly think in meetings.*
2. *I always fully buy into the decisions made in the team and work hard to implement them.*

In the chart below, plot your answer to 1 on the horizontal axis, and that to 2 on the vertical axis.

You as Team Leader

To what extent do these two statements describe your team?
Give yourself a score from 1 to 7 using the scale above.

3. *My team debates issues really well and everyone says what they truly think in meetings.*
4. *Everyone buys into decisions made and works hard to implement them.*

In the chart below, plot your answer to 3 on the horizontal axis, and that to 4 on the vertical axis.

Plot your scores from questions 1 to 4 in the chart below.

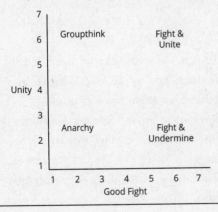

FIGHT AND UNITE

The "Work Harder" Convention

To maximize a team's performance (and by implication, your own), solicit the participation of the best and brightest. Then maximize team effort by scheduling plenty of meetings. If a meeting fails to work, schedule another, and so on.

The New "Work Smarter" Perspective

To maximize performance, maximize team debate and team unity. To have a "good fight" in a team, prioritize diversity over individual talent. When you fight and unite well, you don't need follow-up meetings because your team discussed it well the first time. You meet smart.

Key Points

- A full 80 percent of respondents in our study acknowledged, "Leading teams effectively is really important in my job." Whether as a leader or a participant, you achieve not alone, but with teams.
- Much of a team's joint work occurs in group meetings. Your team's effectiveness and your own individual performance therefore hinge on the quality of those meetings.
- Yet most people—69 percent according to one study—complain that their meetings aren't productive.
- In our study, many people struggled with two important aspects of team meetings. Some failed to hold rigorous "fights" or debates in which they explored ideas and scrutinized assumptions. Some also failed to commit to decisions once they were made and to work hard to implement them (to unite as a team). In either case, team

meetings suffered, and an employee's individual performance diminished.

- To have a productive *fight* in meetings, pursue the following strategies, either as leader or participant:
  - Maximize diversity, not talent
  - Make it safe to speak up
  - Prod the quiet to speak
  - Show up as an advocate, not a salesperson
  - Ask nonleading questions.

- To improve team *unity*, try the following:
  - Ensure everyone has a voice (being heard creates buy-in)
  - Commit, especially when you utterly disagree
  - Confront the prima donna
  - Sharpen the team goal
  - Stop playing office politics and get behind decisions.

EIGHT

THE TWO SINS OF COLLABORATION

Sticks in a bundle are unbreakable.

—Kenyan proverb

It was November 2012, and Tom Wilson (not his real name) was in the hospital—again. At age sixty-eight, the divorced veteran suffered from a long list of ailments, including ischemic cardiomyopathy, which decreased his heart's ability to pump blood; chronic obstructive pulmonary disease, which made breathing difficult; congestive heart failure; diabetes; kidney disease; depression; pulmonary hypertension; and back pain. Over a period of fourteen months, he visited the emergency room six times.

Wilson lived by himself in Fort Dodge, Iowa, a rural farming community of 25,000. Although he enjoyed regular access to medical specialists, getting his caregivers to communicate and coordinate with one another seemed impossible. During his stays at Fort Dodge Hospital, each of which lasted about two weeks, Wilson bounced between his primary care physician, pulmonologist, renal physician, cardiologist, and gastroenterologist, as well as between staff from the outpatient clinic, emergency room, a skilled care unit, and an inpatient hospital unit—nine different medical units in all. No one seemed to know what the others had done. Wilson worried whether he was getting the care he needed to manage his chronic conditions and keep him well.

Unfortunately, Wilson wasn't alone in experiencing the lack of coordination, as we found out in the Harvard Business School case that I wrote on the hospital together with Professor Amy Edmondson and doctoral candidate Ashley-Kay Fryer.[1] A clinic staff explained: "There were times when a patient would show up to their primary care physician for their follow-up hospital visit, two to three weeks after a hospitalization, and the primary care physician had no clue the patient had been recently hospitalized." Another staffer complained that, "No one was looking at the big picture of the patient and taking part of that responsibility . . . every specialist that was working on the patient's case was only looking at their individual piece of the patient." Since care wasn't coordinated, doctors, nurses, physiotherapists, and home aides ordered duplicate tests and examinations and failed to understand the full implications of the courses of treatment they recommended. Patients received lower quality care, and the local health-care system incurred much higher costs.

TWO BAD EXTREMES OF COLLABORATION

These caregivers committed what we might call the First Sin of Collaboration: *undercollaboration*. The health system in Fort Dodge wasn't designed to help people coordinate decision making and share information. Like most hospital systems in the United States, Fort Dodge Hospital was composed of departments that were separated by tall walls—what many call a siloed organization. This phenomenon of siloed care has expanded in recent years. Specialization has exploded: The American Board of Medical Specialties listed 65 specialties in 1985, 124 in 2000, and 136 in 2017.[2] Meanwhile, the fragmentation of care has led to serious problems. A large study of 10,740 patient admissions across nine hospitals in the United States found that poor communication in handoffs from one provider to another resulted in many medical errors. When staff learned to use a simple communication tool, injuries from those errors decreased by 30 percent.[3] When people fail to communicate across silos, bad things happen.

It's hard enough to work well *within* teams, as we saw in the last chapter. But with entrenched silos, many individuals struggle as well to collaborate across boundaries. By collaborating I mean *connecting with people in other groups, obtaining and providing information, and participating in joint projects.* Those groups include other teams, divisions, sales offices, departments, geographic subsidiaries, and business units.

The solution, experts say, is simple: *bust the silos!*[4] Demolish all those walls so individuals and teams can coordinate with one another unhindered. In the name of silo busting, these experts want more interactions, committees, and joint task forces across units. It's a way of thinking typified by former General Electric CEO Jack Welch's famous "boundaryless company."[5] Inevitably, this ideal trickles down to employees, leading to a pervasive belief that collaboration is good, and more of it is even better.

Swayed by this belief, many of us proceed to commit a Second Sin of Collaboration: *overcollaboration.* I remember when this insight first dawned upon me. Martine Haas (then a doctoral student, now a Wharton Business School professor) and I were in my office at Harvard Business School. We were studying data from 182 sales teams in a large information technology consulting firm.[6] Top managers at Centra Consulting (a disguised name) believed that they had to bust all their silos to get the company's 10,000 consultants spread across more than 50 offices to share more knowledge. The managers launched a knowledge management system that consultants could use to look up experts and download past client presentations. They rewarded cooperation across offices. A norm of collaboration took hold. The managers had succeeded in busting their silos.

To test the benefit of the knowledge sharing approach, Martine and I posed a simple question: Did sales teams that collaborated more with colleagues in different offices win more of their client bids? We plugged in data about a bunch of factors in our statistical model. Our first result showed *no* effect. We blinked at the computer screen, dumbfounded. How could more collaboration not have made a difference?

Probing deeper, we discovered that actually, *some* teams that had received input from colleagues from different offices had won their bid, while others lost it. Hmm. That was odd—same collaboration input, vastly different outcomes. We sifted through many possible explanations. Did the number of people on a given team affect the sales outcome? No. How about the competitive situation facing the team? No. How about the size of the deal? No. Then we discovered one factor that *did* influence whether a team won or lost. *Experience.*

Ding! Teams with minuscule experience in either the topic of the bid or the client's industry benefited from outside help. That was obvious—after the fact, of course! By contrast, teams with deep expertise fared *worse* when receiving input from colleagues. The more help they received, the *lower* their chances of winning the sales bid. These teams spent precious time searching for experts and, later, trying to incorporate their advice. They wound up dealing with more conflict and produced more chaotic, less effective sales proposals. These teams *overcollaborated*, because no compelling reason existed for them to seek outside help.

Why did smart, seasoned professionals request help from colleagues across the firm when they didn't need it? Interviewing individual consultants, we learned that they felt pressure to collaborate. "There's a norm around here that you ought to collaborate," they told us. "If you don't ask for help, it can count against you." And so they collaborated, even though they lacked a compelling reason. They applied an old-fashioned "work harder" approach to collaboration, exerting extra effort to obtain and incorporate knowledge, aiming for quantity of collaboration, not quality. As a result, they did worse.[7]

In the study for this book, we found plenty of instances in which over-collaboration compromised performance. Connor, a thirty-one-year-old marketing analyst in a Minnesota retail company, grumbled that "people from other business units constantly ask me for help on trivial things, which prevents me from focusing on my task at hand." That lack of focus in turn caused him to disappoint his bosses.[8]

NOT TOO MUCH, NOT TOO LITTLE

It's clear, then, that *over*collaboration and *under*collaboration can both sty-mie employees and managers trying to perform at their best. Clinging to silos leaves you in the same unhappy situation as Fort Dodge Hospital, while busting silos can swing you to the opposite extreme of too much collaboration, as at Centra Consulting.

My research has uncovered an approach that keeps you within the two extremes of collaboration. *Disciplined collaboration*, as I call it, is a set of practices that allows you first to assess when to collaborate (and when not to) and to implement the effort so that people are both willing and able to commit to it and deliver results.

In my previous book *Collaboration*, I detailed how leaders can design an organization—its structure, incentives, and culture—to promote disci-plined collaboration. In this chapter, I outline how an *individual*—junior or senior—can implement five disciplined collaboration rules to improve *his or her own performance*.

In our 5,000-person dataset, we found that individuals who practiced disciplined collaboration were likely to perform far better than those who didn't. People who mastered disciplined collaboration were likely to rank 14 percentage points higher in their performance ranking than those who scored at the bottom.[9]

Interestingly, women benefited twice as much as men from disci-plined collaboration. Why might women benefit so much more from col-laborating? Our data revealed that a higher proportion of women were good at building trust, ensuring that parties were motivated, and crafting a common goal. More women were also better at seeking information outside their core team. This gender effect is the second among the seven practices in this book: women in our study did better collaborating, while men did better championing forcefully (as discussed in chapter six).

With this gender difference in mind, let's now examine the disciplined

Disciplined Collaborators Perform Better

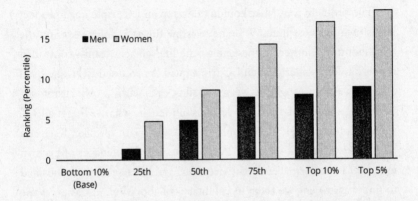

Note:
The chart shows the effect of pursuing disciplined collaboration on performance. For example, a woman who goes from no discipline (bottom 10%) to highly disciplined (top 5%) will likely move up 17 percentiles in the performance ranking (e.g., from 70th to 87th percentile).

collaboration rules to see why they produced better results for both men and women in our study.

FIRST ASK, WHY COLLABORATE?

It was 2003, and Mike had just completed his first eighteen months as manager of the chemical analysis business unit in Agilent Technologies, a 12,000-person large high-tech company at the time. Mike's business developed and sold instrumentation devices used in a variety of markets, including food safety, where the instruments perform sophisticated chemical tests to monitor levels of contaminants in food. The opportunity or "collaboration problem" that had sprung up involved a product idea called "the LC triple quad," an instrument that analyzed chemical liquids. Mike's salespeople had discovered strong customer demand for this product among food testing labs. Yet much to their frustration, Agilent had nothing to offer them. As Mike told me in my interviews for our study, one of his marketing people had taken to knocking on his office door every week, sticking his head in, and asking, "When are we developing a triple quad?!"[10]

The problem was, Mike couldn't develop an LC triple quad product in his own business unit. While he oversaw the sales force covering the food industry, another business unit—the life sciences team—controlled the technology underlying an LC triple quad. A proposed LC triple quad offering was thus caught between two silos, each with its own customers, technology, and profit and loss responsibilities (see chart). To get an LC triple quad to market, Mike would have to work with his peer, Karl, and his team over in "life sciences." While Mike was the manager of his own unit, he had no formal authority over Karl and life sciences. He thus had to find ways to engage them in voluntary collaboration, just as everyone else—senior or junior—has to do when working across organizational boundaries.

Unfortunately, Karl and his life sciences team didn't want to develop an LC triple quad, for good reason. It was perceived as an older technology. As they saw it, the opportunity to sell it into their own market— life sciences companies like pharmaceutical and biotech—had already passed. They didn't know that the LC triple quad could gain traction in other markets such as food testing, as they weren't involved with those

Situation at Agilent in 2003: Two Siloed Units
The LC Triple Quad Opportunity Required Collaboration

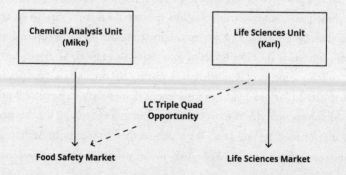

customers. From their perspective, marketing the technology was a potentially costly endeavor, with no real upside.

To secure the life sciences team's participation, Mike set about creating a compelling *business case* for the LC triple quad. He drew on members of the sales team to compile data on specific food-safety customers. If the numbers weren't there, Mike was prepared to drop the idea. Why pursue a project that wouldn't produce financial results? It turned out the numbers were there—big-time. Mike projected that the LC triple quad could earn Agilent more than $150 million in sales within three years. The market was even larger if they also marketed LC triple quad in other markets, such as environmental and forensics. Also, if they took into account the expanding China market, the potential market approached $1 billion in eight years.

With these numbers in hand, Mike approached the life sciences people to solicit their participation. "Before you write off the idea," he said, "please listen to my case. Yes, the LC triple quad is mature in life sciences. But you're missing a big point: these other markets are going through a huge growth as they adopt this technology." Mike showed the life sciences team his numbers. "We have solid market information behind this business case," he argued. He also showed how Agilent could use its intellectual property and technological know-how coupled with strong existing customer relationships to win against the competition. The Agilent field team knew the customers and understood their needs—all that was missing was the product.

Mike had succeeded in getting the life sciences team interested, if not entirely bought in, by dangling a huge carrot—a new $1 billion market they hadn't considered. Adopting an approach that we described in chapter six about forceful champions, he evoked *positive emotions* in addition to presenting a rational argument: he got them excited about *winning* in this market.

Mike undertook the first, fundamental step in disciplined collaboration: building a clear, rigorous business case. Not every collaboration is beneficial. In determining which to choose, managers and employees should focus on one criterion: *value*. What's the compelling benefit of getting together and collaborating on a product, service, project, or cost-cutting exercise? How will the collaboration impact revenues, costs, efficiency, customer satisfaction, or quality of service? In chapter three, I argued that individuals should assess the value they're creating in the course of redesigning their work. That same logic prevails here. If you can't express the value that a proposed collaboration will bring in a clear, compelling way, then do what Agilent's life sciences unit initially did: say no.

During my years studying collaboration in companies, I've found that few people instinctively build business cases for potential collaborations. That's unfortunate: Our study confirmed the strong relationship between selective collaboration and performance. As our data showed, the best performers sought information and expertise from different places in the company, *yet they also resisted collaborating if there was no clear value*. In our 5,000-person dataset, both men and women did equally well at following this principle, with 17 percent receiving a top score on the item "declines requests to collaborate on issues or goals that have unclear value to the company."

Brenda, a thirty-nine-year-old saleswoman in a retail store in a telecommunication company, used to contact some of the other seven stores in her Southwest region to obtain sales advice about new products her company was launching.[11] Over time, Brenda realized that such consultations often weren't worth the trouble. So she came to say "no" more often when a member of her team suggested reaching out to the other sites. Brenda scored a top mark on the aforementioned statement. Yet she didn't isolate herself from her colleagues. She also scored a top mark on the statement: "She actively seeks information and expertise from different places in the company." Brenda had come to discern when to collaborate and when to decline. It was no accident that she ranked among the top 6 percent of performers in our study. To be disciplined about collaboration is to say "no" to the wrong opportunities and only select those few that produce compelling value.

CALCULATE THE PREMIUM

How precisely do you build a "business case"—a compelling reason—for a proposed collaboration? The following equation from my research and consulting provides a useful guide:[12]

Collaboration Premium = Benefit of initiative – opportunity costs
– collaboration costs

Calculate as best you can the "premium" you would gain from working across teams or departmental boundaries. Be sure to consider both the benefits *and* the costs of collaborating. If the premium is positive, then collaboration is a go. If the premium is negative, it's a *no*.

For the people in Agilent's life sciences unit, the LC triple quad collaboration wasn't attractive at the outset. By expanding the opportunity to include food and other markets, it became a $150 million opportunity (that's the *Benefit of initiative* in the equation). The life sciences team should have jumped on it right away, right? But they didn't. They were skeptical. Why?

As the life sciences team saw it, they had already decided to invest in another technology program: proteomics. They didn't have the money to pursue proteomics *and* the LC triple quad at the same time. They faced *opportunity costs*, which are the answer to the question, "What benefits do you forgo if you do the collaboration project?" In life sciences' view, proteomics was a promising program they had to forgo or postpone if they did the LC triple quad. The opportunity costs were too high for them to jump on the triple quad.

At first, Mike wasn't sure how to respond. If Agilent waited a few years to bring the LC triple quad to market, it would be too late—the company's competitors would have jumped on the opportunity. Somehow, Mike had to lower the opportunity costs for life sciences. Otherwise, they wouldn't sign on. Mike examined his budget and hit upon a solution. The life sciences team could pursue both projects *at the same time*, provided that he transfer some additional investment money from his unit to theirs. With those funds, Mike could eliminate the most severe opportunity costs, leaving the life sciences team with no excuse.

But Mike wasn't done. Another problem presented itself: *collaboration costs*. Mike had to determine whether people from his unit and life sciences would dedicate themselves to the project. What if some engineers from life sciences preferred to work on proteomics? Would they put in lackluster efforts on the LC triple quad? And how committed were their managers? What if they assigned their engineers only half time to the project and started to dispute goals and plans? As I wrote in my book *Collaboration*, collaboration costs refer to the hassles of working across units, including "time spent haggling with the other parties over objectives, efforts to solve conflicts, and all the poor results that these complications create: delays, budget overruns, poor quality, and lost sales."[13] As we shall see, Mike took steps to minimize these potential collaboration costs. In all, he had created a favorable collaboration premium, by estimating a $150 million benefit in three years, lowering the opportunity costs, and reducing collaboration costs.

THE FIRST RULE OF DISCIPLINED COLLABORATION

Establish a compelling "why-do-it" case for
every proposed collaboration.
If it's not compelling, don't do it and say "no."

EVALUATING COLLABORATION
OPPORTUNITIES, LARGE AND SMALL

Mike's situation might seem different from the kinds of collaborations you typically consider in your job. He was proposing a significant business initiative, one that would involve dozens of people and millions of dollars in investment, and one that would potentially yield a business worth hundreds of millions of dollars. What about collaborations that are simpler and smaller, and where the stakes are lower? Is it still desirable and practical to calculate a Collaboration Premium in these situations? Absolutely. You may not be able to assign numbers, but you can still use this logic and do a ten-minute calculation to evaluate whether you should collaborate or not.

Let's go back to Centra Consulting. Jack Mason, who held a plum job as a management consultant in the firm's Atlanta office, was part of a four-person team preparing a sales bid for a $6 million contract to help Coca-Cola implement a smaller part of its SAP information technology system.[14] Centra's senior partner in charge of the bid had gathered Mason and two consultants in his office and told them that as a team, the four of them had sound expertise to make the proposal stellar.

Mason put in a lot of effort to make the bid a success. Knowing that other consultants throughout Centra's offices had vast experience with SAP, he thought that tapping into their expertise would help him craft a first-rate sales presentation. He emailed nine colleagues listed as experts on the relevant topic. Three colleagues—from the San Francisco, New York, and Dallas offices, respectively—agreed to fly in to Atlanta to meet in person. Mason was pleased with their willingness to collaborate in the new, silo-flattened culture. It looked as if his team would deliver a terrific sales bid as a result.

Unfortunately, the project soon veered off course. The three experts knew their SAP, all right, and they showed up with the swagger to prove it. During the following three weeks, they offered diverging views on how best to position the Coca-Cola sales bid. The London fellow urged the team to pursue a low-cost bid. The San Francisco techie pressed the team to play up the innovation angle. The New York expert insisted on including extra services. The debate heated up. Mason's two team members in the Atlanta office grumbled that between them, they already had the knowledge they needed to draft the bid—why did they have to spend valuable time listening to these outside experts? "Too many cooks in the kitchen," one of them complained.

Distracted by the conflicting advice and volumes of input, the team struggled to develop a coherent plan in time for the deadline. In the end, the partner described the final proposal as "a mishmash of several approaches." No surprise: they lost the bid.

Let's analyze this case using the collaboration premium equation. What did the Atlanta team stand to gain by soliciting help from the three experts in San Francisco, London, and New York? Not very much. The Atlanta team already possessed significant expertise, so it wouldn't benefit much from getting additional insight. What were the opportunity costs? Large: The team could have spent its limited time working on the proposal instead of interacting with the three experts. What were the collaboration costs? Huge: by insisting on different approaches, the experts created conflict. All in all, the outcome was surely a negative collaboration "premium."

Had Mason paused and spent ten minutes thinking through this logic, he wouldn't have contacted those outside colleagues. There wasn't a compelling business case for it.

If a collaboration premium seems to be negative, don't hesitate to say no. It doesn't matter if others in your company hold the potential collaborators in high regard, or if you like them personally, or if your boss supports your company's collaboration initiative, or if the collaboration's benefits seem attractive at first glance. Buck the pressure. Refuse to engage.

On the other hand, if a compelling case exists, don't just proceed in a casual, thoughtless way—go all in. Make the most of the few collaborations you *do* undertake. Let's examine how.

GET THEM EXCITED

Why might people prove unwilling to collaborate with you? One major reason is the lack of a unifying goal. Consider an example from the global professional services company DNV. A group of six people from two business units formed a collaboration project inside the firm to exploit a nice opportunity. The first business unit delivered consulting services to food companies, helping them lower food risks like E. coli bacteria in their supply chain. The second business unit issued certifications to food companies that verified their supply chains' cleanliness. The consulting and certification units had operated as completely independent entities, each serving different customers in the food industry. In this collaboration project, they sought to approach their customers jointly to cross-sell services. They would sell certification to consulting clients, and consulting to the certification customers.[15] The business case they generated projected a whopping 50 percent growth in combined revenues, so long as the team executed their plan.

Two years later, the collaboration project had failed. Why? One major reason was the lack of a unifying goal. As team members started executing, the consultants had one goal: maximize *consulting* revenues. Likewise, the certification people had their own goal: maximize *certification* revenues. As a result, neither group exerted much effort helping the other land new contracts.

What could the project managers have done differently? They could have articulated a compelling unifying goal, such as "grow *combined* market share in food by 50 percent in three years." That's a *common* goal that could excite each sales force to work toward winning in the market place together.

Mike at Agilent articulated such a unifying goal for the LC triple quad product: *grow revenues from 0 to $150 million in three years*. As we saw, the life sciences team had initially rejected Mike's idea, thinking only about the limited revenue opportunity the LC triple quad represented with their own life sciences customers. Mike's compelling goal considered the *total market*, not just the small life sciences piece. That more comprehensive goal helped unify the interests of the two business units.

Such unifying goals are powerful because they ask people to subordinate their individual interests to the common good. In chapter seven ("Fight and Unite"), I also emphasized the importance of having a team goal to unify team members. These goals are even more important for collaborative projects because they span units with potentially conflicting objectives.

In our study, we scored people on this statement: "When he/she collaborates with others, he/she always makes sure that they have a common goal and are not just pursuing individual agendas." More women in our sample scored higher on this question than men. Almost half of women (47 percent) set common goals, as opposed to just 39 percent of men.

SECOND RULE OF DISCIPLINED COLLABORATION

Craft a unifying goal that excites people so much that
they subordinate their own selfish agendas.

You may throw up your hands and say, "Wait, I am not the top boss, and I am low in the hierarchy. I can't craft a goal for someone else in a different department!" I often hear this objection. But consider Mike's situation at Agilent. He was not the big boss overseeing both the chemical and the life sciences businesses. He had to *convince* his counterparts—his peers—in another business unit. They could have said no—and initially, they did.

Collaboration means working with people over whom you have no formal authority. To motivate and excite them, you can do what Mike did and articulate a compelling unifying goal. We saw how forceful champions employed a similar tactic in chapter six. The goal is to excite people—to evoke their emotions—so that they prioritize the goal of the collaboration over their own departmental agenda.

But beware: not all unifying goals will help. Based on my two decades of studying and advising on unifying goals, I have identified four qualities that can guide you to make them effective. Try to make them *common, concrete, measurable,* and *finite.* The most famous—and successful—unifying goal of all time might well be President Kennedy's dream, articulated in a 1961 speech, "before this decade is out, of landing a man on the moon and returning him safely to Earth." Now, that's a *common* goal: all 400,000 people working on the project—those working on the rockets, the landing vehicle, the space suits, and so on—had to collaborate to accomplish it. The goal was simple and *concrete*: A man on the moon. It was *measurable*: The mission was over when the men returned safely to earth. It was *finite*: within a decade.

Contrast Kennedy's "moon goal" with the goal that then-NASA administrator James Webb wanted: *preeminence in space,*[16] including satellites, science, rockets, a moon landing, and so on. That sounds like many company goals—such as becoming "the best investment bank," or "the premier retailer." Webb's formulation violated all four of my criteria. It wasn't a common goal, bringing together satellite engineers and scientists, for example. It was vague—you needed another page of text to explain it. It was impossible to measure (when have you reached "preeminence")? Finally, it specified no deadline (someday?).

The key to incorporating these four qualities is to *concretize what is vague*. Don't say, "Our objective is to fight malaria in the world." Say, "We want zero deaths from malaria in twenty years," and then track the number of deaths by country.[17] Don't say, "to become the leading provider of IT solutions for companies in Dallas." Say, "Number one by market share in Dallas in three years." Don't say, "Grow revenues of LC triple quad." Say, "Zero to $150 million in three years."

REWARD (YES, BUT WHAT?)

The folks at DNV encountered another problem: their performance incentives didn't align with the collaboration project. The certifiers were rewarded financially based on how well the certification business performed, the consultants based on their unit's performance. Steve Kerr, General Electric's former chief learning officer, summed up this problem in an article with a great title, "On the Folly of Rewarding A, While Hoping for B."[18] Rewarding individual work, hoping for collaboration. It doesn't work.

At Agilent, salespeople in the field loved the LC triple quad product. Their customers in food, environmental, forensics, and in China craved it, and the salespeople would reap big rewards for selling it, as it would become part of their sales quota. But what about salespeople in the life sciences unit? Sales to pharmaceutical and biotech customers would be tiny, so why should they develop this product if they weren't rewarded for it? Mike had thought of that problem, and he had a solution. He decided that *all* revenues from the LC triple quad would roll up to the profit account for the life sciences unit. He wasn't interested in receiving a portion of the profits for his business unit. Life Sciences would get the credit even when the product was sold into food. They thus had *huge* incentives to develop this product. And indeed, when they saw how big the number was, they became very motivated.

When I discussed this case with Mike, I asked him, "It sounds like everyone was incentivized, except you?" To which he answered with a chuckle, "It wasn't completely altruistic on my part." Yes, Mike was first and foremost thinking about what was best for Agilent. But he also had another motive for developing the LC triple quad product. His business unit eventually wanted to develop other products that hinged on the development of the LC triple quad. In Mike's mind, the LC triple quad fed into a longer-term strategy. In addition, Mike's boss had informed him in the previous performance review that he was doing a terrific job as a general manager, but that he wasn't thinking broadly enough. "You're really in your silo," his boss said. "And that often happens with new general managers. And I really want you to think more broadly across the company." Advancing LC triple quad was a way that Mike could help improve results across the company.

The incentives for all three parties—the salespeople in the field, the folks at life sciences, and Mike's team—all lined up. They reinforced the unifying goal. Whenever you can, tinker with the rewards setup so that you can motivate people to channel their effort in pursuit of the unifying goal. In our study, slightly more women excelled at aligning incentives, with 34 percent scoring high on, "She/he always makes sure that the people she/he collaborates with across the company have a great motivation to help out." Only 29 percent of men scored high on this item. As I expected, the men and women who scored high on this item performed better.

Be careful about how exactly you frame incentives. I often see people trying to reward collaboration *activities*, not results. Many managers note whether people participate in collaborative activities such as task forces, committees, and joint visits to customer sites. And so people check the box—"yes, did show up for that committee meeting." When you reward activities, that's what you get—lots of collaboration activities. This leads to overcollaboration and people working long hours (and evenings). Activities are just that—activities—and not accomplishments. What counts is *results*.

GO "ALL IN"

Tammy, a forty-two-year-old maintenance supervisor at a California-based trucking company, told us in an interview that when her department creates a budget, it first funds departmental priorities and only then considers cross-company initiatives in need of staffing.[19] "At that point, we have already allocated most of our money and the best people." As a result, the department had neglected important collaboration projects, like a joint effort with the human resources and logistics departments to better maintain the trucks. Key people on the collaboration project were part-time, and money was too tight. The project floundered.[20]

People often pack their schedules with work they must do for their own department, reserving their remaining time—their "night" shift, so to speak—for collaborative projects. According to one employee in our study, "Finding time is the key problem. Helping someone in another department is always a lower priority than working on your own department's priorities." The result is that people spend too little time honoring their collaboration commitments.

To maximize your collaboration's chances of success, you need a forcing mechanism to assure that your collaboration receives sufficient time, effort, and financial support.

Mike at Agilent wondered whether his life sciences partners would go "all in" on the LC triple quad. With proteomics beckoning, their best people might have dedicated themselves 100 percent to that other project. If they had, the B team would have drifted over to LC triple quad, perhaps only working part-time on it. To lower this risk, Mike made sure that the life sciences unit established two separate teams, one for proteomics and the other for the LC triple quad. As Mike recalled, "I moved some people into [the triple quad team] full-time. I put my best marketing guy, you know, the guy that was sticking his head into my office all the time asking when we were getting the triple. I said, 'Guess what? This is your new job now.'"

On the life sciences side, Mike reviewed and approved the proposed staffing. "I asked for their names. I knew them all well and I chose who I wanted on this team." He also made sure that the staff assigned to the project all had 100 percent of their time allocated to it. "We have a saying in Agilent," he told me. "Part-time people, part-time results." Mike also made sure that the triple quad team had the money it needed (remember, he had transferred some of his own budget to fund it 100 percent). Mike had created what I call a "collaboration time budget," which includes three items: time (how many full-time people or equivalents are on the project); skills (whether the people have the requisite skills); and money (the dollar amount allocated to the project). Disciplined collaboration requires that participants make the necessary time commitments up front. If you can't obtain full resources, reduce the scope of the project, extend the schedule, or kill the project. I've found in my research and consulting that under-resourced collaboration projects are often doomed.

FOURTH RULE OF DISCIPLINED COLLABORATION

Devote full resources (time, skills, money) to a collaboration.
If you can't, scale it back or scrap it.

ENGINEER TRUST, FAST

When we collaborate, we sometimes work with strangers and people we don't know well, in part because we gather people from departments and geographies that are separated from one another. That means that there is a deficit of trust: we haven't had a chance to build trust with strangers, and we haven't yet formed strong relationships with mere acquaintances. We might even distrust partners, if our prior collaborations ended poorly.

Trust is a key issue in collaboration. We can define trust as people's confidence that colleagues will deliver the high-quality work expected of them, on time, every time.[21] In our dataset of 5,000 people, almost half (46 percent) said there was a lack of trust in their collaboration efforts. That's too bad: individuals in our study who fostered the most trust with their fellow collaborators performed much better (the correlation between the measure of "very good at fostering trust with collaboration partners" and performance was a very high 0.70). Slightly more women were better at establishing trust than men. Like Anne, who as a regulatory counsel in a data analysis company based in Watertown, Massachusetts, worked diligently to garner trust in her collaborative efforts: "I work in an office remote from most of the people that I work with. But we spend a lot of time on the phone, and I travel often to meet with them to build relationships and trust. So I trust the folks that I have to rely on to do their jobs in their areas, and they know they can count on me to come through when they have a tight need, and need a quick turnaround."[22]

If you don't trust your partners, or if you actively distrust them, what can you do? Given the hurried nature of modern workplaces, you probably don't have much time to work on relationships prior to kicking off your joint work. So are you doomed to a subpar collaboration? Not at all. As our case studies suggested, you can "engineer" trust quickly using a few techniques.

The first step is to understand *why* so little trust exists. Depending on the answer, you might deploy specific "trust boosters" to improve the relationship (see the sidebar "How to Apply Trust Boosters").

As we've seen, Mike at Agilent feared that some people might not commit. Mike knew he could count on Karl, the life sciences unit head, once he had committed. The problem was people below Karl. As Mike recalls, "There were people at the project level that really didn't agree with our decision to pursue the LC triple quad." So when he and Karl agreed to go ahead with the LC triple quad, they sent out a joint email spelling out their decision and the commitment they had both made. This public commitment signaled a high level of trust between the leaders; if they could trust each other, so should people further down the organization.

Mike also feared that life sciences would put its B team on the project. He lacked confidence in their willingness to staff the project with dedicated first-rate people. So he verified that life sciences had indeed staffed triple quad with excellent people working 100 percent on the project. He did the same on his side, so that the life sciences partners would gain confidence in his team's skills. Now both parties could trust that the project was fully resourced. And Mike went one step further: he conducted rigorous quarterly reviews to confirm that the right people were putting in 100 percent effort and that the project was progressing well according to plan.

FIFTH RULE OF DISCIPLINED COLLABORATION

If you lack confidence in your partners, tailor trust boosters to solve specific trust problems, quickly.

Over time, trust between Mike's unit and his colleagues in the life sciences unit took hold, and the project succeeded. Two and a half years after their collaboration began, Agilent introduced the LC triple quad into its designated markets. Within three years, the LC triple quad accounted for more than $150 million of annual revenues. Goal reached.

How to Apply Trust Boosters

Source of Distrust	Useful Trust Boosters
Lack of competence or resources. You're not certain your partner has the time, money, or skills to deliver high-quality work by the deadline.	Verify (e.g., ask for track record, prior work); Start small (e.g., pilot to test)
Insincere intentions. You're suspicious of your partner's commitment to the unifying goal.	Verify; Start small; Get public commitment (e.g., Mike's email at Agilent)
Misunderstandings. You and your partner may not agree as to what needs to get done, when, and how.	Clarify and educate (e.g., Mike at Agilent educating life sciences about the market size)
Strangers. You and your partner don't know one another well, and you come from different backgrounds (departments, functions, education, nationality, etc.)	Bond up front (team exercise); Share personal information to get to know each other better

As we've seen, Mike's effort with the LC triple quad illustrates all five disciplined collaboration rules: he established a compelling business case (and was prepared to ditch it if it wasn't good enough). He set forth a compelling unifying goal of "$0 to $150 million in 3 years." He aligned incentives well, especially by assigning all the revenues to the life sciences unit. He made sure the project was fully resourced (money, skills, time). And he used trust boosters to build confidence that collaborators would commit to their shared goal. This disciplined approach to collaboration led to great results for the project—and I should add, for Mike as well. In 2009, after his boss retired, Mike was promoted to group president. In 2015, he became CEO of Agilent Technologies. That's right, the Mike in this story is none other than Mike McMullen, chief executive of a global business with revenues in excess of $4 billion.

THE GOAL OF COLLABORATION
IS *NOT* COLLABORATION

At the beginning of this chapter, we saw how physicians and nurses at Fort Dodge Hospital failed to coordinate medical care for Tom Wilson, a chronically ill patient. But that's not the end of the story. In 2012, three leaders at his health system got together: Sue Thomson, president and chief executive officer of UnityPoint Health at Fort Dodge; Pam Halvorson, chief operating officer of the Trimark Physicians Group; and Deb Shriver, chief nursing officer of Trinity Regional Hospital. They launched a radical change program that galvanized large teams of doctors, nurses, and other caregivers to change their behaviors.[23]

While the teams didn't have the disciplined collaboration framework to guide them, they employed the same five rules. Applying the "What's the business case?" logic (rule 1), staff members evaluated whether and where collaboration could yield significant cost and patient benefits. One area in particular passed the "collaboration premium" hurdle: focus on costly patients like Wilson with multiple chronic diseases. These patients claimed a disproportionate part of the hospital's budget, and they also incurred high readmission expenses. If the health-care system could attend to these types of patients in a more coordinated way, they could realize substantial savings and improve the quality of care.

Teams at Trimark and Trinity then embraced a unifying goal (rule 2) in launching their effort: *reduce readmissions below the penalty level*. The government program in which Trimark and Trinity participated penalized high readmission levels. At Fort Dodge, these levels were high—11.3 percent of admitted patients had to come back. By taking the penalty level as its goal, Trimark and Trinity required everyone to understand and prevent costly readmissions. In addition, the teams were motivated by a compelling and common incentive (rule 3): get readmissions down, or pay the penalties.

Teams at the health-care organizations committed full resources (rule 4). Physicians, such as Wilson's primary care doctor, took time to participate in collaboration activities, and the organizations brought on a full-time cross-organization coordinator. To further enhance their collaboration efforts, staff at Trimark and Trinity held weekly meetings to review readmitted patients, inviting nurses, physicians, and specialists as well as staff from other hospitals, clinics, home care, nursing homes, and mental health centers. These meetings helped strangers to get to know each other, boosting trust (rule 5).

By following the rules of disciplined collaboration, staff at Fort Dodge cut their readmission rate from 11.3 percent to 8.6 percent—below the federal demands—in two years. Tom Wilson's life changed, too. Now he could rely on a personal team of doctors, nurses, and social workers, with team members all working to ensure the quality of his care. A home health nurse visited every week or so to check on him, look at his numbers, and review his daily medications.

A more purposeful approach to collaboration allowed the staff at Fort Dodge to cut health-care costs and improve the quality of care. But it also protected them from the opposite ill—too *much* coordination. In our zeal to coordinate efforts, we often lose perspective on collaboration's true value and purpose. We think more collaboration is always better—that the key to success is to be ever more wired, networked, coordinated. This belief is wrong. The goal of collaboration isn't collaboration. It's better performance.

. . .

Disciplined collaboration is the last of our seven practices that you can adopt to transcend the traditional "work harder" mindset and work smarter. One of the greatest tragedies of this old mindset is the assumption that we must sacrifice vital parts of ourselves to excel. We put in more hours and take on more tasks, short-changing family, friends, hobbies, exercise, and sleep. Before long, we wind up burned out, unfulfilled in our personal relationships, and saddled with health issues. A critical question thus emerges: Does pursuing the seven work-smart principles and becoming a top performer mean sacrificing your well-being? As our research proves, it does not. But you will need to take some additional steps to achieve what most people only dream about: becoming great at work *and* at life. The next and final chapter shows you how.

KEY INSIGHTS

THE TWO SINS OF COLLABORATION

The "Work Harder" Convention

The more collaboration, the better.

The New "Work Smarter" Perspective

Overcollaboration is as bad as undercollaboration. Busting silos is not the answer. A different tack—disciplined collaboration—helps you collaborate effectively and perform.

Key Points:

- Organizations and employees struggle with twin sins: undercollaboration and overcollaboration. Some people talk too little across teams and departments, and some people talk too much.
- To avoid the extremes of too little or too much collaboration, top

performers *discipline collaboration*: they carefully select which collaboration activities to participate in (and reject others), and then follow specific rules to make the chosen activities a success.

- In our study, people who practiced disciplined collaboration placed 14 percentage points higher in the performance ranking than people who didn't. Women benefited more than men.
- Disciplined collaboration consists of the following *five rules*:
  1. Establish the business case—a compelling reason—for any proposed collaboration initiative, small or large. If it's questionable, say no.
  2. Craft a unifying goal that excites people, so that they prioritize this project.
  3. Reward people for collaboration results, not activities.
  4. Commit full resources—time, skills, and money—to the collaboration. If you can't obtain those resources, narrow its scope or kill it.
  5. Tailor trust boosters—quickly—to specific trust problems in the partnership.

PART III

MASTERING YOUR
WORK-LIFE

NINE

GREAT AT WORK . . .
AND AT LIFE, TOO

I began the research described in this book by posing a question: why do some people perform better at work than others? As our study progressed, and the answers to this question came into focus, I began to notice an interesting pattern: Many of the top performers we interviewed, the ones who embraced the practices outlined in this book, realized benefits that extended well beyond their work performance. They were less stressed out, more balanced, and more satisfied with their job.

Susan Bishop, the small business owner profiled in chapter two, re-designed her executive search business in line with the principle "Do less, then obsess." She imposed strict rules about which clients and projects she would accept (and what she would reject), and she dedicated herself to the work she took on. As Bishop told us, her life improved dramatically both inside *and* outside of work. Not only did she perform better; she felt more engaged, satisfied, and energized.

Bishop attributed her increased sense of well-being in part to a better work-life balance. Prior to implementing her rules, her work-life balance was, in her words, "horrible." With the rules in place, Bishop still worked hard, but she felt as if "this huge weight had been lifted." She no longer had to deal with "the clients that I hated" as well as the smaller clients whose searches took up so much of her time. Because she and her team weren't bogged down running low-level searches for non-media clients, she could land lucrative assignments, such as a search for an executive position at the Radio City Music Hall Rockettes. Outside of work, Bishop had the energy she needed to steer her family through the sudden death of her daughter's fiancé during the 9/11 terrorist attacks. Years later, she got her Ph.D. and began a second career teaching at a business school.

Bishop was hardly alone in seeing improvements in her personal life. Greg Green, the high school principal featured in chapter three, told us that his stress level tumbled as his redesign of work took off. Before he flipped the teaching model at Clintondale High School, when his school was placed on a list for potential closure, he was "stressed to the max." With a staff of frustrated teachers to manage, he felt uncertain about his future, had trouble sleeping, and endured a range of "health issues." After the redesign, as he regained a sense of control over the school, he became more relaxed, and so did his staff.

Intrigued by examples like Bishop and Green, I wondered whether a statistical link existed between the seven practices and improved work-related well-being. The potential implications would be enormous. Top performance in any field seems to demand personal sacrifice. We presume that rising to the top requires crazy hard work, fortitude, endless practice, long hours—that it entails doing without vacations, neglecting your kids or your spouse, and spending weekends and holidays glued to your computer screen. Because we think this way, we tend to let our job responsibilities balloon out of control. Then, to achieve some semblance of a personal life, we go back in and erect a protective shield around our lives to prevent work from crushing them. We switch off the smartphone at home, or refrain from checking email when watching our kids' baseball games, or leave work early on certain days—all to prevent work from burying our private lives. Such measures only serve to treat the "symptom"—the result of working too much—and not the root cause, the work itself.

If the seven working smart practices contributed to work-related well-being, then work could become part of the solution, not the problem. We could attack the root cause of our diminished private lives by working smarter. We could select very few priorities that maximize value, and then apply intense, targeted effort to master the skills required. We could find and select some work activities that match our passion with a sense of purpose in our work. We could carefully choose a few inspirational and influence tactics to convince others to support our efforts. We could participate in fewer teamwork meetings but foster more intense debates in those meetings we do attend to arrive at better solutions. We could undertake only valuable collaboration efforts and say no to others. Instead of expending so much painful effort trying to rein work in and then complaining when we inevitably fail, we could fix the underlying problem—work.

To test the link between the seven practices and well-being, we created a well-being measure, querying people in our quantitative study about three specific areas related to their jobs: work-life balance, job burnout, and job satisfaction.[1] We ran the numbers and found that proficiency in the seven practices did indeed correlate with both high performance and an improved sense of work-related well-being. It turns out that the way to achieve both better performance and better well-being isn't to put in more hours and then buttress your personal life with ironclad boundaries. It's to concentrate on working *smarter*. *Work on how you work, not on protecting your life from your work.*

How much do the seven practices determine an individual's well-being as defined here? You'll remember from chapter one that the seven practices accounted for a whopping 66 percent of the variation we saw in people's performance. Other factors mattered, too, such as demographics and the number of hours worked. By comparison, the seven practices accounted for 29 percent of the variation in participants' work-related well-being. It makes sense that this effect is not as large as that for performance.

Several factors outside of work affect our well-being on the job, including where we live, the length of our commute, the strength of our collegial relationships, our salary, our bosses' management styles, our health, and so on. Still, 29 percent is considerable. The data shows that mastering just seven practices can substantially improve work-life balance, enthusiasm on the job, and job satisfaction.

There is an important caveat, however. Although the seven practices enhance well-being as I've defined it, a few of them turned out to lower certain parts of well-being. To attain the biggest improvement, you can't just strive to master the seven practices. You must also employ three additional tactics to prevent the negative side effects from occurring. Let's first look at how the seven work-smart practices affect well-being and then examine those extra tactics you need to become truly great at work.

HOW DO YOU *REALLY* GET BETTER WORK-LIFE BALANCE?

To assess whether the seven practices help people achieve better work-life balance, I drew on an approach used by Harvard Business School professor Leslie Perlow.[2] We asked participants to score themselves using a scale from 7 (completely agree) to 1 (completely disagree) on the following statement: "The demands of my work interfere with my family and personal time." Because only a participant can answer this of him or herself, we limited our survey to the 2,000 people (out of 5,000 in our study) who assessed themselves (the others were assessed by their bosses or direct reports).

When our data came back, we found, not surprisingly, that many people were struggling. Almost a quarter (24 percent) of our 2,000 participants completely or strongly agreed that work was interfering with their family and personal time, while a further quarter (27 percent) somewhat agreed. About half (49 percent) reported that work-life balance didn't trouble them much or at all.

Unsurprisingly, many people who worked a lot—between 50 and 65 hours per week on average—reported that work interfered with their personal and family time. At this level, working hours began to eat into evening and weekend time. If you work, say, 50 hours, putting in nine hours per day and five during the weekend, you can just about manage to carve out some good family time. But when you go to 65 hours per week, family time becomes almost impossible.

Two practices did improve work-life balance, most notably "Do less, then obsess." When you narrow your scope of work and jettison less important tasks, you free up time that you can spend outside work. More disciplined collaboration can also improve work-life balance. People who collaborate stand to benefit from the help they receive, allowing them to work less. Meanwhile, those who *discipline* their collaboration don't

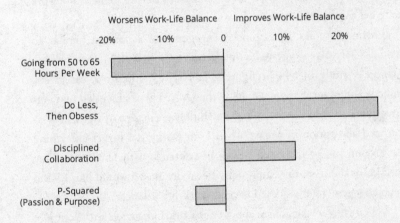

Smart Work Improves Work-Life Balance
Key Practices That Affect Work-Life Balance

Notes:
The chart shows results from a regression analysis of 2,000 people, predicting the effects of the seven practices and hours worked per week on the work-life balance item, measured on a 7-point scale: "The demands of my work interfere with my family and personal time." Answers were reversed so that a high score (7) means no interference—that is, a good balance between work and private/family life.

A positive score on the horizontal axis indicates improvement in work-life balance, a negative score deterioration of work-life balance. For each practice, the chart reveals the effect of moving from a poor position (bottom 10%) to mastery (scoring in the top 10% in that practice), while other practices are average. For example, by mastering "do less, then obsess," people are likely to move up 26 points in the work-life balance ranking (e.g., from the 60th to the 86th percentile).

get roped into unnecessary working groups and nighttime conference calls. They minimize the extra time required to collaborate, reducing the chances that work will bog down their private lives.

Our analysis also turned up a surprising result: one practice—infusing work with passion and purpose—*worsened* work-life balance. Many people think of passion at work as exclusively positive, but our study suggests that passion makes it harder for us to sustain boundaries around our work.

Kate, a forty-three-year-old administrative assistant in our study, loved her job at an advertising sales company in Oklahoma City.[3] In our study, she scored high on both passion and purpose. She felt excited to go to work most days because of the learning opportunities her job offered, and she felt that she contributed in important ways by supporting the sales staff with travel, reports, and other paperwork. Her performance placed her in the top 11th percentile of all participants. But she ranked her work-life balance as poor, in part because her excitement for work made her think about it when she was home.

Previous studies of employee engagement—a concept similar to passion—have also suggested a link between passion and poor work-life balance. A study of 844 firefighters, hairstylists, educators, caregivers, bankers, and other working adults in the United States revealed that employee engagement—measured by an employee's degree of vigor, dedication, and absorption in work ("when I am working, I forget everything else around me")—increased work's interference with family life ("my work keeps me from my family activities more than I would like").[4] Too much engagement at work led to poor work-life balance.[5]

When you feel passionate about your work and engage with your job, you can short other parts of your life. You're so engrossed that you tack an extra hour on to your workday. Before you know it, it's 7 p.m. and you're arriving home too late for your family dinner. Or you end up making your family dinner, but you're distracted and thinking about work. Or you're so focused on specific work tasks that priorities like sleep or exercise lose out.

HOW DO YOU PREVENT BURNING OUT?

The Mayo Clinic defines job burnout as a "special type of job stress—a state of physical, emotional or mental exhaustion combined with doubts about your competence and the value of your work."[6] Such job stress is quite common in the workplace. We asked the 2,000 self-respondents in our sample to rate their level of work-related burnout. Many experienced some level of mental and emotional exhaustion. About a fifth (19 percent) strongly or completely agreed that they felt burned out. Another quarter (25 percent) agreed somewhat, with the remaining 56 percent reporting little or no sense of burnout.

Burnout is serious. Research has tied it to ills such as cardiovascular disease, marital dissatisfaction, and depression.[7] Fortunately, our study found that several practices lower the chances of burning out. "Do less, then obsess" can protect people from becoming exhausted at work because it leaves them with fewer priorities to handle and track. Likewise, if you take a more disciplined approach to collaboration, your partnerships enable you to accomplish more in less time, thus preventing exhaustion. Both of these practices prevent you from being physically and mentally exhausted at work.

There is another part of burnout—emotional exhaustion. As the Mayo Clinic's definition suggests, burnout can stem from a sense that work is stressful, bristling with interpersonal friction, and lacking in meaning. The smart-work practices also regulated this emotional aspect of burnout. P-squared—matching passion and purpose—helps prevent emotional fatigue. People who experience passion and purpose go to work excited about what they do every day, perpetually reacquainting themselves with work's deeper meaning. When my colleagues and I interviewed principal Greg Green and his staff in 2016, they still faced the same challenges of dealing with a disadvantaged student population that they had before "flipping" Clintondale High School. But whereas before their work enervated them, now it energized and inspired them, not least because it allowed them to devote more of their time to teaching students, rather than disciplining them and breaking up fights. For hours when we

Smart Work Lowers Burnout

Key Practices That Affect Feeling Burned Out at Work

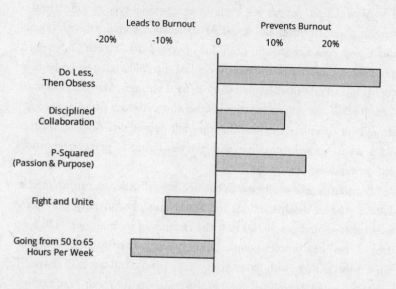

Note:
The horizontal axis indicates the gain or loss in percentile ranking of feeling burned out in our sample of 2,000 people (based on a regression analysis). For each practice, the chart shows the effect of moving from a poor position (bottom 10%) to mastery (scoring in the top 10% in that practice), while other practices are average. For example, by mastering "do less, then obsess," people are likely to move up 29 points in the "preventing burnout" ranking (e.g., from the 60th to the 89th percentile in preventing burnout).

visited, Green and his staff talked with us about the flipped model, what new technologies they were excited to try, and most of all, how the flipped model was impacting the students. They felt deep passion and purpose. They were still working hard, but they were accomplishing more and feeling less burned out.

I was surprised that one of our seven practices—"fight and unite"—*increased* the chance of burning out. Upon reflection, I came up with a possible explanation. Vigorous debates during meetings may produce better decisions, but they can also wear you down —all that frowning and head-shaking, all those moderately raised voices, all those attacks and counterattacks. Research has shown that a good intellectual fight (what scientists call "cognitive conflict") often accompanies interpersonal friction or "emotional conflict."[8] In a study of 612 employees working in industries like manufacturing, telecommunications, pharmaceutical, and governmental defense, an increase in cognitive conflict (for example, "how often did the members of your team debate different ideas") predicted higher levels of emotional conflict, as measured by interpersonal clashes, anger, tension, and intrateam rivalry.[9] Friction between colleagues can in turn lead to burnout.

HOW DO YOU ENHANCE YOUR JOB SATISFACTION?

As for job satisfaction, our last well-being factor, four out of our seven practices enhance this benefit, two of them strongly. Passion and purpose

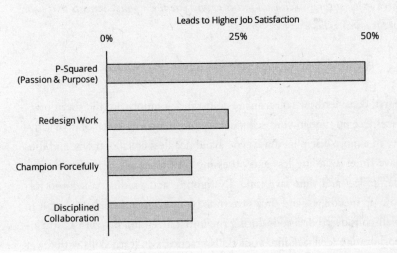

Smart Work Improves Job Satisfaction

Key Practices That Affect Job Satisfaction

Leads to Higher Job Satisfaction

Note:
The horizontal axis indicates the gain in percentile ranking of job satisfaction in our sample of 2,000 people (based on a regression analysis). For each practice, the chart shows the effect of moving from a poor position (bottom 10%) to mastery (scoring in the top 10% in that practice), while other practices are average. For example, by mastering P-squared, people are likely to move up 49 points in the job satisfaction ranking (e.g., from the 40th to the 89th percentile in job satisfaction).

loom large. People who are deeply passionate and feel a strong sense of purpose feel far more satisfied in their jobs than those who aren't. One study of 271 working men and women in the United States showed that those who felt very passionate about their jobs were much more satisfied with them.[10] Another study of 260 university employees demonstrated that those who felt that their work contributed to the greater good ("I know my work makes a positive difference in the world") also reported much higher job satisfaction than those who didn't.

In our study, people who redesigned their job tasks also felt much more satisfied, perhaps because they got a chance to work on more valuable activities, or because they appreciated the autonomy or discretion they had to reimagine their role.

Overall, our analysis demonstrates that different smart-work practices affect well-being differently. It's not the case that one or two of the seven practices produce well-being, nor are all the effects positive. As a result, simply mastering all seven practices won't yield the greatest performance and well-being gains. You do need to master them, *but you also need to adopt three additional tactics to mitigate the negative impacts that some of the practices have on well-being.*

SPEND YOUR TIME DIVIDEND

First, consider how you manage your time. A number of the seven practices free up time in your schedule. By pursuing your collaborative activity in a more disciplined way, you avoid needless collaborations, and thus save time. By doing less and obsessing, you focus your efforts on a few key tasks—and thus save time. By fighting and uniting, you forgo follow-up meetings—and thus save time (your productive debates result in well-considered decisions during the initial meeting). By consistently incorporating feedback into your skills practice, you learn skills with fewer repetitions—and thus save time. By redesigning work, you work more effectively to achieve the same or better results—and thus, yet again, you save time.

All of this time-saving piles up. Review your schedule over the past two weeks and remove all the assignments, phone calls, email tasks, and meetings you wouldn't have had to bother with if you had followed these practices. Chances are, that's a lot of time! I think of this newfound time as a "time dividend" you generate by practicing the seven practices. The question is what to do with this dividend.

You have two choices: You can reinvest that extra time in work, or you can spend it on outside personal and family time. Think about a company that earns a profit: It can invest that money back into the business, or it can distribute some of it as a cash dividend to shareholders. You are in an analogous situation. You may need to reinvest *some* of that time back into your work; the "do less, then obsess" practice requires you to spend time obsessing in your few chosen focus areas. Some people put *all* their time dividend back into their jobs, enjoying little in the way of work-life balance. The great sushi chef Jiro Ono from chapter two lives for work and doesn't like public holidays because they keep him away from his restaurant. But other people we've met do split their time dividends, reserving some extra time for their personal life.

Susan Bishop realized a substantial time dividend upon applying "Do less, then obsess." By setting rules regarding which clients to accept and which to reject, she was able to work only in industries where she possessed expertise. As a result, she and her team saved time that they otherwise would have spent learning about new industries. She could have poured all of her time dividend into her remaining client work. Instead, she channeled a portion of that time back into her personal life, being there for her daughter and going back to school.

In our larger data set of 5,000 managers and employees, most people who were great at work split their time dividends as well. As we've seen, top performers who excelled at "do less, then obsess" didn't work longer hours. They were more effective when they *did* work. In general, as we saw in chapter three, working beyond 50 to 55 hours a week didn't yield significantly higher performance.

The traditional "work harder" mentality runs deep. We think we *have* to attend that extra meeting, agree to that extra collaboration, or put that extra hour into tweaking that presentation. Don't fall into that trap. You need to break your work-harder pattern, setting some clear limits. Obsessing so as to excel in what you do means working up to 50 to 55 hours per week, infusing your work with passion and purpose during those hours, and then taking a break. Spend any hours beyond that—your time dividend—on your personal commitments.

KEEP YOUR PASSION IN CHECK

As we saw earlier, the practice of infusing work with passion and purpose increases job satisfaction and reduces feelings of burnout, but it also worsens work-life balance. To avoid this trap, keep your passion in check. Even if you're working a reasonable number of hours, don't let your passion for work seep into your leisure time. If you're thinking about work while you're having dinner with friends or watching your kid's baseball game, you're *too* passionate about work. If you have trouble falling asleep at night because you're thinking about work, or you find yourself checking your email in the bathroom at 3 a.m., you're too passionate about your job.

Top performers in our study pursued passions for sure, but they also kept those passions in perspective. Hartmut Goeritz, who spent years redesigning operations at Maersk's Tangiers shipping terminal (chapter three), devoted his off hours to his three kids and to hobbies such as squash and scuba diving. When I asked whether he could forget about his work during leisure hours, he said, "Absolutely! My brain switches over to family mode. I'm very good about that." He noted that he takes time to drop his son off at school each morning, leaves work at around 5 p.m., and works only occasional weekends. When I asked him if he would ever work 70 to 80 hours a week, he told me that he would "refuse to do that. That would kill me and it would kill my work-life balance." You, too, can be extremely, wonderfully passionate about work and *not* let it consume you.

DON'T TAKE IT PERSONALLY—
AND DON'T FIGHT NASTY

People who reap the full well-being benefits of the seven practices contain the *emotional* turmoil that work can create. Emotional conflict at work wears people down. One study of fifty-two staff in a small private hospital in Northern California found that nurses who experienced more unpleasant interactions with colleagues and supervisors were more emotionally exhausted from work and suffered from much higher burnout levels.[11] For introverts and those who tend to avoid conflict, heated debates might prove especially taxing.

Don't shy away from "mental" fights in meetings, but be sure to fight in the right way. As we discussed in chapter seven, don't make your fighting in team meetings personal, and don't take the comments cast in your direction personally, either. Avoid inflammatory language ("that's a stupid idea"), because such toxic language upsets people. Likewise, when other people make disputes personal in a meeting, try to reorient them. One great tactic is to get more objective, highlighting impersonal data, facts, and numbers as opposed to emotion-laden opinions. Another is to play "devil's advocate," a tactic that reduces interpersonal conflict by allowing you to play a *role* rather than speaking for yourself ("for the sake of argument, I am going to disagree"). Make fights about ideas, not people. The quality of your debates will improve, the emotional conflict will subside, and your sense of well-being will be better.

WORK SMARTER, NOT HARDER

With the seven practices and these three additional tactics in place, I have now presented in full our scientifically validated path to greater work performance and well-being. Most of us think we need a strong "work ethic" and pure "grit" to achieve greatness. If someone has emerged as a superstar, we assume that he or she works harder than everyone else. Yet the idea that working harder—longer hours—beyond some threshold will yield superior performance is flawed. The best performers don't work harder. They work *smarter*. They maximize the value of their work by choosing a few priorities and applying targeted, intense effort to excel.

I began this book by observing that "work smart" is a cliché and that no one wants to work dumb. Yet as we've seen, employees and managers have lacked a clear framework for *how* to work smart. They haven't parsed out what this phrase really means, nor have they had at their disposal concrete guidelines for what to do on a daily basis. The preceding chapters have provided a framework for working smart.

I've focused on individual performance, but the project of improving how we work extends beyond that. As you proceed in your career and take on leadership positions, look around you. Does your organization support working smarter? Many do not. Why do many medical interns work twenty-four hours straight, when that's not the best way of adding value? Why do some McKinsey consultants work seventy to eighty hours a week instead of fifty? Almost everything about our organizations supports the "work harder" mentality, from compensation to the structuring of work processes to the way hiring decisions and promotions are made. Leaders sustain the "work crazy hard" mentality, expecting more effort from their employees and failing to applaud employees for setting boundaries and performing *smart* work. The sad part, of course, is that this imperative to work harder reduces the collective performance of a company's employees, which in turn most likely lowers financial results.

Some leaders do get it. Facebook cofounder Dustin Moskovitz, reputed to be the youngest self-made billionaire in history, has reflected on his time at Facebook and lamented the excessive time he put in. "I wish I had slept more hours, and exercised regularly," he wrote in a 2015 blog posting. "I wish I had made better decisions about what to eat or drink—at times I consumed more soda and energy drinks than water. I wish I had made more time for other experiences that helped me grow incredibly quickly once I gave them a chance."[12]

You might think, "Well, easy for him to say. His breakneck pace helped make Facebook what it is today." That's not Moskovitz's conclusion. As he said, "I believe I would have been *more* effective [if he had prioritized other parts of life]: a better leader and a more focused employee." He goes on to explain: "I would have picked fewer petty fights with my peers in the organization, because I would have been generally more centered and self-reflective. I would have been less frustrated and resentful when things went wrong, and required me to put in even more hours to deal with a local crisis. In short, I would have had more energy and spent it in smarter ways . . . AND I would have been happier."

Let's learn from Moscovitz's experience. And let's learn from our study of 5,000 people drawn from many industries and all kinds of jobs, senior and junior. We can all become great at work—and in life—by working smarter, not harder. Focus on just seven core practices (and three tactics to improve well-being). Understand them. Apply yourself to these seven. Master them. Your performance will likely improve, and you'll feel less stressed and more fulfilled. One day, you might even notice something strange and wonderful happening. You know that colleague who outperforms everyone else, yet who mysteriously leaves the office at a decent hour at the end of every day? The "Natalie" that I mentioned in chapter one and whom I encountered while working at the Boston Consulting Group in London?

That could be you.

SMALL CHANGES,
BIG RESULTS

When I was a junior in high school, I was an accomplished track-and-field runner in my hometown of Oslo, Norway, where I had won four regional championships. One competition, the Norwegian national junior championship, stands out in my mind. The event started well with a bronze medal in the 4x400 meter. The following day, I anchored the 4x1500 meter race. For much of the race, everything went well. I had positioned myself in the front group as the bell rang for the final lap in the race. With 300 meters to go, I accelerated to the front. Then another runner overtook me. No problem, I thought. I usually did well in the final sprints. I figured that I could position myself behind him and wait. With fifty yards left, I'd make my move and win.

As we went into the finish, I accelerated to pass him. But I miscalculated, advancing too late. As I tried to overtake him, I met a huge headwind. My legs fatigued from earlier races, I didn't have enough strength left. I threw myself at the finish line. The photo finish showed that I lost by 2/100 of a second. It sure felt more like losing the gold than winning the silver.

Looking back on it all these years later, I am struck by how a tiny miscalculation led to such a different outcome. I lost the championship because I made my move a fraction too late. That's often how it works in sports. Just a bit too much topspin on a basketball free shot, or a football wide receiver who breaks a split second too late—these miscues make all the difference. But is that also true at work? As the data and stories in this book demonstrate, small changes in behaviors can have a disproportionate effect on outcomes. In chapter three, I used the Archimedes lever to make that point, invoking the phrase "give me a lever and a place to stand, I can move the earth." Dr. Michael Bennick, the senior doctor described in that chapter, did "move the earth," so to speak. Wanting to help hospital patients sleep better at night, he didn't launch some large-scale bureaucratic transformation to make the hospital quieter. Rather, he told the attending nurses and physicians that they should wake him first if they wanted to wake a patient during the night to take a blood sample. No one did. That small alteration changed hospital care and led to a dramatic improvement in the patients' "quiet at night" score from the 16th to 47th percentile. A minute lever, with a big outcome.

That insight—that tiny changes can yield big results—has vast implications for how we choose to work. We don't have to make massive changes in our work to lift our performance. Small changes can be just as effective. That's a hopeful message: start with small steps. That's working smart, not hard.

To close out this book, I highlight a few of those smaller changes from each chapter that can be just right for you as you embark on your journey of becoming great at work.

In chapter two ("Do Less, Then Obsess"), we saw that the best performers chose a few key areas to work on and then obsessed to excel in those. They went narrow and deep, not broad and shallow. Of course, sometimes you must cut out substantial areas of work—a big project, a large customer, or even a job—to get to that level of intense focus. But just as often, small changes—one by one—can free up enough time to do less and obsess. Start by learning to say "no" to new requests for your time. Give yourself a buffer: The next time someone asks you for something, respond with, "Let me think about it, and I will get back to you tomorrow." In the meantime, ask your spouse or a colleague to play the role of naysayer for you. Why might committing to the request be a bad idea? What do you have to lose by taking on the additional work?

You can also do what Susan Bishop, the small business manager of the executive search firm, did: she set clear rules ahead of time for which clients to accept ("only in media" and a "minimum fee of $50,000") and which to reject. You can set a rule such as "only attend meetings where I *must* be present." Still another small change you can make is to apply "Occam's razor" and start chopping away work you don't have to do. Do you *really* have to answer those emails, create those extra PowerPoint slides, schedule premeetings to prepare for a meeting, or return that phone call? *Everything* takes time, so chopping off even small tasks can free you up to zoom in and obsess over the few key areas that matter.

That brings up the question of *what*, exactly, you should focus on and obsess over. Not all work is created equal: some tasks produce far more impact than others, as we discussed in the "Redesign Work" chapter. The answer, we found in our research, is to redesign your work so that you add more activities that create value, and stop or reject work that doesn't. Value creation differs from goals: remember the Hewlett-Packard manager who submitted the quarterly report on time (achieving his goal), but no one read his report (zero value creation). In contrast, Principal Greg Green of Clintondale High School in Detroit flipped the entire method of teaching (doing homework at school and lecturing via video at home) and thereby transformed student learning and created tremendous value.

Now, you might say, "That's not a tiny change, that's a huge one!" True, but Green started with tiny changes. First he performed a small experiment with one class, then a few more, and so on, until he was confident that he had the new model right. You, too, can start small, keeping an eye out for tiny but meaningful redesigns. Try to find just one way to reduce the time you spend on activities of little value (like furnishing those reports that no one reads) and to increase an activity that will yield value (returning those customer calls more quickly). Start by looking at your calendar the past two weeks: Circle each item that you think created very good value, and cross out those that yielded little or no value. Now do the same for the next two weeks. Confront yourself: have the courage to get rid of some of those crossed-out upcoming items!

Once you focus on activities that have an impact, improve them bit by bit by applying the learning loop, as we discussed in chapter four. You'll recall from the story of hospital food supervisor Brittany Gavin that a learning loop is about making small changes to achieve a big impact over time: tweak a way of doing your job, measure the outcome, get feedback on it, modify the approach, and so on, in an upward cycle of improvement. When you're just getting started, keep the risk low: If you're a salesperson tweaking your pitch, modify the pitch with a not-so-important customer. Then observe the impact and tweak it some more. Over time, you might just see a huge uptake in your sales performance.

Pursuing this kind of intense, sustained effort requires a high degree of commitment, so how can you turn up your motivation? As we saw in chapter five ("P-Squared"), top performers became energized by tapping into their *passion* and a strong sense of *purpose*. We witnessed how hotel concierge Genevieve Guay matched her passion ("I love interacting with people") with her sense of purpose (helping and caring for hotel guests). As a result, she poured energy into every hour she worked and thereby performed exceptionally well. Unfortunately, the convention is that you need to make a huge change in your life to achieve what Genevieve accomplished—you must quit your job and find a new career that gives you both passion and purpose at work. But as this chapter showed, that's not true. You can make small changes to expand your passions at work. Join a new project that taps into creative passions. Seek out competitive job situations (like sales pitches) to tap into a passion you might have for competition and winning. Join a training workshop to fuel your passion for personal growth. Have lunch more often with colleagues who make you excited about work. To gain more purpose, look for small ways to add value for your team or organization. Find assignments that are meaningful to you. Spend a few minutes this week reflecting on the ways you're *already* contributing, perhaps without realizing it. Become more active in social causes your organization might support. Step by step, you're increasing your sense of passion and purpose at work.

As we turn to the second half of the book, which focuses on how we can master working with others, here, too, we can make small changes in how we work. Our top performers were forceful champions (chapter six). They inspired people by evoking their *emotions*. They didn't rely on charisma but rather on clever tactics. Celebrity chef Jamie Oliver used a giant, jiggling mountain of fat to convince parents to improve their kids' diets. Agilent executive Jacob Thaysen excited an audience of managers by playing a heartfelt video of a young cancer patient who had survived thanks in part to the company's products. Look for creative ways to inspire by evoking strong emotions. Let's say you work at a hotel and you want your colleagues to focus more on customer service. Go to yelp.com, find negative comments left by customers ("the reception staff was rude, gave us the wrong key, and the concierge never returned our phone calls"), print them out, and circulate them. That should spark emotions (guilt, disgust, anger, frustration) and compel people to improve.

Forceful champions also circumvented resistance by deploying *smart grit*, which means persevering in the face of difficulty (grit) and deploying tailored tactics to circumvent opposition (smart). Lorenza Pasetti used smart grit to combat the attack that the powerful Consorzio del Prosciutto di Parma lobbed at her company, Volpi Foods. She took time to understand the Consorzio's concerns, and then used that insight to devise a clever strategy to convince her opponents to rescind their advance. To apply smart grit, identify a colleague whose support you need and who does not support your agenda. On a piece of paper, write down your best guess at what her agenda might be. Try to understand the issues from her point of view (cognitive empathy). Then craft one or two influencing tactics to overcome her resistance. Small steps such as these help you champion your agenda more forcefully.

The other way to work better with others is to revamp all those lame meetings. Whether you're participating in or running the meeting, take small steps to fight and unite better (chapter seven). Remember the lessons we drew from Reckitt Benckiser, a manufacturer of dishwasher soap that is one of the world's top-performing companies. When teams have a good *fight* in their meetings, people debate, consider alternatives, challenge one another, and listen to minority views. In teams that *unite*, people commit to the decision taken (even if they disagree) and work hard to implement it. You can take those small steps in your next meeting: make a better effort to listen (put away that smartphone); articulate your own dissenting views; invite a colleague to argue an opposite position; prompt quiet colleagues to speak up; and pose a good question instead of telling others what you think. Then forge unity: tell yourself to support a decision even if you disagree, and ask a colleague to do the same. As you get better at this, you will find that meetings become more productive. And the good news is that, once you're on that path, you need fewer meetings!

You can also take small, incremental steps to discipline how you collaborate with people across organizational boundaries (chapter eight). The doctors, nurses, and administrators at Fort Dodge hospital changed how they collaborated across the emergency room, outpatient clinics, and in-hospital departments to better coordinate patient care without overdoing their collaboration. The results were impressive: they reduced healthcare costs *and* improved quality of care. In the coming week, challenge yourself to say no to three unnecessary collaborations: Eliminate interactions that seem least likely to add value (that phone meeting late at night where you're just listening in anyway). You're not being a bad team player by saying no—you're just optimizing your time. Once you do decide to collaborate, do it better. For every collaboration, take a few minutes to examine the unifying goal. Is there one? If so, write it down and share it with others to keep everyone focused. If there isn't, then spend a bit of time in your next meeting clarifying what it might be.

You can start small on each of the seven practices that make up the work-smart framework in this book. Pick just a few small steps, and start practicing. If you're a young professional looking to move up in your company, apply the learning loop to improve just one skill at a time—say, prioritizing and becoming better at saying "no." Over time, you'll find that you're working fewer hours, because you're working on the right things in the right way. That frees up time you can spend outside of work, giving you a better work-life balance, less chance of burnout, and higher job satisfaction (as we discussed in chapter nine).

Our discussion of small steps returns us to a major theme in this book: the potential we all have to become not just good at work, but great. Experts have attributed top performance to factors like talent, effort, or luck. Although these play some role, my research has statistically linked superior performance to daily practice of the seven principles. That means that anybody can become a top performer—you don't have to work crazy hours, be a genius, or be unusually lucky. You *can* become much better over time at working smart. Get started with small steps and keep at it, and someday you can win that gold medal in your line of work—and have a great life, too.

Research Appendix

This appendix provides a detailed explanation of our study of 5,000 managers and employees, and it also shows how we developed the seven-factor conceptual framework. Although some of the language I use here contains technical statistical terms, most of the appendix can be read without knowledge of statistics.

At the outset, I would like to acknowledge several people who helped with the design and execution of this study. Warren Cormier, Robert Tafet, and David Volpe of Boston Research Technologies helped design the survey instrument and execute the population sample. Professor Emeritus James Watt of the University of Connecticut carried out the statistical analysis, and Nana von Bernuth worked on the analysis and conducted subsequent interviews. Many others contributed (see the acknowledgments).

1. FRAMEWORK

Organizational scholars have long studied various dimensions of a person's job and the relationship between the person and the job. A few classic accounts include professor Richard Scott's book *Organizations and Organizing* (now updated by coauthor professor Gerald Davis, 2016) as well as professors Richard Hackman and Greg Oldham's theory of job design (Hackman and Oldham, 1976). The early approaches from the 1960s and 1970s were mainly concerned with how to enhance motivation and performance in monotonous factory and clerical jobs; they included factors like job enrichment, enlargement, variety, and rotations.

For modern "knowledge workers," however, other dimensions have become more salient, reflecting a broader change in the nature of work. As many organizations have moved from a strictly formal command-and-control structure to more decentralized forms wherein the informal organization plays a more significant role, relational factors such as teamwork and collaboration have become significant aspects of work roles. In addition, as work roles, tasks, and skills seem to change more quickly now than before, the processes of learning new skills and improving on skills have received increased scholarly attention. Motivational factors have also changed. Whereas earlier scholarship was mainly concerned with crafting jobs that weren't too boring and repetitive for industrial workers, recent scholarship has shifted to other dimensions of work, and notably to more intrinsic and intangible dimensions such as whether work is understood as meaningful.

In light of these developments, I have developed a framework that builds on the early ideas of job design and that also incorporates the three trends of relations, learning, and new motivators. This approach yields four broad categories corresponding to *what* a person should work on (job design); *how* the person should improve over time (learning); *why* a person should exert effort (motivation); and with *whom* a person should interact at work (relation). Put colloquially, these four categories represent the *what, how, why*, and *who* of work.

It is important to note how I proceeded. First, I used these four categories to articulate eight plausible ideas about how work-practices affect performance (e.g., the idea of "focusing"). Second, I tested those ideas in the 300-person pilot study and examined them through the lens of numerous case studies and interviews. Based on these insights, we revised those ideas in important respects and turned them into specific hypotheses that reflected additional insights into what leads to performance (e.g., "focusing" is an insufficient explanation and needs to be specified differently; see below). Also, the statistical factor analysis from the pilot study showed that two of the eight ideas (influence and change agent) were in fact one concept, so we turned those into one practice (forceful champions). That left us with seven conceptual factors. *In summary, this was a discovery-driven process, where I began with a set of broad ideas and ended up with a different set of specific hypotheses.*

1.1. Job design category (the "what" of work)

If we want to understand why some people perform better in their jobs than others, we need to examine first the nature of their job design. As mentioned above, early scholarship discussed several aspects of job design, including dimensions like task variety and job enlargement, both of which were seen as important for improving motivation and job satisfaction. More recently, scholars have examined characteristics of job tasks within the context of modern knowledge work, where the basic issue is not monotony but rather information and work overload. Scholars have described how knowledge workers such as consultants are overwhelmed with work, including not only the absolute volume of work but also the fragmentation and dispersion of tasks (e.g., Gardner 2012, Reid 2015). This has led scholars to examine the role of job scope—the extent to which people select and pursue many versus few tasks, along with goals and responsibilities. Scholars have examined the lack of focus (e.g., Hallowell 2015) and the inefficiencies of multi-tasking or more precisely task switching at work (e.g., Rubinstein, Meyer and Evans, 2001; Coviello et al., 2015). Popular books like *Driven to Distraction at Work* by Hallowell (2015), *Focus* by Goleman (2015), and *Essentialism* by McKeown (2014) have picked up on this research trend and argued for the need to focus (i.e., for a more narrow scope of work activities).

The scope of someone's job is likely to influence how effectively that person will carry out the job. I therefore included that dimension of job design as a key factor in our framework. Job scope is here defined as the extent to which a person is able to focus on a few key priorities. The greater the focus, the more narrow the scope.

As described in chapters one and two, the pilot of 300 people and the many case studies produced a surprise finding in this respect: "focusing" is not simply about *choosing* a few tasks; it is also about making huge efforts to excel in those selected tasks ("obsessing"). Thus, once we had tested the initial framework of focus (choosing) in the 300-person pilot sample (see the methods section below), our further investigation of the answers from the pilot and the case studies indicated that we needed to incorporate the obsession (effort) part in our hypothesis. Those two form the first principle or hypothesis that we formulated after the pilot and to be tested in the 5,000-person study:

HYPOTHESIS 1: Individuals who do less (i.e., focus on a few key priorities) and then obsess (i.e., make great efforts within those chosen areas of focus) will perform better at work than those who don't.

Note that I stated this practice as a hypothesis. It was quite possible that the data would not support this hypothesis. In fact, we can reasonably suggest that someone who "does more" (i.e., does not focus, which is the same as taking on many tasks) will do better, because she accomplishes more.

The second feature of job design that I analyze is the extent of and change in a person's tasks and work goals. This dimension was also a key aspect in seminal research on work design, such as in Hackman and Oldham's early work. The idea was that job tasks and goals could be changed so as to maximize worker satisfaction and performance. Jobs could thus be "designed" in better ways. That in turn raises the issue of what kind of change most improves individual performance.

In our case studies, we analyzed why some job redesigns seemed more effective than others and came to the realization that the better ones had one aspect in common: they increased the *value* that the person created through his/her job (as we describe in chapter three). The idea of value relates partially to the idea of *task* significance from the old job design literature, i.e., the extent to which a job produces output of any significance.

The idea of redesigning one's job to create more value aligns well with recent scholarship on work and management innovation. Julian Birkinshaw's *Reinventing Management* (2012), Thomas Malone's *The Future of Work* (2004), and Lynda Gratton's *The Shift* (2011), for example, outline how individuals and teams innovate their core work tasks.

The second hypothesis regarding job design that I tested is as follows:

HYPOTHESIS 2: Individuals who have redesigned their work and created new opportunities in an effort to add more value perform better at work than those who have not.

1.2. Continuous learning (the "how" of working)

Two different strands of research inform this category. The concepts of organizational and team learning have featured prominently in organization theory for several decades (e.g., Argyris and Schön, 1978; Argote and Epple, 1990; Edmondson, 1999, Gibson and Vermeulen, 2003). Stan and Vermeulen (2013) describe the process of a learning cycle, while others have examined learning curves (Argote and Epple, 1990). Most studies, however, have been conducted at the organizational or team level of analysis.

In the second research trajectory, psychologists have focused on the acquisition of individual expertise. Ericsson et al. (1993) posited the theory of deliberate practice, which is described in chapter four of this book. The popular notion that it takes 10,000 hours of practices to master a skill comes from this research, although Ericsson and colleagues underscore that deliberate practice comprises two elements—many repetitions (hours) and deliberation (the quality of learning, including feedback from coaching). The research in this domain has mainly studied sports, the performing arts, spelling bees, and memory tests, and not people working in companies.

Given the volume of research in this area and the strong links to performance that studies have demonstrated, I felt it important to include a learning category in my framework for this book.

However, as we discovered in our case studies and pilot study, learning at the individual level at work differs from Ericsson's deliberate practice approach. Thus, we have one strand of research that is at the organizational level and one strand that is at the individual level but not about work. My framework combines these two lines of research and considers *the quality of learning at the individual employee level.* Thus my third hypothesis:

HYPOTHESIS 3: Individuals who focus on the quality of their learning (trying out new things, reviewing how they work, getting helpful feedback, learning from failures) will perform better at work than those who don't.

Professor James March's highly influential article, "Exploration and Exploitation in Organizational Learning" (1991), argued that any entity—individual or organization—needs to both engage in major redesign of how it works (exploration) and engage in continuous refinement (exploitation) in order to survive and prosper. My framework covers both: work redesign refers to exploration (hypothesis 2), while refinement concerns exploitation in the form of the learning loop (hypothesis 3).

1.3. Motivational dimensions (the "why" of work)

A long trajectory of research in organizational behavior focuses on the topic of employee motivation, including Herzberg's (1966) classic account of motivation-hygiene theory. I could not do justice to all theories of employee motivation in my framework, as this would require volumes. However, a substantial trend among scholars in recent years has been to move beyond financial compensation and job design as motivators and analyze more intangible dimensions of motivation, including the categories of meaningful or purposeful work, intrinsic motivation, and the role of passion or engagement as a motivator to exert effort while at work (e.g., Amabile and Kramer, 2011; Grant, 2013; Berg, Dutton, and Wrzesniewski, 2013). The basic argument in some of this research is a job-fit theory—people who find a job where they experience passion and purpose will exert more effort and hence perform better. Other researchers postulate a "job crafting" alternative, whereby individuals augment their existing job to experience more purpose and passion (Berg, Dutton, and Wrzesniewski 2013).

Given the prominent role that the concepts of passion and purpose play in recent research, I incorporated those dimensions in my framework. As I detail in chapter five, we learned through our case studies and the pilot study that it wasn't as straightforward as analyzing the effect of "do what you love" (passion) on performance, as passion can lead to poor results, too. We learned that it is the matching of one's desires (passion) with one's ability to contribute beyond oneself (purpose) that produces the best performance:

HYPOTHESIS 4: Individuals who experience high levels of both passion and purpose ("P-squared") will perform better at work than people who don't.

As I discuss in detail in chapter five, "purpose" is a multifaceted aspect, including both "contributions to society" and "contributions to the company and colleagues" (value creation). The latter is in part derived from Hackman and Oldham's job design theory, where "task significance" assessed the extent to which employees *perceive* that what they do matters to colleagues and their organization.

1.4. Relational dimensions (the "who" of work)

1.4.1. Inspiration and Influence

A burgeoning volume of research exists on the topic of how employees relate to one another at work and how they use influence tactics, inspirational tactics, political maneuvering, and sheer grit or persistence to overcome opposition. These lines of research have recognized that individual achievement in today's workplace requires the ability to "get things done with and through others"—that is, to solicit and obtain support, help, expertise, information, and political cover in order to accomplish one's work. While this entire body of research comprises not one but multiple strands of inquiries, I think we can reasonably compile them under the umbrella of "advocacy," as all this research essentially focuses on the same aspect: an individual's ability to obtain support from others.

First, the "influence" school of thought, mostly tied to Professor Robert Cialdini and all the research that is summarized in his book *Influence* (Cialdini, 2008), argues that individuals who use cunning influence tactics (such as mobilizing support and using peer pressure) obtain more support.

Second, closely related is Professor Jeffrey Pfeffer's "power and politics" school, which maintains that individuals need to read the political landscape of their workplace and use cunning political tactics (such as co-opting enemies) to gain support for their agenda (Pfeffer, 2010).

Third, the "grit" school associated with psychologist and Professor Angela Duckworth advances the argument that individuals' perseverance and passion for long-term goals enable employees to overcome setbacks and opposition and thereby improve performance (Duckworth, 2016).

In chapter six, I bring these ideas together to form a "smart grit" concept, arguing that it is the *combination* of Duckworth's grit concept and Pfeffer and Cialdini's political influence tactics that explain performance.

Scholars have also examined the emotional side to persuasion, asserting that individuals who appeal to others' emotions are more likely to make change happen and gain support for their efforts (e.g., Heath and Heath, 2010). This line of inquiry relates to research on leading change (Kotter, 1996). The core idea is that individuals who inspire others by evoking their emotions are better able to gain support for their efforts.

I combined these various dimensions into an overall *advocacy practice*, yielding the following hypothesis about forceful champions:

HYPOTHESIS 5: Individuals who are able to inspire others and deploy smart grit will perform better at work than those who don't.

I originally thought that there were two separate practices here, one around inspiration/grit (advocacy) and another around using political change tactics (change agent). If so, we would have had eight practices in the smartwork framework and not seven. But our empirical analysis (factor analysis) from our 300-person pilot study revealed that these were similar constructs, so I combined them into one. That makes sense: "change agents"—those who use political tactics to get change adopted in the organization (such as Ian Telford, discussed in chapter six)—need to rely heavily on influence and inspirational tactics (i.e., advocacy) as well as sheer grit to get their change through.

1.4.2. Teamwork

If there has ever been one major thrust in organization behavior research over the past two decades, it's teamwork. This emphasis goes hand in hand with the rise of teamwork in organizations. One part of this line of research concerns the design of teams. Richard Hackman proposed a five-factor teamwork model (2002) that has been widely used to organize teams. However, because the present book deals with individual performance and not the design of entire teams, I did not include all the elements in his comprehensive framework. Instead, I included research that focuses on who's on a team (composition) and behaviors in team settings. Here, too, there is a large body of research focused on group conflict (e.g., de Wit, Greer, and Jehn, 2012). The essential conclusion from decades of this research is that diverse teams with talented people who can debate issues well and then commit to actions once a course has been decided do much better than other teams (Amason, 1996; Edmondson, 1999). Thus, for individuals, the key issue is to promote diversity of perspectives (i.e., different backgrounds and not just skills), debate, and then commit, either as a participant or leader. As chapter seven details, this is not easy to accomplish. Teams frequently get trapped in dysfunctional behavior and dynamics such as groupthink (Janis, 1983).

Our case studies, and especially of Reckitt Benckiser (detailed in chapter seven) sharpened these ideas, which I synthesize under the rubric of "fight and unite." Fighting involves rigorous debate among a diverse group of talented individuals who have the right values and attitudes, while uniting involves deciding on an action and committing to it. My hypothesis is as follows:

> HYPOTHESIS 6: Individuals who participate in and lead teams that fight and unite will perform better at work than those who don't.

1.4.3. Collaboration

In recent years, collaboration has become as salient a topic as teamwork. Both topics feed into the larger scholarly trend toward studying more relational (as opposed to strictly individual) dimensions of work. Collaboration differs from teamwork: whereas teamwork focuses on stable teams within a department or across functions, collaboration is a more fleeting activity organized around ad hoc projects and informal knowledge sharing that spans teams and departments. Granted, a gray zone between the two exists. Conceptually though, the two are distinct. Both are extremely important for most employees (although not all), and our survey showed that most individuals frequently engage in both activities.

As chapter eight details, collaboration is fraught with problems, and I will not rehash them here. As research shows, some teams and individuals over- or under-collaborate (Haas and Hansen, 2005; Cross and Parker, 2004; Cross et al., 2016; Gardner, 2017). The key therefore is for employees to engage in "disciplined collaboration." This behavior consists of a set of rules designed to encourage collaboration only on activities of high value (and say no to others) and then to implement them well by finding common goals, building trust, making sure people are motivated to collaborate, and by fully resourcing the effort:

HYPOTHESIS 7: Individuals who engage in disciplined collaboration will perform better at work than those who don't.

This seven-part framework is based on key categories that research has documented as crucial for job performance, including job design (scope and redesign), motivation, learning, advocacy, teamwork, and collaboration. I focused on these categories because of the importance given to them by prior research. Yet my framework extends beyond prior findings. When we conducted the pilot study of 300 people and analyzed numerous cases studies, we discovered several additional or different aspects to the basic findings that seemed to make a large difference in explaining why some people performed and others didn't, namely: that you need to obsess (and not just choose to focus); that the key to redesign is value creation and not just changing goals and tasks; that individuals can apply deliberate practice in most work situations (provided they follow certain tactics as described in chapter four); that following one's passion can be dangerous and that one needs to match it with purpose; that we need to go beyond the notion of sheer grit to include smart grit in the workplace; that a certain kind of fighting in teams is good; and that more collaboration is not necessarily good and that we need to embrace disciplined collaboration. These additional aspects are crucial to understanding the difference between great and merely good individual performance.

The seven hypotheses form a "work-smarter" theory of work. *To work smart means to maximize the value of work by selecting a few activities and applying intense targeted effort.* First, people who work smarter select a few activities that produce high value: They redesign work (hypothesis 2), do less and then obsess (hypothesis 1), and also choose a few collaborations and reject others (hypothesis 7).

Second, people who work smart apply *intense, targeted effort* toward those activities. They create tremendous motivation by tapping into their passion and purpose (hypothesis 4), which is a more effective way to gain motivation than to rely on some outside force like pay. They then make their work productive by improving it through high-quality learning loops (hypothesis 3), intense but effective team meetings (hypothesis 6), well-executed collaborations (hypothesis 7), targeted channeling of efforts (the obsess part of hypothesis 1), work redesigns that improve efficiency and quality (hypothesis 2), and inspirational and persuasive acts that lead others to support the work (hypothesis 5).

In conclusion, this theory postulates a different way of working from the traditional way of "working harder" or "doing more," which is based on taking on as many responsibilities as you can to get more done (vs. selecting only a few tasks), and then working crazy-long hours to be able to complete all that work if at all possible (vs. applying targeted, intense effort toward a few tasks and doing them exceptionally well).

At the end of the day, it's a testable framework: do the seven hypotheses as outlined here explain a substantial part of individual performance or not? And do people who pursue this approach to work outperform those who pursue the "work harder" approach of working many hours and taking on many responsibilities? The second half of this appendix details how I tested the hypotheses and the framework.

2. THE 5,000-PERSON STUDY

2.1. Main objective of the quantitative study

The purpose of undertaking the quantitative study was to test how the seven (or previously eight) factors outlined above affected performance and our well-being index. We used statistical techniques, including regression analysis and structural equation modeling (SEM), to analyze these effects. The purpose of the statistical study was not mainly to gauge the percentage of people reporting a certain behavior (e.g., "x percent reported that they have a rigorous debate in meetings"), but rather to test whether a high score on the seven factors predicted an improvement in performance and well-being. For this reason, this study constitutes an analytical study and not simply a survey.

2.2. Population selection

Initially, we considered a number of populations, including employees in large and small companies, nonprofits, governmental agencies, hospitals, educational institutions, as well as employees residing in the United States, Europe, Asia, and Latin America. While I would have liked to have incorporated these data, doing so would have increased the complexity of the study tremendously (e.g., we would have had to translate the survey instrument into different languages and tailor it to different types of institutions). Instead, we applied "Occam's razor," as discussed in chapter two. What population *must* we have to be able to test the framework? We decided to include employees who met the following criteria:

- they worked in the United States
- they worked in for-profit companies
- their company employs at least 2,000 people
- they are employed full-time (at least 30 hours per week)

Note that we tested the framework in midsize to large, established companies. We reasoned that if the framework worked in these settings, it would likely work in other organizational settings as well (e.g., in large governmental bureaucracies), although we did not confirm that in this study.

We spread the sample across industries to obtain a representative sample (see below).

We divided the total number of survey respondents (5,000) into three subsamples:

a. Self-report (2,000)
b. Rating the boss (1,500)
c. Rating a direct report (1,500)

Each survey respondent was asked to rate one person: self, the boss, or a direct report. The study is about the person being rated ("ratee") and not the rater or respondent (if different). These are not three different ratings of the same person, but rather three different ways of administering the survey.

For the "direct report" version, in which a boss rates a direct report, we asked the boss to pick one of three direct reports as predetermined by us: top-third performer, middle-third, or bottom-third. This procedure ensured that the bosses wouldn't just pick top performers all the time.

We conducted the three different surveys to minimize the potential for what academic researchers call *attribution bias*; such bias often occurs when survey respondents answer questions to cast themselves in the best possible light. Although the survey was anonymous, respondents could still engage in this bias, most likely in the "self-report" sample, in which the respondent was rating herself. Attribution bias was less likely to occur in the other two samples, however, where the respondent was rating someone he or she knew well (the boss, or a direct report), and thus there was no reason for self-serving biases to arise.

We decided to conduct the study on 5,000 people, as we needed sufficient numbers in all three categories and different industries.

2.3. Measurement scales

2.3.1. 7 practices

In a first iteration, we developed a number of survey items to measure each of the eight practices (recall that the initial framework had eight and not seven practices), then tested them on a pilot data set of 300 respondents. Based on that analysis, we kept only those items that properly measured each practice and excluded those questions that had ambiguous or wrong meanings.

Some items were reversed (expressed in the negative) in order to avoid scale use bias in which the respondents simply checked high (or low) on many questions presented in the survey. For example, one item for the "do less, then obsess" practice reads, "Often let themselves get pulled in too many directions." We then reversed this item before doing our analysis, so that it would be stated in the positive for the statistical analysis.

The respondents scored the ratee on each item, using the scale from 1 to 7 (see Table 1 for a list of the items).

Consistent with academic protocol, we used multiple items for each scale, with each item representing a slight variation of the same underlying construct. For example, "does a poor job focusing his/her time and effort on a few key things" and "often lets himself/herself get pulled in too many directions" measure slight variations in "do less." Multiple scales are more robust measurements because they do not depend on the respondent's interpretation of one single item. The internal consistency of items for a single construct was measured with the Cronbach Alpha (CA) statistic. This is a measure of whether the items in a scale co-vary—that they go together and don't measure completely different dimensions. CAs of 0.7 or more are considered good. All seven of the practice scales met this criterion.

Some of the scales have two subdimensions. For example, the "do less, then obsess" practice contain both "do less" and "then obsess." As I discussed in chapter two, it was possible to score differently on these two. When relevant, we conducted an additional analysis where we split the various dimensions underlying one practice.

To complement the quantitative scores, we asked for some qualitative assessments. For the "do less" practice, we asked two questions, with an open-ended space to record comments: "What key factors make it difficult for [you, your direct report, your boss] to focus and simplify [your, his/her] work?" And "What key factors make it easier for [you, your direct report, your boss] to focus and simplify [your, his/her] work?" We also asked, "Please tell us in a few words about the value that [you, your direct report, your boss] is adding to the company."

We initially performed a Principal Components factor analysis to see how distinct these practices were from one another. A factor analysis uses the data to report the extent to which some of the practices were in fact the same or similar construct. In our first iteration, using the pilot data, we determined that a number of items didn't load on the right factor and took them out. Also, the factor analysis revealed that a number of the "advocacy" and "change agent" items under the forceful champion loaded on the same factor and thus represented a similar construct. We resolved this overlap by combining "advocacy" and "change agent" into one construct and thereby reducing the set of factors from eight to seven. The final factor analysis revealed that these seven constructs load on distinct dimensions and thus are different dimensions of work.

To compute the final variable for each practice, we used the factor coefficient weights from the Principal Components analysis for each item. The factor analysis procedure computes a factor score by adding the weighted

List of Items Used for Each Scale

Completely Agree 7	Strongly Agree 6	Somewhat Agree 5	Neither Agree Nor Disagree 4	Somewhat Disagree 3	Strongly Disagree 2	Completely Disagree 1

Table 1. Seven Work-Smart Practices

Practice	Items	Cronbach Alpha**
Do Less, Then Obsess	1. Is extremely good at focusing on key priorities, no matter how much work and how many things he/she has to do	0.80
	2. Does a poor job focusing his/her time and effort on a few key things (reversed)	
	3. Often lets him/herself get pulled in too many directions (reversed)	
	4. Seems to have a habit of making things more complicated than they have to be (reversed)	
	5. Puts a lot of effort into his/her job	
	Note: 1-4 for "do less," and 5 for "obsess."	
Redesign Work	1. Created new opportunities in his/her work — new activities, new projects, new ways of doing things	0.93
	2. Reinvented his/her job to add more value to the company's performance	
	3. Redefined his/her work from doing something typical to something big to pursue	
	4. Strives to do something big in his/her job — to have a huge impact	
	5. Carved out an area of work where he/she is doing something really big and impactful	
	Note: 1-3 for redesign in general; 4-5 for value (impact).	
Learning Loop	1. Doesn't believe that he/she knows best	0.89
	2. Is a very curious person in general	
	3. Often tries out new approaches to see if they will work	
	4. Experiments a lot — trying out things on a small scale to see if they work before doing more	
	5. Constantly changes how he/she works in order to learn and improve	
	6. Constantly reviews how he/she is working and makes changes in an effort to improve	
	7. Is excellent at learning well from failures to avoid repeating the same mistakes	
	Note: 1-2 for learning attitude; 3-5 for trying new practices; 6-7 for feedback and modification.	

Practice	Items	Cronbach Alpha**
P-Squared (Match Passion and Purpose)	1. Is extremely passionate about his/her work 2. Contributes a lot of value to his/her company 3. I feel that my work makes contributions to society beyond just making money Note: 2 measures first base of the purpose pyramid (value); 3 only included for self-report sample (n=2,000), as it measures a feeling which others cannot know.	0.80
Forceful Champion	1. Is very good at inspiring others 2. Is extremely good at getting people fired up in their work 3. Frequently taps into people's emotions to get them excited about their work 4. Relentlessly pursues his/her objectives, no matter the obstacles he/she faces 5. In the face of a setback, he/she keeps going, undeterred 6. Very effective in mobilizing people to make change happen* 7. Uses peer pressure to get people to change* 8. Finds influential people who agree to change and then lets them influence others* Note: 1-3 is inspiration; 4-8 is smart grit (scale omitted a statement about cognitive empathy). *Statement that was combined from "change agent" scale (the 8th factor).	0.86
Fight and Unite	1. Is successful at making sure a team debates issues really well 2. Is extremely good at making people feel it is safe to speak up in meetings 3. Is very successful in getting really skilled and talented people on his/her teams 4. Is very good at picking team members who have the right attitude and values, not just the right skills 5. Makes sure everyone buys into decisions, once they are made 6. Goes to great lengths to eliminate politics that would prevent a decision from being implemented 7. Encourages debate for an appropriate amount of time, but if the team can't agree, he/she will make the decision Note: 1-4 for "fight" (3-4 for staffing diverse teams as part of the "fight" dimension), and 5-7 for "unite."	0.93

Practice	Items	Cronbach Alpha**
Disciplined Collaboration	1. Actively seeks information and expertise from different places in the company that are outside his/her core team	0.80
	2. Often gives help to others outside his/her core team	
	3. Is extremely effective in working across groups in the company to accomplish goals	
	4. Never collaborates with people outside his/her team if there is no compelling reason to do so	
	5. Declines requests to collaborate on issue or goals that have unclear value to the company	
	6. Is very good at fostering trust with the people he/she collaborates with in the company	
	7. Always makes sure that the people he/she collaborates with in the company have a great motivation to help out	
	8. When he/she collaborates with others, he/she always makes sure that they have a common goal and are not just pursuing individual agendas	
	Note: 1-3 measure activity, 4-5 "no" rules, 6-8 quality of collaborations.	

** The Cronbach Alpha ranges from 0.0 to 1.0 and higher values indicate the reliability of the items to measure the practice.

questionnaire item responses on each of the seven dimensions for each respondent.[1] The resulting factor score is a standard z-score whose mean is 0.0 and whose standard deviation is 1.0. For example, for "do less, then obsess," each of the 5 items in table 1 was used to compute the standard score for the "do less, then obsess" practice.

2.3.2. Performance scale

We created a performance index comprised of four questions, as we didn't want to rely on just one item. We used four different formats for the questions. As seen in table 2, the Cronbach Alpha for this measure was 0.92 (very good). A principal components factor analysis was used to create a single standard score for performance in the same way as the factor scores for the 7 dimensions were created.

(In a further analysis that we used to ease interpretation, we transformed the factor score for performance into a placement on the percentile distribution in the 5,000 person data set; this way we could analyze the effect of moving from say the 40th to the 50th percentile on a practice's variable to the practice's movement on the performance variable. We use this analysis to report the effect sizes in each chapter.)

The four performance questions were:

QUESTION 1. Compared to his/her peer group, please indicate his/her level of performance at work.

1. Bottom 0–10 percent (worst)
2. 11–20
3. 21–30
4. 31–40
5. 41–50
6. 51–60
7. 61–70
8. 71–80
9. 81–90
10. Top 91–100 percentile (best)

QUESTION 2. Which category comes closest to describing his/her performance, relative to his/her peer group?

Outstanding: clearly among the very best performers among peers   7
Excellent: consistently performs far better than peers   6
Clearly Above Average: consistently performs better than peers   5
Average: performance falls in the middle of peer group   4
Clearly Below Average: often performs worse than peers   3
Poor: Consistently performs far below peers   2
Very poor: one of the very worst performers among peers   1

Question 3-4. How strongly would you agree or disagree with these statements?

Completely Agree	Strongly Agree	Somewhat Agree	Neither Agree Nor Disagree	Somewhat Disagree	Strongly Disagree	Completely Disagree
7	6	5	4	3	2	1

QUESTION 3. He/she performs exceptionally well at work.

QUESTION 4. He/she produces extremely high-quality work.

Table 2. Performance Factor

Measure	Items	Cronbach Alpha**
Performance	1. Best performance, relative to his/her peer group	0.92
	2. Compared to peer group, level of performance at work	
	3. Performs exceptionally well at work	
	4. Produces extremely high-quality work	

** The Cronbach Alpha ranges from 0.0 to 1.0 and higher values indicate the reliability of the items to measure the practice.

2.3.3. Well-being Scale

This was a composite measure of three constructs: work-life balance, burnout, and job satisfaction. While we combined them into one scale that measured well-being, we also ran separate analyses of the three (as reported in chapter nine). It should be noted that only the self-reported data (n = 2000) were used, as it is impossible for direct reports and bosses to rate those deeply personal experiences.

Table 3. Well-Being Factor

Completely Agree 7	Strongly Agree 6	Somewhat Agree 5	Neither Agree Nor Disagree 4	Somewhat Disagree 3	Strongly Disagree 2	Completely Disagree 1

Measure	Dimension	Items	Cronbach Alpha**
Well-Being	Work-Life Balance	1. The demands of my work interfere with my family or personal time (reversed)	0.92
	Burnout	2. I am feeling burned out at work (reversed)	
	Job Satisfaction	3. I feel that the actual work I do is rewarding in and of itself	
	Job Satisfaction	4. I am very satisfied with my job	

** The Cronbach Alpha ranges from 0.0 to 1.0 and higher values indicate the reliability of the items to measure the practice.

2.3.4. Other variables

We captured the industry in which the person being rated worked (see Table 4). A good mix of industries is represented in the sample. We also asked the rater to check the box that best describes the ratee's department or role (Table 5), which also shows a good mix. Table 6 shows that there is a good mix with respect to gender, age, company tenure, company size, and job levels.

Finally, we used the StrengthFinders 2.0's approach to job fit to ask the key question about whether a person's strengths match the job he or she has, using the scale from 7 (completely agree) to 1 (completely disagree): "His/her current job gives him/her the opportunity to do what he/she does best every day." We used this measure in our further analysis of passion and purpose (see section 3.2.5).

Table 4. Industry Categories

Items	Percent
Manufacturing	15.7
Financial Services incl. Insurance and Real Estate	14.0
Retail	11.1
Information Technology	8.2
Health-care Other, incl. Pharmaceutical and Biotech	5.7
Transportation	5.7
Consumer Goods and Services	5.0
Telecommunication	4.7
Energy	3.1
Utilities	1.9
Health-care Delivery	1.8
Industrial Products and Services	1.7
Construction	1.0
Materials	0.5
Other	19.9
N=4,964	100.0%

Table 5. Department or Role

	Percent
Accounting / Finance	7.6
Administration	4.3
Advertising / Media / PR	0.7
Consultant	2.1
Corporate Development	0.4
Customer Service / Retail	7.1
Design & Technology	1.1
Doctor / Nurse / Care Giver / Social Work	0.4
Education & Training	1.4
Engineering	7.3
General Management	3.9
Human Resources	4.8
Information Management	1.5
Information Technology	7.4
Legal Services	1.6
Logistics & Distribution	1.8
Marketing	2.6
Operations / Project Management	9.6
Planning	1.1
Production	3.4
Purchasing	1.6
Quality Assurance	3.4
Research & Development	3.6
Sales	9.2
Maintenance	1.5
Other Job Function	10.6
Total	100.0%

Table 6. Distribution of Sample by Various Variables

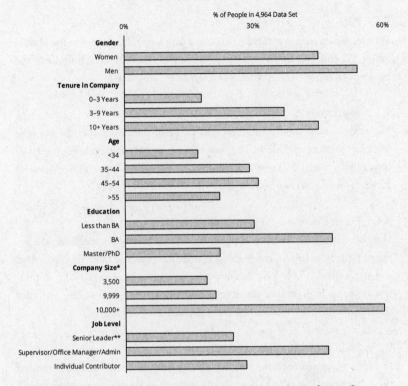

% of People in 4,964 Data Set

* Company size denotes number of employees (the data also included a supplement of very small companies).
** Senior leader: CEO, president, vice president, general manager.

2.4. Data Collection

2.4.1. Pilot

We used a data service company that uses a database of employees in the United States. We collected 300 self-reported surveys for the pilot. The purpose of the pilot was to refine the hypotheses and the survey instrument.

2.4.2. Main study

We used the same service to collect data for 5,000 individuals (people from the pilot sample were excluded). The targets were set for 2,000 self-reports, 1,500 boss-ratings, and 1,500 direct report ratings. We ended up with 4,964 useful surveys (rounded to n=5,000 throughout the text in the book).[2]

2.4.3. Phone interviews for case studies (N= 51)

We also did follow-up phone interviews with 51 survey respondents. We selected those who had scored high on a particular practice. They were recorded and transcribed. These gave us qualitative insights into what they did in their work to score high on specific survey items. We use their data as case examples throughout the book (names and other details have been altered).

2.4.4. Additional case studies (N=72)

In addition, we searched for case subjects beyond the survey sample. We used the survey measurement as a guide to determine that the protagonist scored high on a particular quality practice. We followed up with qualitative interviews to gain deeper insight into what they did to do well on that particular practice. These cases are reported throughout the book.

3. MAIN RESULTS

3.1. Predicting performance

To estimate the main effect of all the seven practices, we created a variable, *Score on 7 Factors Combined*, by summing the scores on the seven factors. Not all ratees who scored high on the seven practice factors performed well, of course, but the overwhelming majority did. Neither did all high-performers score high on the seven factors. The correlation plot in chapter one and included here shows the dispersion of the two variables.

For the main test, we used ordinary least square regression analysis. (Although there is some correlation among the predictor measures—i.e., multicollinearity—all practice variables had tolerance levels high enough to permit isolation of the independent effects of the variables.)

Table 7 shows the main results from the regression analysis. Model 1 shows the effects of the control variables. Model 2 adds average hours worked per week. We also entered the squared term of hours worked to control for the curvilinear effect described below.[3] The plot of these two variables is reported in chapter three.

In Model 3 we add the seven practices to show the impact of these variables after the effects of the control variables and hours worked are taken into

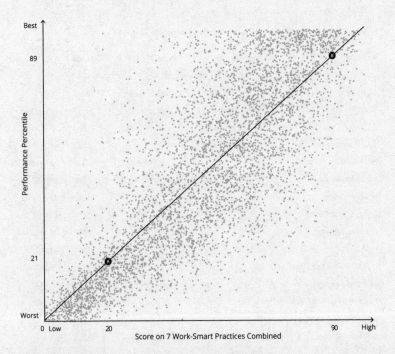

Lifting Individual Performance

The Positive Effect of the Seven Practices Combined on Individual Performance

Note:
These 4,964 data points representing people in our study show a pattern: The inserted line represents a statistical regression prediction of how the seven practices combined affect individual performance. Score low on the seven practices (point A in the chart) and your performance likely will be mediocre. Score high (point B) and your performance likely will be excellent.

account. All seven variables show significant and positive effects in predicting performance at the p<.001 level (that is, they are statistically highly significant).

Table 7 also reveals the incremental increase in variance in performance explained (R-squared) across the models. The control variables account for only 4 percent of the variance in the performance scores. The two hours-worked variables explain an additional 6 percent, after the effect of the control variables are removed. *The seven practices then show an additional R-square change of 0.66, which means that they explain 66 percent of the total variance of performance in the sample after the effects of the control variables and hours worked are removed.* The residual variance of 24 percent is not explained in this model and is the effect of all other unmeasured variables.

For the control variables, education, increased job tenure, and being female predict higher performance ratings. Increased hours worked also predicts higher performance in a curvilinear fashion (as described in chapter three).

Table 7. Performance (All Respondents, N=4,964)

Variable	Model 1	Model 2	Model 3
	Standardized Coefficients, Beta (t-stat in Parenthesis)		
Age (Years)	0.003 (0.189)	-0.006 (-0.401)	-0.002 (-0.311)
Gender	-0.063*** (-4.487)	-0.083*** (-6.086)	-0.014** (-1.980)
Job Tenure (Years)	0.074*** (4.909)	0.054*** (3.687)	0.043*** (5.583)
Education (Years)	0.176*** (12.586)	0.132*** (9.595)	0.032*** (4.343)
Hours Worked Per Week		0.910*** (9.521)	0.128*** (2.541)
Hours Squared		-0.687*** (-7.207)	-0.089* (-1.788)
Redesign Work			0.063*** (4.671)
Do Less, Then Obsess			0.276*** (27.544)
Forceful Champion			0.109*** (7.437)
Fight and Unite			0.063*** (4.303)
Disciplined Collaboration			0.134*** (9.316)
Learning Loop			0.153*** (11.784)
P-Squared (Passion & Purpose)			0.194*** (14.886)
R-Squared	0.04	0.10	0.76
R-Squared Change		0.06	0.66
N	4,964	4,964	4,964

Note:
6 observations with missing information.
***p <0.001; **p<0.05; *p<0.10.

In terms of coefficients, the total standardized effect of the seven practices factors is the sum of the Beta weights, 0.99. In a hypothetical case, that means that a simultaneous one standard deviation increase in factor scores for all seven practices would lead to a 0.99 standard deviation increase in performance, independent of the effects of the control variables and hours worked variables. (It's a coincidence that there is a nearly a one-to-one ratio here.) This effect is substantial and is much larger than the effects of hours worked and the other control variables.

Overall, this statistical analysis lends very strong support to the main argument in the book: the higher the score on the seven "work smarter" practices, the higher the likely performance.

3.2. Predicting well-being

3.2.1. Predicting work-life balance (self-report respondents, N=2,000)
Table 8 shows the results for work-life balance (i.e., the reverse score of "the demands of my work interfere with my family or personal time"). The results show the following significant effects: "do less, then obsess" and "disciplined collaboration" are significant positive predictors, as is increased age, while hours worked, length of job tenure, and passion and purpose are negative predictors, as detailed in chapter nine.

3.2.2. Predicting NO burnout (self-report respondents, N=2,000)
The model in table 9 predicts lower chances of burnout (i.e., the opposite of survey item of feeling burned out). The significant and positive effects were: "do less, then obsess," "P-squared (passion and purpose)," "redesign work," and "disciplined collaboration" lower chances of burnout, as does increasing age and being male, while "fight and unite," long hours, and longer job tenure increase the risk of burning out.

3.2.3. Predicting job satisfaction (self-report respondents, N=2,000)
The model in table 10 predicts job satisfaction. The significant effects: "redesign work," "forceful champion," "disciplined collaboration," and "P-squared (passion and purpose)" all positively predict job satisfaction. Hours worked had no significant impact on job satisfaction. Older respondents also had higher job satisfaction. "P-squared (passion and purpose)" is a very strong predictor, more than twice as powerful as any of the other significant predictors.

Table 8. Predictors of Positive Work-Life Balance (Self-Report Respondents, N=2,000)

Variable	Standardized Coefficients, Beta (t-stat in Parenthesis)
Age (Years)	0.058** (2.548)
Gender	0.011 (0.531)
Job Tenure (Years)	-0.050** (-2.213)
Education (Years)	-0.052** (-2.510)
Hours Worked Per Week	-0.945*** (-6.383)
Hours Squared	0.621*** (4.205)
Redesign Work	0.032 (1.088)
Do Less, Then Obsess	0.221*** (10.051)
Forceful Champion	-0.030 (-0.965)
Fight and Unite	-0.046 (-1.475)
Disciplined Collaboration	0.083** (2.738)
Learning Loop	-0.002 (-0.061)
P-Squared (Passion & Purpose)	-0.055* (-1.930)
N	2,000

***p <0.001; **p<0.05; *p<0.10.

Table 9. Predictors of Low Burnout (Self-Report Respondents, N=2,000)

Variable	Standardized Coefficients, Beta (t-stat in Parenthesis)
Age (Years)	0.096*** (4.155)
Gender	0.087*** (4.068)
Job Tenure (Years)	-0.110*** (-4.835)
Education (Years)	-0.028 (-1.307)
Hours Worked Per Week	-0.621*** (-4.127)
Hours Squared	0.478** (3.182)
Redesign Work	0.094** (3.117)
Do Less, Then Obsess	0.227*** (10.136)
Forceful Champion	0.006 (0.181)
Fight and Unite	-0.070** (-2.227)
Disciplined Collaboration	0.098** (3.175)
Learning Loop	-0.026 (-0.934)
P-Squared (Passion & Purpose)	0.097** (3.341)
N	2,000

***p <0.001; **p<0.05; *p<0.10.

Table 10. Predicting Job Satisfaction (Self-Report Respondents, N=2,000)

Variable	Standardized Coefficients, Beta (t-stat in Parenthesis)	
Age (Years)	0.067**	(3.364)
Gender	0.008	(0.444)
Job Tenure (Years)	-0.012	(-0.611)
Education (Years)	-0.024	(-1.311)
Hours Worked Per Week	-0.003	(-0.022)
Hours Squared	-0.029	(-0.219)
Redesign Work	0.199***	(7.589)
Do Less, Then Obsess	-0.008	(-0.392)
Forceful Champion	0.071**	(2.598)
Fight and Unite	-0.052*	(-1.908)
Disciplined Collaboration	0.061**	(2.285)
Learning Loop	0.024	(1.013)
P-Squared (Passion & Purpose)	0.392***	(15.559)
N	2,000	

***p <0.001; **p<0.05; *p<0.10.

3.2.4. Analyzing the relationship between hours worked and performance

In chapter 3, we included an analysis showing that there is an inverted U-relationship between hours worked and performance. To measure hours worked, we asked the respondents to ask how many hours the ratee worked on average over the past six months. That would be self-report for those who assessed themselves.

This estimate is of course a subjective assessment. It is quite possible that people overestimated the hours people worked. However, that does not change the main conclusion of this analysis, as the inverted U-relationship will still hold although the peak point of 65 hours would move to the left, i.e., be slightly lower if there was a systematic overestimation.

Developing the best representation of this nonlinear relationship between hours worked and performance was an iterative process. The first test was to see if there was a simple linear relationship (more hours, better performance) or if performance was related to hours worked in a nonlinear form (diminishing returns or a reversal after a peak).[4]

We found that a model with an inverted-U component that resulted from the addition of hours squared as a predictor was significantly better at predicting performance than a simple straight line. This is called the combined quadratic model, in which the predicted values increase to one maximum point, then begin falling off.[5]

However, the rate at which performance fell off after the peak was slower than predicted by a simple squared parabola. The solution was to fit two functions to the data, one for lower values of the predictor variable and a different one for higher values, joining at a value of the predictor variable called the "knot." This is called a *spline fit*.[6]

The value of the knot was found by methodically testing values near the maximum of the quadratic function, in the range of 50–70 hours. The best fit to the data with the lowest error in prediction was found with the knot set at 65 hours. The predictive function from 30 to 65 hours is the combined quadratic function, with the subsequent 65–90 hours function represented by a linear function. The resulting spline fit that minimizes error between hours worked and performance prediction is shown in the graph. This analysis is described in chapter three in the section "squeezing the orange."

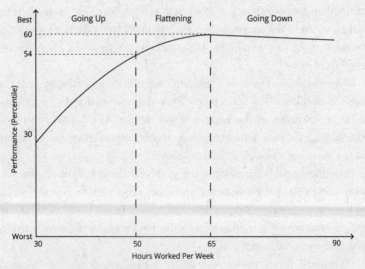

Squeezing the Orange
Less Performance Juice Per Hour Worked

Note:
Based on regression analysis of 4,964 people.

In a further analysis to try to understand why the curve flattens and then decreases with hours worked, we isolated one of the performance items—quality of work ("produces extremely high-quality work")—to see if we would get the same answer. Perhaps hours worked reduced overall work-quality at very high numbers of hours? That turned out to be the case. Up to about 50 hours, adding more hours increased quality of work. Between 50 and 65 hours, work-quality still went up but at a decreasing rate. Beyond 65 hours, work-quality decreased, just as the performance percentile did in the chart above. Thus it is possible that the real driver of the inverted U-shaped curve is that a person's quality of work begins to suffer at very long hours of work (perhaps because of increased error rates), and that causes overall work-performance to decline.

3.2.5. Further analysis of the effect of passion on hours worked, effort and performance

As discussed in chapter five, we found that passion and purpose didn't lead to that many more hours of work (i.e., only seven more hours), but rather to more effort per hour worked. We can think of a person's total effort as consisting of two components:

Total effort at work = number of hours worked × effort-per-hour

If we can remove the effect of number of hours worked ("controlled for" in statistical parlance), then we can isolate the effect of effort-per-hour. As I argue in chapter five, passion and purpose make a person have more energy at work, and that leads to *greater effort per hour of work*.

We used a method called Structural Equation Modeling (SEM) to tease apart these various effects of effort. SEM models the flow of hypothetical cause-and-effect relationships among variables, and tests the hypothetical model against the actual data to see if the flow is a plausible explanation. It does not prove causality, but does provide statistical evidence to reject implausible models (see this endnote for more details[7]).

The diagram below shows the model that resulted from tests of a number of theoretically justified models (most of which were rejected as implausible after SEM analysis). It is a very good model that fits the data very well, with only 0.3 percent error. The probability that this error was random ($p = .37$) is well above the criterion for a good fit. The model is a plausible explanation of the relationships among Passion and Purpose, hours worked, and performance.

The arrows in the diagram indicate the direction of influence between variables, and numbers near the arrows show the path coefficients. These are the estimate of the strength of the influence, which can range from -1.0 (perfect negative relationship) to 0.0 (no influence) to 1.0 (perfect positive relationship).

First, what drives passion in this model? As the diagram shows, the key variable is the StrengthsFinder approach to job-fit ("opportunity to do what I do best every day"), which drives passion. That makes sense. People are passionate about jobs that tap into their natural strengths.

Second, higher passion and purpose predicts a small increase in hours worked (.08), but a very much larger increase in effort ("makes a huge effort on the job") put into their job (.81). This higher effort is associated with a moderate increase in working hours, too (.22), but this increase in working hours then has only a tiny impact on performance (.03). Both passion and purpose (.49) and effort (.30) are much stronger predictors of performance.

We can conclude from this analysis that passion and purpose primarily drives effort during working hours (effort-per-hour), as distinct from effort through working long hours.

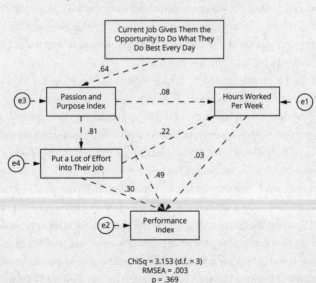

Job Fit, Passion, and Hours as Performance Predictors

ChiSq = 3.153 (d.f. = 3)
RMSEA = .003
p = .369

4. STRENGTHS AND LIMITATIONS

4.1. Strengths of this method

All research methods have strengths and limitations, and this study is no exception. On the strength side, several benefits accrue from using a large sample of 4,964 managers and employees (rounded up to 5,000 in the text). First, a large sample allows us to verify the framework statistically and demonstrate its effects on performance and well-being. It holds up well against statistical scrutiny.

Second, the statistical tests are conducted across respondents drawn from different companies and industries. Thus they generalize to a larger population and are not confined within a few industries or job roles.

This large-scale analysis allows us to verify the seven-practice model of working smart and to provide an empirically derived framework to the work-productivity field of books and articles that have been lacking in the use of data and statistical analysis.

4.2. Limitations

Large sample vs. in-depth insight. On the limitations side, one issue is that a survey instrument does not allow us to gain in-depth information on each study participant. That's the trade-off: the greater the number of participants in the study (which allows for a better statistical test), the less in-depth information on each person. I opted for large numbers so as to enable a robust statistical test of the framework. To complement this approach, we conducted interviews with 120 case studies to gain in-depth information.

Common methods problem. Another limitation is that we use the survey instrument to measure both the outcomes (performance and well-being) and the input factors (the seven or eight practices). This is known in academic studies as the "common methods" problem. Because a respondent is asked to fill in information for both input and outcomes, a bias might occur. For example, a boss-respondent may personally like the ratee, leading him to give high ratings on both the input and outcome variables.

I mitigated this problem in the following ways: a) by asking specific behavioral questions (e.g., "he/she puts a lot of effort into his/her job"); b) by putting the performance questions in a separate final segment of the survey so as not to bias the other questions, and c) by framing the overall survey as one about work habits and not about a performance evaluation, which should alleviate the tendency to always associate an answer to a survey question with overall performance evaluation. These mitigations seem to have been effective. In our data, we identified numerous negative correlations between variables, which should not occur if the respondent rated everything high (e.g., because the respondent liked the person) or everything low (e.g., because the respondent disliked the person). Thus I am reasonably confident that we avoided significant common methods problems.

Reverse causality. The other issue in all studies of this type is the potential problem of reverse causality. For example, the study tested whether "do less, then obsess" predicted higher performance. It's a cause-and-effect statement. By doing less, people perform better. But the causality could run the other way: high performance caused the person to practice the "do less, then obsess." Such reverse causalities are quite possible. The only way to disentangle this would be to measure the impact of changes in a practice over the course of one or more years.

However, part of this issue can be dealt with. Some of the reverse causalities are theoretically less plausible: it's unlikely that high performance would cause someone to do less. Rather, high performance may lead the boss to load more work onto the person (who becomes a "go-to" person), thus leading the person to do more, not less. In addition, we have statements from the interviews that buttress arguments that the causality runs as we predicted in the model, for example, that the person's ability to prioritize (do less) contributed to better performance.

In addition, some of the reverse causalities are compatible with the main argument in this book (that the seven factors led to higher performance). Two-way causalities can coexist. For example, passion leads to greater performance, which leads to greater passion, which leads to greater performance, and so on, creating an upward cycle.

Determinism. The final issue concerns probability versus determinism. The model I present in this book does not state that the seven factors *determine* performance, if determination (or cause) here is construed to mean "guaranteed." Nothing in work productivity is guaranteed. The only statement we can make is that *a person stands a much higher chance of achieving better performance to the extent that he or she practices the seven practices*. It's a probabilistic and not a deterministic statement. It is always possible to identify people who score very high on the seven practices, *yet who do not perform well*. The chart in chapter one and on page 237 showing the 4,964 data points reveals such instances: there are people who scored highly on the seven practices yet did not perform so well (toward bottom-right of the chart). There may be other reasons for why they failed to perform. Likewise, some people in the chart who performed extremely well did not practice the seven practices (top-left corner). As the outliers indicate, the seven-factor framework is not the only road to success.

In conclusion, this study overwhelmingly demonstrates that the work-smart framework that I present in this book substantially improves people's chances of becoming a top performer in their line of work.

Bibliography

Agle, Bradley R., Nandu J. Nagarajan, Jeffrey A. Sonnenfeld, and Dhinu Srinivasan. "Does CEO Charisma Matter? An Empirical Analysis of the Relationships Among Organizational Performance, Environmental Uncertainty, and Top Management Team Perceptions of CEO Charisma." *Academy of Management Journal 49*, no. 1 (2006): 161–174.

Alexander, Caroline. "The Race to the South Pole." *National Geographic*, September 2011.

Amabile, Teresa M., and Steven J. Kramer. "The Power of Small Wins." *Harvard Business Review 89*, no. 5 (2011): 70–80.

Amason, Allen C. "Distinguishing the Effects of Functional and Dysfunctional Conflict on Strategic Decision Making: Resolving a Paradox for Top Management Teams." *Academy of Management 39*, no. 1 (1996): 123–148.

Amundsen, Roald. *The South Pole: An Account of the Norwegian Antarctic Expedition in the Fram, 1910–1912*. New York: Cooper Square Press, 2000.

Argote, Linda, and Dennis Epple. "Learning Curves in Manufacturing." *Science 247*, no. 4945 (1990): 920–924.

Argyris, Chris, and Donald A. Schön. *Organizational Learning. A Theory of Action Perspective*. Reading: Addison Wesley, 1978.

Ariely, Dan. *Predictably Irrational: The Hidden Forces That Shape Our Decisions*. New York: HarperCollins, 2008.

Barclay, Laurie. "Better Handoffs Cut Medical Errors 30% in Multicenter Trial." *Medscape*, November 6, 2014.

Berg, Justin M., Jane E. Dutton, and Amy Wrzesniewski. "Job Crafting and Meaningful Work" in *Purpose and Meaning in the Workplace*. Ed. Bryan J. Dik, Zinta S. Byrne, and Michael F. Steger. Washington, DC: American Psychological Association, 2013, 81–104.

Berger, Jonah A. *Contagious: Why Things Catch On*. New York: Simon & Schuster, 2016.

Berger, Jonah A., and Katherine L. Milkman. "What Makes Online Content Viral?" *Journal of Marketing Research 49*, no. 2 (2012): 192–205.

Biciunaite, Audre. "Economic Growth and Life Expectancy: Do Wealthier Countries Live Longer?" *Euromonitor International*, March 14, 2014. Accessed June 22, 2017, http://blog.euromonitor.com/2014/03/economic growth-and-life-expectancy-do-wealthier-countries-live-longer.html.

Birkinshaw, Julian. *Reinventing Management: Smarter Choices for Getting Work Done*. San Francisco: Jossey-Bass, 2012.

Bishop, Susan. "The Strategic Power of Saying No." *Harvard Business Review 77*, no. 6 (1999): 50–61.

Bissel, Richard M. Jr. *Reflections of a Cold Warrior: From Yalta to the Bay of Pigs*. New Haven: Yale University Press, 1996.

Black, Jane. "Jamie Oliver Improves Huntington, W.Va.'s Eating Habits." *Washington Post*, April 21, 2010.

Bluedorn, Allen C., Daniel B. Turban, and Mary Sue Love. "The Effects of Stand-Up and Sit-Down Meeting Formats on Meeting Outcomes." *Journal of Applied Psychology 84*, no. 2 (1999): 277–285.

Bohmer, Richard, Laura Feldman, Erika Ferlins, Amy C. Edmondson, and Michael Roberto. "*Columbia*'s Final Mission." Case 304-090. Boston: Harvard Business School, April 2004.

Bolino, Mark C., and William H. Turnley. "Counternormative Impression Management, Likeability, and Performance Ratings: The Use of Intimidation in an Organizational Setting." *Journal of Organizational Behavior 24*, no. 2 (2003): 237–250.

Bono, Joyce E., and Remus Ilies. "Charisma, Positive Emotions, and Mood Contagion." *Leadership Quarterly 17*, no. 4 (2006): 317–334.

Breashears, David, Morten T. Hansen, Ludo Van der Heyden, and Elin Williams. "Tragedy on Everest." Case 5519 (Fontainebleau: INSEAD, September 2014).

Breen, Richard, and Inkwan Chung. "Income Inequality and Education." *Sociological Science 2* (2015): 454–477.

Brennan, Paul, et al. "High Cumulative Risk of Lung Cancer Death among Smokers and Nonsmokers in Central and Eastern Europe." *American Journal of Epidemiology 164*, no. 12 (2006): 1233–1241.

Buckingham, Marcus. *Now, Discover your Strengths*. New York: Gallup Press, 2001.

Bunderson, J. Stuart, and Jeffrey A. Thompson. "The Call of the Wild: Zookeepers, Callings, and the Dual Edges of Deeply Meaningful Work." *Administrative Science Quarterly 54* (2009): 32–57.

Burke, Ronald J., and Esther R. Greenglass. "Hospital Restructuring, Work-Family Conflict and Psychological Burnout Among Nursing Staff." *Psychology and Health 16*, no. 5 (2001): 583–594.

Cain, Susan. *Quiet: The Power of Introverts in a World That Can't Stop Talking*. New York: Broadway Books, 2013.

Chaikin, Andrew. "White House Tapes Shed Light on JFK Space Race Legend." *Space & Science*, August 22, 2001.

Chakravarthy, Bala, and Hans Huber. "Internal Entrepreneurship at the Dow Chemical Co." Case 1117. Lausanne: IMD, July 2003.

Chen, Patricia, Phoebe C. Ellsworth, and Norbert Schwarz. "Finding a Fit or Developing It: Implicit Theories About Achieving Passion for Work." *Personality and Social Psychology Bulletin 41*, no. 10 (2015): 1411–1424.

Christensen, Clayton, Michael E. Raynor, and Rory McDonald. "What Is Disruptive Innovation?" *Harvard Business Review 93*, no. 12 (2015): 44–53.

Cialdini, Robert B. *Influence: The Psychology of Persuasion*. New York: HarperCollins, 2006.

Clotfelter, Charles T., Helen F. Ladd, and Jacob L. Vigdor. "Teacher Credentials and Student Achievement in High School: A Cross-Subject Analysis with Student Fixed Effects." *NBER Working Paper No. 13617*, November 2007, last revision March 2008.

Coens, Tom, and Mary Jenkins. *Abolishing Performance Appraisals: Why They Backfire and What to Do Instead*. San Francisco: Berrett-Koehler, 2000.

Cohen-Charash, Youchi, and Paul E. Spector. "The Role of Justice in Organizations: A Meta-analysis." *Organizational Behavior and Human Decision Processes 86*, no. 2 (2001): 278–321.

Collins, Jim. *Good to Great: Why Some Companies Make the Leap . . . and Others Don't*. New York: HarperBusiness, 2001.

Collins, Jim, and Morten T. Hansen. *Great by Choice: Uncertainty, Chaos and Luck—Why Some Thrive Despite Them All*. New York: HarperBusiness, 2011.

Collins, Jim, and Jerry I. Porras. *Built to Last*. New York: HarperCollins, 1994.

Colvin, Geoff. *Talent Is Overrated: What Really Separates World-Class Performers from Everybody Else*. New York: Portfolio, 2008.

Covey, Stephen R. *The 7 Habits of Highly Effective People: Powerful Lessons in Personal Change*. New York: Simon & Schuster, 2013.

Coviello, Decio, Andrea Ichino, and Nicola Persico. "The Inefficiency of Worker Time Use." *Journal of the European Economic Association 13*, no. 5 (2015): 906–947.

Coyle, Daniel. *The Talent Code: Greatness Isn't Born. It's Grown*. New York: Bantam, 2009.

Cross, Rob, and Andrew Parker. *The Hidden Power of Social Networks: Understanding How Work Really Gets Done in Organizations*. Boston: Harvard Business Review Press, 2004.

Cross, Rob, Reb Rebele, and Adam Grant. "Collaborative Overload." *Harvard Business Review 94*, no. 1 (2016): 74–79.

Crveni17. "1994 Bulls Knicks Game 3 Buzzer Beating Game Winner (The Story Behind)." Sole Records. Posted August 20, 2011. https://www.youtube.com/watch?feature=player_detailpage&v=c7SbG-8Bvgk.

Csikszentmihalyi, Mihaly. *Flow: The Psychology of Optimal Experience*. New York: Harper & Row, 1990.

Cuddy, Amy J. C., Peter Glick, and Anna Beninger. "The Dynamics of Warmth and Competence Judgments, and Their Outcomes in Organizations." *Research in Organizational Behavior 31* (2011): 73–98.

De Saint-Exupéry, Antoine. *Terre des Hommes* (1939). Trans. Lewis Galantière. *Wind, Sand and Stars*. New York: Harcourt Brace & Company, 1967.

De Wit, Frank R. C., Lindred L. Greer, and Karen A. Jehn. "The Paradox of Intragroup Conflict: A Meta-Analysis." *Journal of Applied Psychology 97*, no. 2 (2012): 360–390.

Donini-Lenhoff, Fred G., and Hannah L. Hedrick. "Growth of Specialization in Graduate Medical Education." *JAMA: The Journal of the American Medical Association 284*, no. 10 (2000): 1284–1289.

Drucker, Peter. *The Effective Executive: The Definitive Guide to Getting the Right Things Done*. New York: HarperBusiness, 2006.

Duckworth, Angela L. *Grit: The Power of Passion and Perseverance*. New York: Scribner, 2016.

Duckworth, Angela L., and Christopher Peterson. "Grit: Perseverance and Passion for Long-Term Goals." *Journal of Personality and Social Psychology 92*, no. 6 (2007): 1087–1101.

Dweck, Carol. *Mindset: The New Psychology of Success*. New York: Random House, 2007.

Edmondson, Amy C. "Psychological Safety and Learning Behavior in Work Teams." *Administrative Science Quarterly 44*, no. 2 (1999): 350–383.

Edmondson, Amy C., Richard M. Bohmer, and Gary P. Pisano. "Disrupted Routines: Team Learning and New Technology Implementation in Hospitals." *Administrative Science Quarterly 46* (2001): 685–716.

Edmondson, Amy C., and Kathryn Roloff. "Leveraging Diversity Through Psychological Safety." *Rotman Magazine* (Fall 2009): 47–51.

Edmondson, Amy C., Ashley-Kay Fryer, and Morten T. Hansen. "Transforming Care at UnityPoint Health—Fort Dodge." Case 615-052. Boston: Harvard Business School, March 2015.

Eisenhardt, Kathleen M., and Mark J. Zbaracki. "Strategic Decision Making." *Strategic Management Journal 13*, no. 52 (1992): 17–37.

Ericsson, K. Anders, Ralf Th. Krampe, and Clemens Tesch-Roemer. "The role of deliberate practice in the acquisition of expert performance." *Psychological Review 100* (1993): 363–406.

Ericsson, K. Anders. "The Influence of Experience and Deliberate Practice on the Development of Superior Expert Performance." In *Cambridge Handbook of Expertise and Expert Performance*, edited by K. Anders Ericsson, Neil Charness, Paul J. Feltovich, and Robert R. Hoffman, 685–70. Cambridge: Cambridge University Press, 2006

Ericsson, K. Anders, and Jim Pool. *Peak: Secrets from the New Science of Expertise*. New York: Houghton Mifflin Harcourt, 2016.

Forbes Healthcare Summit 2014. "At Age 22, DNA Sequencing Put My Cancer on Pause." Forbes Video. December 15, 2014. https://www.forbes.com/video/3930262661001.

Freeman, Rebecca. "Labour Productivity Indicators: Comparison of two OECD Databases, Productivity Differentials & The Balassa-Samuelson Effect." OECD, July 2008. Accessed August 3, 2015. http://www.oecd.org/std/labour-stats/41354425.pdf.

Gardner, Heidi K. "Performance Pressure as a Double-edged Sword." *Administrative Science Quarterly 57*, no. 1 (2012): 1–46.

Gardner, Heidi K. *Smart Collaboration: How Professionals and Their Firms Succeed by Breaking Down Silos*. Boston: Harvard Business Review Press, 2017.

Garrad, Lewis, and Tomas Chamorro-Premuzic. "The Dark Side of High Employee Engagement." *Harvard Business Review*, August 16, 2016. Accessed

February 24, 2017. https://hbr.org/2016/08/the-dark-side-of-high-employee
-engagement.

Gawande, Atul. "The Bell Curve." *The New Yorker*, December 6, 2004.

Gelb, David. *Jiro Dreams of Sushi*. New York: Magnolia Home Entertainment: 2012. DVD.

Gerace, Adam, Andrew Day, Sharon Casey, and Philip Mohr. "An Exploratory Investigation of the Process of Perspective Taking in Interpersonal Situations." *Journal of Relationships Research 4*, no. e6 (2013): 1–12.

Gibson, Cristina, and Freek Vermeulen. "A Healthy Divide: Subgroups as a Stimulus for Team Learning Behavior." *Administrative Science Quarterly 48*, no. 2 (2003): 202–239.

Gladwell, Malcolm. *Outliers: The Story of Success*. New York: Little, Brown & Company, 2008.

Gleijeses, Piero. "Ships in the Night: The CIA, the White House and the Bay of Pigs." *Journal of Latin American Studies 27*, no. 1 (February 1995): 1–42.

Goleman, Daniel. *Focus: The Hidden Driver of Excellence*. New York: HarperCollins, 2013.

Golkar, Armita, Emilia Johansson, Maki Kasahara, Walter Osika, Aleksander Perski, and and Ivanca Savic. "The Influence of Work-Related Chronic Stress on the Regulation of Emotion and on Functional Connectivity in the Brain." *PLoS One 9, no. 9* (2014). doi: 10.1371/journal.pone0104550.

Govindarajan, Vijay. "The First Two Steps Toward Breaking Down Silos in Your Organization." *Harvard Business Review*, August 9, 2011. Accessed February 24, 2017. https://hbr.org/2011/08/the-first-two-steps-toward -breaking-down-silos/.

Grant, Adam. *Give and Take: Why Helping Others Drives Our Success*. New York: Viking, 2013.

Grant, Adam. *Originals: How Non-Conformists Move the World*. New York: Viking, 2016.

Grant, Adam M., Elizabeth M. Campbell, Grace Chen, Keenan Cottone, David Lapedis, and Karen Lee. "Impact and the Art of Motivation Maintenance: The Effects of Contact with Beneficiaries on Persistence Behavior." *Organizational Behavior and Human Decision Processes 103* (2007): 53–67.

Gratton, Lynda. *The Shift: The Future of Work Is Already Here*. New York: HarperCollins, 2011.

Gulati, Ranjay. "Silo Busting: How to Execute on the Promise of Customer Focus." *Harvard Business Review 85*, no. 5 (2007): 98–108.

Haas, Martine R., and Morten T. Hansen. "Competing for Attention in Knowledge Markets: Electronic Document Dissemination in a Management Consulting Company." *Administrative Science Quarterly 46* (2001): 1–28.

Haas, Martine R. and Morten T. Hansen. "When Using Knowledge Can Hurt Performance: An Empirical Test of Competitive Bidding in a Management Consulting Company." *Strategic Management Journal 26* (2005): 1–24.

Hackman, J. Richard. *Leading Teams: Setting the Stage for Great Performances.* Boston, Harvard Business Press, 2002.

Hackman, J. Richard, and Greg R. Oldham. "Motivation through the Design of Work: Test of a Theory." *Organizational Behavior and Human Performance 16*, no. 2 (1976): 250–279.

Halberstam, David. "The Vantage Point; Perspectives of the Presidency 1963–1969. By Lyndon Baines Johnson. Illustrated. 636 pp. New York: Holt, Rinehart and Winston. $15." *New York Times*, October 31, 1971.

Halberstam, David. *The Best and the Brightest.* New York: Ballantine Books, 1992.

Halbesleben, Jonathon R. B., Harvey Jaron, and Mark C. Bolino. "Too Engaged? A Conservation of Resources View of the Relationship Between Work Engagement and Work Interference with Family." *Journal of Applied Psychology 94*, no. 6 (2009): 1452–1465.

Hansen, Morten T. "Transforming DNV: From Silos to Disciplined Collaboration Across Business Units—Food Business in 2005." Case 5458. Fontainebleau: INSEAD, August 2007.

Hansen, Morten T. *Collaboration: How Leaders Avoid the Traps, Build Common Ground, and Reap Big Results.* Boston: Harvard Business Press, 2009.

Hansen, Morten T., Herminia Ibarra, and Nana von Bernuth. "Transforming Reckitt Benckiser." Case 5686. Fontainebleau: INSEAD, April 2011.

Hansen, Morten T., Herminia Ibarra, and Urs Peyer. "The Best-Performing CEOs in the World." *Harvard Business Review 88*, no. 1 (2010): 104–113.

Hansen, Morten T., Herminia Ibarra, and Urs Peyer. "The Best-Performing CEOs in the World." *Harvard Business Review 91*, no. 1/2 (2013): 81–95.

Hansen, Morten T., Michelle Rogan, Dickson Louie, and Nana von Bernuth. "Corporate Entrepreneurship: Steven Birdsall at SAP." Case 6022. Fontainebleau: INSEAD, December 2013.

Heath, Chip, and Dan Heath. *Switch: How to Change Things When Change Is Hard.* New York: Crown Business, 2010.

Hemingway, Ernest. "A Man's Credo." *Playboy 10*, no. 1 (1963): 120–124.

Herzberg, Frederick. *Work and the Nature of Man*. Cleveland: World Publishing Company, 1966.

Hewlett, Sylvia Ann, and Carolyn Buck Luce. "Extreme Jobs: The Dangerous Allure of the 70-Hour Workweek." *Harvard Business Review 48*, no.12 (2006): 49–59.

Hirschhorn, Larry, and Thomas Gilmore. "The New Boundaries of the 'Boundaryless' Company." *Harvard Business Review 70*, no. 3 (1992): 104–115.

Ho, Violet, Sze-Sze Wong, and Chay Hoon Lee. "A Tale of Passion: Linking Job Passion and Cognitive Engagement to Employee Work Performance." *Journal of Management Studies 48*, no. 1 (2011): 26–47.

Huntford, Roland. *Scott and Amundsen: The Last Place on Earth*. New York: Modern Library, 1999.

Isidore, Chris. "Death Toll for GM Ignition Switch: 124." *CNN Money*, December 10, 2015. Accessed February 23, 2017. http://money.cnn.com/2015/12/10/news/companies/gm-recall-ignition-switch-death-toll.

Jacobs, Emma. "Kill the Passion for Work." *Financial Times*, May 13, 2015.

Janis, Irving L. *Groupthink: Psychological Studies of Policy Decisions and Fiascoes*. New York: Houghton Mifflin, 1983.

Kappel, Frank. "Bop Invasion First Hand Account—May 1961." Cuban Information Archives, May 29, 1961. Dade County OCB file #153-D. Accessed December 18, 2014. http://cuban-exile.com/doc_026-050/doc0041.html.

Kellaway, Lucy. "And the Golden Flannel of the Year Award Goes to . . ." *Financial Times*, January 4, 2015.

Kellaway, Lucy. "Endless Digital Feedback Will Make Us Needy and Unkind." *Financial Times*, March 8, 2015.

Kerr, Stephen. "On the Folly of Rewarding A, While Hoping for B." *The Academy of Management Executive 9*, no. 1 (1995): 7–14.

Knight, Andrew P., and Markus Baer. "Get Up, Stand Up: The Effects of a Non-Sedentary Workspace on Information Elaboration and Group Performance." *Social Psychological and Personality Science 5*, no. 8 (2014): 910–917.

Kolata, Gina. "Doctors Strive to Do Less Harm by Inattentive Care," *New York Times*, February 17, 2017. Accessed June 23, 2017. https://www.nytimes.com/2015/02/18/health/doctors-strive-to-do-less-harm-by-inattentive-care.html?_r=0.

Kotter, John P. *Leading Change*. Boston: Harvard Business Press, 1996.

Kotter, John P., and Dan S. Cohen. *The Heart of Change: Real-life Stories of How People Change Their Organizations*. Boston: Harvard Business Review Press, 2012.

Kramer, Roderick. *Organizational Trust: A Reader*. New York: Oxford Management Readers, 2006.

Lawrence, Paul R., and Nitin Nohria. *Drive: How Human Nature Shapes Our Choices*. San Francisco: Jossey-Bass, 2002.

Lebowitz, Shana. "A Yale Professor Explains How to Turn a Boring Job into a Meaningful Career." *Business Insider*, December 1, 2015. Accessed February 23, 2017. http://uk.businessinsider.com/turn-a-boring-job-into-a-meaningful -career-job-crafting-2015-12?r=US&IR=T.

Lebowitz, Shana. "One of the Most Influential Silicon Valley Investors Reveals How His Firm Decides Whether to Back a Company." *Business Insider*, June 2, 2016. Accessed February 24, 2017. http://uk.businessinsider.com /how-andreessen-horowitz-decides-to-back-a-company-2016-6?r=US &IR=T.

Leiter, Michael P., and Christina Maslach. "The Impact of Interpersonal Environment on Burnout and Organizational Commitment." *Journal of Organizational Behavior 9*, no. 4 (1988): 297–308.

Linkner, Josh. "Is Your Company Selling Aspirin, or Vitamins?" *FastCompany*, March 27, 2012. Accessed February 18, 2017. http://www.fastcompany .com/1826271/your-company-selling-aspirin-or-vitamins.

Malone, Thomas W. *The Future of Work: How the New Order of Business Will Shape Your Organization, Your Management Style and Your Life*. Boston: Harvard Business Review Press, 2004.

March, James G. "Exploration and Exploitation in Organizational Learning." *Organization Science 2*, no. 1 (1991): 71–87.

McKeown, Greg. *Essentialism: The Disciplined Pursuit of Less*. New York: Crown Business, 2014.

Melamed, Samuel, Arie Shirom, Sharon Toker, Shlomo Berliner, and Itzhak Shapira. "Burnout and Risk of Cardiovascular Disease: Evidence, Possible Causal Paths, and Promising Research Directions." *Psychological Bulletin 132*, no. 3 (2006): 327–353.

Meyer, Erin. "Negotiating Across Cultures." HBR Video, February 25, 2016. https://hbr.org/video/4773888299001/negotiating-across-cultures.

Michaels, Ed, Helen Handfield-Jones, and Beth Axelrod. *The War for Talent*. Boston: Harvard Business Review Press, 2001.

Mooney, Ann C., Patricia J. Holahan, and Allen C. Amason. "Don't Take It Personally: Exploring Cognitive Conflict as Mediator of Effective Conflict." *Journal of Management Studies 44*, no. 5 (2007): 733–758.

Moran, Michael. *The British Regulatory State: High Modernism and Hyper-Innovation*. New York: Oxford University Press, 2007.

Newport, Cal. *So Good They Can't Ignore You: Why Skills Trump Passion in the Quest for Work You Love*. New York: Grand Central Publishing, 2012.

O'Connell, Andrew. "The Pros and Cons of Doing One Thing at a Time." *Harvard Business Review*, January 20, 2015.

Page, Scott E. *The Difference: How the Power of Diversity Creates Better Groups, Firms, Schools, and Societies*. Princeton: Princeton University Press, 2007.

Pencavel, John. "The Productivity of Working Hours." *Economic Journal 125*, no. 589 (2015): 2052–2076.

Pentland, Alex Sandy. "The New Science of Building Great Teams." *Harvard Business Review 90*, no. 4 (2012): 60–70.

Perlow, Leslie A., and Jessica L. Porter. "Making Time Off Predictable—and Required." *Harvard Business Review 87*, no. 10 (2009): 102–109.

Pfeffer, Jeffrey. *Power: Why Some People Have It and Others Don't*. New York: HarperCollins, 2010.

Phillips, Katherine. "How Diversity Makes Us Smarter." *Scientific American*, October 1, 2014.

Pink, Dan. "The Puzzle of Motivation." TED Video, July 2009. https://www.ted.com/talks/dan_pink_on_motivation.

Plous, Scott. *The Psychology of Judgment and Decision Making*. New York: McGraw-Hill, 1993.

Preston, Diana. *A First Rate Tragedy: Captain Scott's Antarctic Expeditions*. London: Constable, paperback ed., 1999.

Rasinger, Jim. *The Brilliant Disaster: JFK, Castro, and America's Doomed Invasion of Cuba's Bay of Pigs*. New York: Scribner, 2012.

Rath, Tom. *StrengthsFinder 2.0*. New York: Gallup Press, 2007.

Reid, Erin. "Embracing, Passing, Revealing, and the Ideal Worker Image: How People Navigate Expected and Experienced Professional Identities." *Organization Science 26*, no. 4 (2015): 997–1017.

Rejcek, Peter. "Shipwreck: Remains of Scott's Vessel Terra Nova Found off Greenland Coast." *Antarctic Sun*, August 24, 2012, updated August 29, 2012. Accessed May 27, 2017. https://antarcticsun.usap.gov/features/contenthandler.cfm?id=2725.

Roberto, Michael A. *Why Great Leaders Don't Take Yes for an Answer: Managing for Conflict and Consensus*. Upper Saddle River: Wharton School Publishing, 2005.

Robson, David. "The Scott Expedition: How Science Gained the Pole Position." *Telegraph*, June 21, 2011. Accessed May 27, 2017. http://www.telegraph.co.uk/news/science/science-news/8587530/The-Scott-expedition-how-science-gained-the-pole-position.html.

Rosen, Rebecca J. "What Jobs Do People Find Most Meaningful?" *Atlantic*, June 24, 2014.

Rubinstein, Joshua S., David E. Meyer, and Jeffrey E. Evans. "Executive Control of Cognitive Processes in Task Switching." *Journal of Experimental Psychology: Human Perception and Performance* 27, no. 4 (2001): 763–797.

Rudman, Laurie A., and Julie E. Phelan. "Backlash Effects for Disconfirming Gender Stereotypes in Organizations." *Research in Organizational Behavior* 28 (2008): 61–79.

Schlesinger, Arthur M., Jr. *Thousand Days: John F. Kennedy in the White House.* New York: Mariner Books, 2002.

Scott, W. Richard, and Gerald F. Davis. *Organizations and Organizing: Rational, Natural, and Open Systems Perspectives.* New York: Routledge, 2016.

Shannon, Sarah. "Britain's Reckitt Benckiser Goes Shopping." *Bloomberg Businessweek*, July 29, 2010. Accessed June 23, 2017. https://www.bloomberg.com/news/articles/2010-07-29/britains-reckitt-benckiser-goes-shopping.

Shin, Jiwoong, and Dan Ariely. "Keeping Doors Open: The Effect of Unavailability on Incentives to Keep Options Viable." *Management Science* 50, no. 5 (May 2004): 575–586.

Simon, Herbert A. "Rational Choice and the Structure of the Environment." *Psychological Review* 63, no. 2 (1956): 129–138.

Simon, Herbert A. "Designing Organizations for an Information-Rich World." In *Computers, Communication, and the Public Interest*, edited by Martin Greenberger, 40–41. Baltimore: Johns Hopkins University Press, 1971.

Sobel, David. "I Never Should Have Followed my Dreams." *Salon*, September 1, 2014. Accessed February 23, 2017. http://www.salon.com/2014/09/01/i_never_should_have_followed_my_dreams.

Sobh, Rana, and Brett Martin. "Hoped-for Selves and Feared Selves: How Positive and Negative Reference Values in Self-Regulation Moderate Consumer Goal-Directed Efforts." *European Advances in Consumer Research* 8 (2008): 350–352.

Stan, Mihaela, and Freek Vermeulen. "Selection at the Gate: Difficult Cases, Spillovers, and Organizational Learning." *Organization Science* 24, no. 3 (2013): 796–812.

Starmer, Amy J., Nancy D. Spector, Rajendu Srivastava, et al. "Changes in Medical Errors after Implementation of a Handoff Program." *New England Journal of Medicine 371* (2014): 1803–1812

Steger, Michael F., Bryan J. Dik, and Ryan D. Duffy. "Measuring Meaningful Work: The Work and Meaning Inventory." *Journal of Career Assessment 20*, no. 3 (2012): 322–337.

Stobbe, Mike. "Appalachian Town Shrugs at Poorest Health Ranking." *Herald-Dispatch*, November 16, 2008. Accessed February 24, 2017. http://www.herald-dispatch.com/news/appalachian-town-shrugs-at-poorest-health-ranking/article_c50a30c5-f55c-5a3a-8fad-2285c119e104.html.

Sull, Donald, and Kathleen M. Eisenhardt. *Simple Rules: How to Thrive in a Complex World.* London: John Murray Publishers, 2015.

Swartz, Aimee. "Beating Cystic Fibrosis." *Atlantic*, September 27, 2013.

Tenney, Matt. "Why Empowering Employees to Be Compassionate Is Great for Business." *Huffington Post*, September 6, 2016.

Tett, Gilian. *The Silo Effect: The Peril of Expertise and the Promise of Breaking Down Barriers.* New York: Simon & Schuster, 2015.

Thaler, Richard, and Cass Sunstein. *Nudge: Improving Decisions About Health, Wealth, and Happiness.* New York: Penguin Books, 2009.

Tichy, Noel, and Ram Charan. "Speed, Simplicity, Self-Confidence: An Interview with Jack Welch." *Harvard Business Review 67*, no. 5 (1989): 112–120.

Toker, Sharon, and Michal Biron. "Job Burnout and Depression: Unraveling Their Temporal Relationship and Considering the Role of Physical Activity." *Journal of Applied Psychology 97*, no. 3 (2012): 699–710.

Toussaint, John, and Roger A. Gerard. *On the Mend: Revolutionizing Healthcare to Save Lives and Transform the Industry.* Cambridge: Lean Enterprise Institute, 2010.

Van Gorder, Chris. *The Front-Line Leader: Building a High-Performance Organization from the Ground Up.* San Francisco: Jossey-Bass, 2015.

Venema, Vibeke. "The Indian Sanitary Pad Revolutionary." *BBC News*, March 4, 2014. Accessed June 23, 2017. http://www.bbc.com/news/magazine-26260978.

Whelan, Fred, and Gladys Stone. "James Dyson: How Persistence Leads to Success." *Huffington Post*, December 15, 2009.

Wilcox, Laura. "Huntington Area Labeled as Nation's Most Unhealthy." *Herald-Dispatch*, November 16, 2008.

Wile, Rob. "Marc Andreessen Gives the Career Advice That Nobody Wants to Hear." *Business Insider*, May 27, 2014.

Wrzesniewski, Amy, Jane E. Dutton, and Gelaye Debebe. "Interpersonal Sense-making and the Meaning of Work." *Research in Organizational Behavior 25* (2003): 93–135.

Zetlin, Minda. "17 Percent of Employees Would Rather Watch Paint Dry than Attend Meetings." *Inc.* January 30, 2015. Accessed February 23, 2017. http://www.inc.com/minda-zetlin/17-percent-of-employees-would-rather -watch-paint-dry-than-attend-team-meetings.html.

Notes

ONE: THE SECRETS TO GREAT PERFORMANCE

1　Jim Collins and Morten T. Hansen, *Great by Choice: Uncertainty, Chaos and Luck—Why Some Thrive Despite Them All* (New York: HarperBusiness, 2011); Jim Collins, *Good to Great: Why Some Companies Make the Leap . . . and Others Don't* (New York: HarperBusiness, 2001).

2　Ed Michaels, Helen Handfield-Jones, and Beth Axelrod, *The War for Talent* (Boston: Harvard Business Review Press, 2001).

3　Tom Rath, *StrengthsFinder 2.0* (New York: Gallup Press, 2007) and Marcus Buckingham, *Now, Discover Your Strengths* (New York: Gallup Press, 2001).

4　See for example, Anders K. Ericsson and Jim Pool, *Peak: Secrets from the New Science of Expertise* (New York: Houghton Mifflin Harcourt, 2016); Geoff Colvin, *Talent Is Overrated: What Really Separates World-Class Performers from Everybody Else* (New York: Portfolio, 2008); Daniel Coyle, *The Talent Code: Greatness Isn't Born. It's Grown* (Bantam, 2009).

5　Angela L. Duckworth, *Grit: The Power of Passion and Perseverance* (New York: Scribner, 2016).

6　For example, in a *60 Minutes/Vanity Fair* poll, people rated "hard-working" as the second most important factor in hiring a new employee, behind "honesty" and ahead of "intelligence." The question asked: "Which of the following qualities would you think is most important if you were hiring a new employee—intelligence, being hard-working, personality, experience, or honesty?" "The 60 Minutes/Vanity Fair Poll," *Vanity Fair,* January 2010, accessed May 29, 2017, http://www.vanityfair.com/magazine/2010/03/60-minutes-poll-201003.

7   Malcolm Gladwell popularized the idea of 10,000 hours of practice in his book *Outliers: The Story of Success.* (New York: Little, Brown & Company, 2008).

8   Our statistical analysis showed that men benefitted more from the practice of forceful champion, while women benefitted more from the practice of disciplined collaboration. These differences are statically significant results in our regression models. (New York: Back Bay Books, 2011).

9   This number denoted the R-squared from a regression analysis, which is the additional variance explained by adding the seven factors to the regression analysis. See the research appendix for details.

10 Audre Biciunaite, "Economic Growth and Life Expectancy: Do Wealthier Countries Live Longer?" *Euromonitor International,* March 14, 2014, accessed June 22, 2017. http://blog.euromonitor.com/2014/03/economic-growth-and-life-expectancy-do-wealthier-countries-live-longer.html. The study reveals a correlation of -0.42 between smoking and life expectancy, which means an r-squared of 0.18 to make this study somewhat compatible to our regression results.

11 PK, "The Older You Get, the More Discipline Helps Your Net Worth," Don't Quit Your Day Job, March 11, 2016, accessed June 22, 2017, https://dqydj.com/correlation-of-wealth-and-income-by-age computed as average across age groups. See also PK, "Income Is Not Net Worth: The Raw Data," Don't Quit Your Day Job, March 11, 2016, accessed June 22, 2017, https://dqydj.com/income-is-not-net-worth-the-raw-data.

12 I use "just" in quotation marks, as his 3-point percentage rate is just amazing. "Stephen Curry," NBA, accessed October 12, 2016, http://www.nba.com/players/stephen/curry/201939. Admittedly, this comparison is not strictly correct, since our results show variance among people (using the r-squared result from a regression result), while Curry's score is a simple percentage stats. Still, it is an informative comparison.

13 Stephen R. Covey, *The 7 Habits of Highly Effective People: Powerful Lessons in Personal Change* (New York: Simon & Schuster, 2013).

14 See, for example, Samuel Melamed, Arie Shirom, Sharon Toker, Shlomo Berliner, and Itzhak Shapira, "Burnout and Risk of Cardiovascular Disease: Evidence, Possible Causal Paths, and Promising Research Directions,"

Psychological Bulletin 132, no. 3 (2006): 327–353. See also chapter nine for more details on research on this topic.

TWO: DO LESS, THEN OBSESS

1 Translated from Norwegian. From the play *Brand*. Several translations of this quote from Norwegian to English exist, and I like this one the best. The original quote in Norwegian: *"Det som du er, vær fullt og helt, og ikke stykkevis og delt."*

2 Diana Preston, *A First Rate Tragedy: Captain Scott's Antarctic Expeditions* (London: Constable, paperback ed., 1999), 83–84.

3 Caroline Alexander, "The Race to the South Pole," *National Geographic*, September 2011.

4 Length of Terra Nova: Peter Rejcek, "Shipwreck: Remains of Scott's vessel Terra Nova found off Greenland coast," *Antarctic Sun*, August 24, 2012, updated August 29, 2012, accessed May 27, 2017, https://antarcticsun .usap.gov/features/contenthandler.cfm?id=2725; length of Fram: Roald Amundsen, *The South Pole: An Account of the Norwegian Antarctic Expedition in the Fram, 1910–1912* (New York: Cooper Square Press, 2000): 437; budget Scott: "Robert Falcon Scott 1868–1912: The TERRA NOVA Expedition 1910–13," accessed May 27, 2017, http://www.south-pole.com/ p0000090.htm; budget Amundsen: Roland Huntford, *Scott and Amundsen: The Last Place on Earth* (New York: Modern Library, 1999): 200 and 245; crew Scott: David Robson, "The Scott Expedition: How Science Gained the Pole Position," *Telegraph*, June 21, 2011, accessed May 27, 2017, http:// www.telegraph.co.uk/news/science/science-news/8587530/The-Scott -expedition-how-science-gained-the-pole-position.html; crew Amundsen: Roald Amundsen, *The South Pole: An Account of the Norwegian Antarctic Expedition in the Fram, 1910–1912* (New York: Cooper Square Press, 2000), 392.

5 "Greenland Dog," Dogbreedslist, accessed February 20, 2017, http://www .dogbreedslist.info/all-dog-breeds/Greenland-Dog.html#.VvgRjMtf0dU and "Siberian Husky–Flat-Lying Outer," Pet Paw, accessed February 20, 2017, www.petpaw.com.au/breeds/siberian-husky.

6 Quoted in Roland Huntford, "The Last Place on Earth," p. 209.

7 Ibid., p. 279.

8 Ibid., p. 309.

9 Ibid., 407.

10   See ibid., p. 412, for example.

11   Daniel Goleman, *Focus: The Hidden Driver of Excellence* (New York: Harper-Collins, 2013) and Stephen R. Covey, *The 7 Habits of Highly Effective People: Powerful Lessons in Personal Change* (New York: Simon & Schuster, 2013).

12   This effect was computed by comparing those who scored in the top 10 percent on "do less, then obsess" to those who scored in the bottom 10 percent. The predicted effect was obtained by running a regression analysis where the other variables (apart from do less, then obsess) were held constant at their mean values. We transformed the standard scores into percentiles to ease interpretation.

13   Throughout the book, we have altered the names and settings of the stories of the study participants. "Maria" and "Cathy," for example, are not their real names.

14   Susan Bishop, "The Strategic Power of Saying No," *Harvard Business Review* 77, no. 6 (1999): 50–61. The quotes and data for this story are based on two author interviews with Susan Bishop as well as this *HBR* article.

15   We asked Bishop to retrospectively complete the survey scores for two periods—one for this point in time, and one for a later time.

16   Herbert A. Simon, "Designing Organizations for an Information-Rich World," in *Computers, Communication, and the Public Interest*, ed. Martin Greenberger (Baltimore: Johns Hopkins Press, 1971), 40–41.

17   Specifically, they estimated that an 8 percent decrease in multitasking led to a 3 percent improvement in completion time (fewer days to close case). They wrote: "At the mean of the distribution of new opened cases (127), ten fewer newly opened cases in a quarter (an 8% decrease of this indicator of task juggling) reduce the duration of assigned cases by 8.6 days (a 3% improvement, given a mean duration of 290 days)." Extrapolating from their results, we can enlarge those numbers six-fold from 8 percent to 50 percent (i.e., cutting toggling in half), which corresponds to a six-fold increase in gain from 3 percent to about 19 percent (nearly 20 percent) in completion time. Decio Coviello, Andrea Ichino, and Nicola Persico, "The Inefficiency of Worker Time Use," *Journal of the European Economic Association 13*, no. 5 (2015): 906–947. See also Andrew O'Connell, "The Pros and Cons of Doing One Thing at a Time," *Harvard Business Review*, January 20, 2015.

18   Joshua S. Rubinstein, David E. Meyer, and Jeffrey E. Evans, "Executive

Control of Cognitive Processes in Task Switching," *Journal of Experimental Psychology: Human Perception and Performance 27*, no. 4 (2001): 763–797. They found that it took students far longer to solve complicated mathematics problems when they had to switch to other tasks. According to Meyer multitasking could reduce speed by 40 percent. See "Multitasking: Switching Costs," *American Psychological Association*, March 20, 2006, accessed February 20, 2017, https://www.apa.org/research/action/multitask.aspx/.

19 "2 photos for Sukiyabashi Jiro," Yelp, last modified January 22, 2016, http://www.yelp.com/biz_photos/%E3%81%99%E3%81%8D%E3%82%84%E3%81%B0%E3%81%97%E6%AC%A1%E9%83%8E-%E4%B8%AD%E5%A4%AE%E5%8C%BA?select=AVt9FtTaOvRic25kRNptCA&reviewid=INi0Hf2mbjYnVTe6OdDPiw.

20 Jiro Ono, *Jiro Dreams of Sushi*, directed by David Gelb (New York: Magnolia Home Entertainment, DVD: 2012). Jiro Ono was eighty-five years old at the time of the movie.

21 Upon embarking on my research, I didn't understand the obsession aspect of work. I had published an academic article with my colleague Martine Haas in the *Administrative Science Quarterly* that showed the benefits of focus. Studying forty-three practice groups in a large management consultancy, we found that teams that published fewer electronic documents on fewer topics in the company's knowledge management database achieved more hits from users, and we concluded that the additional hits were driven by the authors' reputation for quality. We called it a "less-is-more" strategy. But we missed the crucial part of obsessing. After learning about Jiro's sushi and Amundsen's trip to the South Pole, I went back and reexamined our research. I found that the consultants who focused and excelled also obsessed over quality. They scrutinized every document they uploaded and ditched many more, with one group rejecting 80 percent of all submissions. Morten Hansen and Martine Haas, "Competing for Attention in Knowledge Markets: Electronic Document Dissemination in a Management Consulting Company," *Administrative Science Quarterly 46* (2001): 1–28.

22 Ernest Hemingway, "A Man's Credo," *Playboy 10*, no. 1 (1963): 120.

23 "Nail-Biting Allowed: Alfred Hitchcock's 10 Most Memorable Scenes," *Time*, November 16, 2011, accessed March 4, 2017, http://entertainment.time.com/2012/11/19/spellbinder-hitchcocks-10-most-memorable-scenes/slide/the-shower-scene-in-psycho/.

24   Fred Whelan and Gladys Stone, "James Dyson: How Persistence Leads to Success," *Huffington Post*, December 15, 2009.

25   We also asked the same question for a boss evaluating a subordinate, and for a subordinate evaluating a boss.

26   This story is based on interviews with the nurse manager and previous published versions. I have altered the names in this story.

27   The name of the Occam's razor is spelled differently and differs sometimes from his name.

28   He is often quoted in a slightly different way: "Perfection is achieved, not when there is nothing more to add, but when there is nothing left to take away." This quote is from Saint-Exupéry's book *Terre des Hommes* (1939), translated into English by Lewis Galantière as *Wind, Sand and Stars* (1967).

29   For a terrific treatment of the idea of "simple rules," see Donald Sull and Kathleen M. Eisenhardt, *Simple Rules: How to Thrive in a Complex World* (London: John Murray Publishers 2015).

30   Subjects, in this case smart MIT students, were invited to play a computer game where they could earn money by clicking three doors—one blue, one green, and one red. The first click opened the room, and they earned money clicking inside. Most realized that the green one offered more money for each click. The game had a total of 100 clicks, so the right strategy was to explore the three options at first (hedging), then stick with the green room (focusing). Then came the intriguing part. When they were in the green room, the doors to the other rooms started to vanish. The options were fading away, and the only way to keep them was to go back and click on the blue and red doors again. Now, once you had learned that the green door was best, you shouldn't care about the red and blue anymore. But that's not what happened! The subjects went back and forth, wasting clicks, just to keep the red and blue doors alive. Green-green-green-blue, green-green-green-red, green-green-green-blue. Jiwoong Shin and Dan Ariely, "Keeping Doors Open: The Effect of Unavailability on Incentives to Keep Options Viable," *Management Science 50*, no. 5 (May 2004): 575–586.

31   Dan Ariely, *Predictably Irrational: The Hidden Forces That Shape Our Decisions* (New York: HarperCollins, 2008), p. 354.

32   Adam Grant, *Originals: How Non-Conformists Move the World* (New York: Viking, 2016).

33 Jim Collins and Morten T. Hansen, *Great by Choice: Uncertainty, Chaos and Luck—Why Some Thrive Despite Them All* (New York: HarperBusiness, 2011).

34 As portfolio theory in financial decision-making suggests, when great uncertainty exists about the outcomes of existing options, you should hedge your bets until you feel confident that one option is likely to prove the best. At that point, you should select that option, go all in, and obsess to excel.

35 Sue Shellenbarger, "What to Do When Co-Workers Won't Leave You Alone," *Wall Street Journal*, blog, September 11, 2013, http://blogs.wsj.com/atwork/2013/09/11/what-to-do-when-co-workers-wont-leave-you-alone.

36 When saying no, be sure to take into account the cultural dimensions. Erin Meyer, "Negotiating Across Cultures," HBR Video, February 25, 2016, https://hbr.org/video/4773888299001/negotiating-across-cultures.

37 Name and details have been disguised.

THREE: REDESIGN YOUR WORK

1 Naomi Shihab Nye is an American-Palestinian poet. Poetry Foundation, last modified 2010, accessed February 20, 2017, https://www.poetryfoundation.org/poems-and-poets/poets/detail/naomi-shihab-nye.

2 We interviewed Greg Green three times for this story from 2014 to 2016. Three of us also traveled to Clintondale in 2016 and spent a day there where we observed two classrooms in session, interviewed two teachers and two administrators in addition to Greg Green, and conducted an interview session with five students. The Clintondale story has also been covered by media, including a segment in *NewsHour* at PBS: http://www.pbs.org/newshour/rundown/what-does-a-flipped-classroom-look-like-2/

3 Leslie A. Perlow and Jessica L. Porter, "Making Time Off Predictable—and Required," *Harvard Business Review 87*, no. 10 (2009): 102–109.

4 Sylvia Ann Hewlett and Carolyn Buck Luce, "Extreme Jobs: The Dangerous Allure of the 70-Hour Workweek," *Harvard Business Review 48*, no. 12 (2006): 49–59.

5 We let the people in our study decide what constituted working hours. Clearly, they may be biased in their estimates, perhaps reporting higher numbers than they actually work. If so, the peak point in our chart (65 hours) would move slightly to the left and be lower, say 55 hours, but the

shape of the curve should be the same if everyone is either underreporting or overreporting their hours.

6   You may think that this makes no sense, as you do get some more work done when you add hours beyond 65 hours per week; you may not be very productive but still, you're doing additional work. This logic is based on a sequential view of work—that you do get extra work done as you add more hours late in the day. There are two reasons why the sequential model may not hold. First, as you add those extra hours at night, poor-quality work may detract from what you did earlier in the day, as when errors in a software code creep in and destroy the computer program. Second, when you add extra hours late at night, you detract from your ability to work better the next day, as you're getting tired. So extra hours impede the productivity of subsequent hours.

7   John Pencavel, "The Productivity of Working Hours," *Economic Journal* *125*, no. 589 (2015): 2052–2076.

8   Name and other details have been altered.

9   I thank Jim Collins for suggesting this table.

10 According to the OECD: "Labour productivity is equal to the ratio between a volume measure of output (gross domestic product or gross value added) and a measure of input use (the total number of hours worked or total employment). Labour productivity = volume measure of output / measure of input use." See Rebecca Freeman, "Labour Productivity Indicators: Comparison of Two OECD Databases, Productivity Differentials & the Balassa-Samuelson Effect," OECD, July 2008, accessed August 3, 2015. http://www.oecd.org/std/labour-stats/41354425.pdf.

11 http://www.maersk.com/en/the-maersk-group/about-us#stream_2_ctl00 _header.

12 APM Credit for photo: APM Terminals, Terminals, Tangier, Morocco, accessed February 20, 2017, http://apmterminalsphotos.com/famain .asp?customerId=573&sKey=EHT4NWGE&action=viewimage&cid= 111&imageid=10292.

13 We interviewed Hartmut Goeritz in 2015 and 2016 for this story.

14 More precisely, its throughput was 1.3 million 20-foot container equivalent units, a standard measure in the industry that takes into account the size of the containers.

15 This distinction is to some extent based on the distinction drawn by Peter Drucker, who apparently said that management is doing the things right,

while leadership is doing the right things. See https://www.goodreads.com /author/quotes/12008.Peter_F_Drucker (accessed August 27, 2017). In his book, *The Effective Executive*, Drucker states that the job of the executive is "to get the right things done," which is close to the first part here of "doing the right things," which requires a definition of what those "right things" are, namely those that create value as defined here. Peter Drucker, *The Effective Executive: The Definitive Guide to Getting the Right Things Done* (New York: HarperBusiness, 2006).

16 Gina Kolata, "Doctors Strive to Do Less Harm by Inattentive Care," *New York Times*, February 17, 2017, accessed June 23, 2017, https://www.nytimes .com/2015/02/18/health/doctors-strive-to-do-less-harm-by-inattentive -care.html?_r=0.

17 This concept of small redesigns is similar to the idea of "nudges." Richard Thaler and Cass Sunstein revealed in their book *Nudge* that small changes—mere nudges—can lead to surprisingly big impacts. Richard Thaler and Cass Sunstein, *Nudge: Improving Decisions About Health, Wealth, and Happiness* (New York: Penguin Books, 2009).

18 Allen C. Bluedorn, Daniel B. Turban, and Mary Sue Love, "The Effects of Stand-Up and Sit-Down Meeting Formats on Meeting Outcomes," *Journal of Applied Psychology 84*, no. 2 (1999): 277-285. In a different study published in 2014 in *Social Psychological and Personality Science*, researchers at Washington University in St. Louis report that groups working together on a project while standing are measurably more engaged and less territorial than while seated. Andrew P. Knight and Markus Baer, "Get Up, Stand Up: The Effects of a Non-Sedentary Workspace on Information Elaboration and Group Performance," *Social Psychological and Personality Science 5*, no. 8 (2014): 910–917.

19 Alex "Sandy" Pentland, "The New Science of Building Great Teams," *Harvard Business Review 90*, no. 4 (2012): 60–70.

20 Name and other details have been altered.

21 Josh Linkner, "Is Your Company Selling Aspirin, or Vitamins?," *FastCompany*, March 27, 2012, accessed February 18, 2017, http://www.fastcompany .com/1826271/your-company-selling-aspirin-or-vitamins.

22 The writer Dan Pink has a TED talk, viewed 18 million times, in which he describes the "candle experiment," conducted by Karl Duncker in 1945. In it, people were given a candle, a box of thumbtacks, and some matches. Then they were told to attach the candle to the wall so that wax wouldn't

drip onto a table below. Some people tried to thumbtack the candle to the wall. Some tried lighting one side of the candle in order to stick it to the wall. Neither of these acts worked. Finally, people began to see a new way: They took the box the thumbtacks were in and tacked it to the wall, creating a makeshift candleholder and placed the candle within it. The functional fixedness in this case was the inability to see the box as serving any purpose other than containing the tacks. Dan Pink, "The Puzzle of Motivation," TED video, July 2009, https://www.ted.com/talks/dan_pink_on_motivation

23 Tom Coens and Mary Jenkins, *Abolishing Performance Appraisals: Why They Backfire and What to Do Instead* (San Francisco: Berrett-Koehler, 2000): 35.

24 Michael Moran, *The British Regulatory State: High Modernism and Hyper-Innovation* (New York: Oxford University Press, 2007), 38–66.

FOUR: DON'T JUST LEARN, LOOP

1 See https://www.brainyquote.com/quotes/quotes/w/williampol163253.html. Accessed August 27, 2017.

2 The Dan Plan, accessed February 20, 2017, http://thedanplan.com/about/.

3 See www.thedanplan.com.

4 "How Do You Stack Up?," Golf Digest, March 17, 2014, accessed February 21, 2017, http://www.golfdigest.com/story/comparing-your-handicap-index.

5 "Men's Handicap Index® Statistics," USGA, accessed February 27, 2017, http://www.usga.org/Handicapping/handicap-index-statistics/mens-handicap-index-statistics-d24e6096.html, and "Golf Participation in the U.S.," National Golf Foundation, accessed February 27, 2017, http://www.ngf.org/pages/golf-participation-us.

6 K. Anders Ericsson and Jim Pool define deliberate practice more precisely in *Peak: Secrets from the New Science of Expertise* (New York: Houghton Mifflin Harcourt, 2016), 98–99.

7 http://thedanplan.com/statistics-2/.

8 During the 1950s and 1960s in Japan and the 1980s in the United States, experts like W. Edwards Deming advocated for a "plan-do-check-act" cycle of manufacturing and process improvement whereby planners would systematically keep what worked and identify opportunities for improvements. This effort sparked a movement in organizational learning, whereby organizations strive to improve by incorporating new routines

into their processes. Such approaches have given rise to a host of specialist roles in companies such as "quality engineers" and "six sigma" professionals. However, their efforts have by and large stayed within the purview of company-specific processes. They haven't cascaded to lots of jobs where employees—and not quality experts—take charge of their own improvements. See "PDSA Cycle," W. Edwards Deming Institute, accessed February 21, 2017, https://deming.org/management-system/pdsacycle.

9 Interestingly, women in our study succeeded more than men at parlaying learning into performance. Women who mastered learning leaped 21 points in the percentile performance ranking compared to those who didn't learn, whereas men only moved up 13 percent. (We ran separate regression analyses for women and men. The difference in the coefficient estimates were significant in some models but not in others, and henceforth I am not using this analysis to reveal a significant difference between men and women. Two other practices showed that: men reaped greater benefit from practicing "champion forcefully" while women benefited more from practicing disciplined collaboration.) Our data doesn't reveal why there was this difference, but I can use some data points to speculate. While only 24 percent of men scored high on the statement "he/she constantly changes how he/she works in order to learn and improve," a full 33 percent of women did so. Thus women seemed to have put in more effort to learn.

Women may also have improved more because they learned from failure more readily. Somewhat more women (56 percent) scored higher than men (48 percent) on the statement: "He/she is excellent at learning well from failures to avoid repeating the same mistakes." People who learn from mistakes modify how they work and perform better as a result. No surprise that those who placed high on this failure statement also scored very high on performance.

10 This compares the top 10 percent on the learning scorecard to those who scored in the bottom 10 percent, holding all other variables at their average level (50th percentile).

11 We interviewed Gavin several times over the phone for this study, and she responded to several email questions. Her boss scored her on the learning and performance survey instruments.

12 Lucy Kellaway, "Endless Digital Feedback Will Make Us Needy and Unkind," *Financial Times*, March 8, 2015, accessed February 21, 2017,

http://www.ft.com/cms/s/0/2476806e-c32c-11e4-9c27-00144feab7de
.html#axzz3sQcCuhC4.

13   Mihaela Stan and Freek Vermeulen, "Selection at the Gate: Difficult
     Cases, Spillovers, and Organizational Learning," *Organization Science 24*,
     no. 3 (2013): 796–812.

14   Name and details have been altered.

15   Low score is denoted as 4 or less; high score is 7 out of 7 on the scale.

16   Mads A. Andersen, VG TV interview with Magnus Carlsen, December 21,
     2013, translated from Norwegian by author, accessed February 21, 2017,
     http://www.vgtv.no/#!/video/75947/intervjuet-magnus-carlsen.

17   Carol Dweck, *Mindset: The New Psychology of Success* (Random House,
     2007).

18   Charles T. Clotfelter, Helen F. Ladd, and Jacob L. Vigdor, "Teacher
     Credentials and Student Achievement in High School: A Cross-Subject
     Analysis with Student Fixed Effects," NBER Working Paper No. 13617,
     November 2007, last revision March 2008.

19   Of course, we don't know how many hours those teachers were actually
     in the classroom teaching. Even those with twenty-seven years of experi-
     ence may have far fewer hours teaching. But, teaching and improvement
     in teaching skills, is not just about being in the classroom. It also involves
     drawing lesson plans, correcting homework, etc. One labor bureau study
     found that teachers work about 40 hours per week. Jill Hare, "When,
     Where, and How Much Do U.S. Teachers Work?," Teaching.monster
     .com, accessed February 17, 2017, http://teaching.monster.com/careers
     /articles/4039-when-where-and-how-much-do-us-teachers-work. So if we
     give them 3 months off on vacation, that's still about 40 weeks * 40 = 1,600
     hours per year * 27 = 43,200 hours of teaching experience.

20   Herbert A. Simon, "Rational Choice and the Structure of the Environ-
     ment," *Psychological Review 63*, no. 2 (1956): 129–138.

21   K. Anders Ericsson, "The Influence of Experience and Deliberate Prac-
     tice on the Development of Superior Expert Performance," in *Cambridge
     Handbook of Expertise and Expert Performance*, ed. K. Anders Ericsson, Neil
     Charness, Paul J. Feltovich, and Robert R. Hoffman (Cambridge: Cam-
     bridge University Press, 2006): 685–706.

22   Top performance is here defined as top 10 percent in performance, while
     underperformance is defined as below-average performance. "Constantly
     reviewed" is scored as placing 6 or 7 out of 7 on that scale system.

23 This trend in disruption of work is akin to the disruption of product technologies in the marketplace. According to Harvard Business School professor Clayton Christensen's theory of "disruptive innovation," this occurs when a new technology arrives, offering a unique solution at far lower cost. This kind of innovation tends to be inferior at first but, as it is revised and enhanced, it progresses beyond the current technology and surpasses it. The personal computer, for instance, was a toy compared to the "old" mainframe computers when it first came out but has since, of course, overtaken them. See for example Clayton Christensen, Michael E. Raynor, and Rory McDonald, "What Is Disruptive Innovation?," *Harvard Business Review 93*, no. 12 (2015): 44–53.

24 Amy C. Edmondson, Richard M. Bohmer, and Gary P. Pisano, "Disrupted Routines: Team Learning and New Technology Implementation in Hospitals," *Administrative Science Quarterly 46* (2001): 685–716.

25 "Mastered both" means that they scored in top 10 percent on both redesign and learning loop, while "did neither" means falling below median on both practices.

FIVE: P-SQUARED

1 Ninetieth birthday celebration of Walter Sisulu, Walter Sisulu Hall, Randburg, Johannesburg, South Africa, May 18, 2002. From *Nelson Mandela by Himself: The Authorised Book of Quotations*, https://www.nelsonmandela.org/content/page/selected-quotes, accessed December 16, 2014.

2 "Oprah Talks to Graduates About Feelings, Failure and Finding Happiness," *Stanford Report*, June 15, 2008, accessed 10 February 2017, http://news.stanford.edu/news/2008/june18/como-061808.html.

3 Matt Tenney, "Why Empowering Employees to Be Compassionate Is Great for Business," *Huffington Post*, September 6, 2016.

4 Emma Jacobs, "Kill the Passion for Work," *Financial Times*, May 13, 2015.

5 Caitlin Riegel, "The Key to Success: Loving What You Do," *Huffington Post*, Blog, last modified January 18, 2017, accessed February 21, 2017, http://www.huffingtonpost.com/caitlin-riegel/the-key-to-success-loving_b_8998760.html.

6 Rob Wile, "Marc Andreessen Gives the Career Advice That Nobody Wants to Hear," *Business Insider*, May 27, 2014.

7 David Sobel, "I Never Should Have Followed My Dreams," *Salon*,

September 1, 2014, accessed February 23, 2017, http://www.salon.com /2014/09/01/i_never_should_have_followed_my_dreams/.

8   Transcript of Full Commencement Address by Jim Carrey, Maharishi University of Management, May 24, 2014, Maharishi University of Management, accessed February 23, 2017, https://www.mum.edu/whats-hap pening/graduation-2014/full-jim-carrey-address-video-and-transcript/.

9   Passion is related to what Mihaly Csikszentmihalyi (don't even try to pronounce it) calls "flow," a state where you are immersed in an activity with complete involvement, energy, and enjoyment. Mihaly Csikszentmihalyi, *Flow: The Psychology of Optimal Experience* (New York: Harper & Row, 1990).

10 This way of viewing purpose and passion resembles that proposed by David Brooks in "The Moral Bucket List," *New York Times*, April 11, 2015. "Commencement speakers are always telling young people to follow their passions. Be true to yourself. This is a vision of life that begins with self and ends with self. But people on the road to inner light do not find their vocations by asking, what do I want from life? They ask, what is life asking of me? How can I match my intrinsic talent with one of the world's deep needs?"

11 Names and details have been altered in the Theresa and Marianne stories.

12 This effect contrasts those who scored in the top 10 percent on the passion-purpose score with those in the bottom 10 percent, while all other factors and variables are assumed average.

13 Although those cases of long hours did exist in our data set, they also existed for people void of passion. If we look at people who worked 70 hours or more per week in our data, highly passionate people put in on average 75 hours per week compared to 76 for nonpassionate people, so no meaningful difference.

14 Adding 7 hours per week to persons with low passion-purpose predicts an addition of 1.5 percent to their performance ranking.

15 Les Clefs d'Or, www.lesclefsdor.org. Accessed October 29, 2017.

16 Violet Ho, Sze-Sze Wong, and Chay Hoon Lee have linked harmonious passion to higher performance mediated by intensity of focus and immersion. See "A Tale of Passion: Linking Job Passion and Cognitive Engagement to Employee Work Performance," *Journal of Management Studies 48*, no. 1 (2011): 26–47.

17 Being absorbed, as in "I am completely engrossed in my work," is similar to the idea of "flow," as proposed by Mihaly Csikszentmihalyi in *Flow: The Psychology of Optimal Experience* (New York: Harper & Row, 1990).

18   Rebecca J. Rosen, "What Jobs Do People Find Most Meaningful?," *Atlantic*, June 24, 2014.

19   Shana Lebowitz, "A Yale Professor Explains How to Turn a Boring Job into a Meaningful Career," *Business Insider*, December 1, 2015, accessed February 23, 2017, http://uk.businessinsider.com/turn-a-boring-job-into -a-meaningful-career-job-crafting-2015-12?r=US&IR=T.

20   This story is based on several interviews of Birdsall by the author. It is also based on the INSEAD business school case: Morten Hansen, Michelle Rogan, Dickson Louie, and Nana von Bernuth, "Corporate Entrepreneurship: Steven Birdsall at SAP," Case 6022 (Fontainebleau: INSEAD, December, 2013).

21   See Patricia Chen, Phoebe C. Ellsworth, and Norbert Schwarz, "Finding a Fit or Developing It: Implicit Theories About Achieving Passion for Work," *Personality and Social Psychology Bulletin 41*, no. 10 (2015): 1411–1424.

22   This aspect is one of the fundamental human drives discussed in Paul R. Lawrence and Nitin Nohria, *Drive: How Human Nature Shapes Our Choices* (San Francisco: Jossey-Bass, 2002).

23   Name and other details have been altered.

24   Tom Rath, *StrengthsFinder 2.0* (New York: Gallup Press, 2007). We also performed an analysis where we analyzed the effect of the StrengthsFinder key question ("gives me an opportunity to do what I do best every day") on passion and performance (see section 3.2.5 in the appendix). It showed that the StrengthsFinder item—the job-fit argument—affects performance *indirectly* via passion. That is, it is passion that drives performance and not job fit. Job fit only affects passion.

25   In our study, people who reported that their job allowed them to "do what they do best every day" reported much higher passion (see the appendix for details on this analysis). The idea that mastery of a skill leads to passion for that skill has been explored by Georgetown University professor Cal Newport in his book *So Good They Can't Ignore You: Why Skills Trump Passion In The Quest For Work You Love* (New York: Grand Central Publishing, 2012).

26   https://www.nytimes.com/2014/03/03/business/in-general-motors-recalls -inaction-and-trail-of-fatal-crashes.html?_r=0. It should be noted that according to *The New York Times*, Rose was under the influence of alcohol and speeding when she had her accident; even so, her death was linked to the failure of the airbag to deploy.

27 Chris Isidore, "Death Toll for GM Ignition Switch: 124," CNN Money, December 10, 2015, accessed February 23, 2017, http://money.cnn.com /2015/12/10/news/companies/gm-recall-ignition-switch-death-toll.

28 There are many other clear-cut cases where performance on the inside of a company harms people on the outside. Yet this gets tricky in the gray area. Can a McDonald's store manager have a strong sense of purpose if he sells burgers that contribute to obesity? Can a supervisor at a Coca-Cola plant have purpose if those sugary drinks contribute to diabetes? Critics say these companies harm people, while defenders argue that they sell products that consumers want.

29 J. Stuart Bunderson and Jeffrey A. Thompson, "The Call of the Wild: Zookeepers, Callings, and the Dual Edges of Deeply Meaningful Work," *Administrative Science Quarterly 54* (2009): 32–57.

30 Name and demographic information have been altered.

31 Amy Wrzesniwski, Jane E. Dutton, and Gelaye Debebe, "Interpersonal Sensemaking and the Meaning of Work," *Research in Organizational Behavior 25* (2003): 93–135.

32 Atul Gawande, "The Bell Curve," *The New Yorker* (December 6, 2004); Aimee Swartz, "Beating Cystic Fibrosis," *Atlantic*, September 27, 2013.

33 Chris Van Gorder, *The Front-Line Leader: Building a High-Performance Organization from the Ground Up* (San Francisco: Jossey-Bass, 2015).

SIX: FORCEFUL CHAMPIONS

1 Quote Investigator: Exploring Origins of Quotations, last modified April 6, 2014, http://quoteinvestigator.com/2014/04/06/they-feel.

2 The information for this story is obtained from the IMD case on the epoxy business, Bala Chakravarthy and Hans Huber, "Internal Entrepreneurship at the Dow Chemical Co.," Case 1117 (Lausanne: IMD, July 2003) and from four interviews conducted with Ian Telford and from three interviews conducted with three of his ex-employees (Isabelle Lomba, John Everett, Arantxa Olivares).

3 Bala Chakravarthy and Hans Huber, "Internal Entrepreneurship at the Dow Chemical Co.," Case 1117 (Lausanne: IMD, July 2003).

4 Ibid.

5 "IBM CEO Study: Command & Control Meets Collaboration," May 22, 2012, http://www-03.ibm.com/press/us/en/pressrelease/37793.wss.

6 John Kotter and Dan Cohen make this point in their book on change, *The*

Heart of Change: Real-Life Stories of How People Change Their Organizations (Boston: Harvard Business Review Press, 2012). See also Chip Heath and Dan Heath, *Switch: How to Change Things When Change Is Hard* (New York: Crown Business, 2010).

7   For the role of charisma, see Joyce Bono and Remus Ilies, "Charisma, Positive Emotions, and Mood Contagion," *Leadership Quarterly 17*, no. 4 (2006): 317–334. The relationship between leader charisma and performance is more complicated; see Bradley R. Agle, Nandu J. Nagarajan, Jeffrey A. Sonnenfeld, and Dhinu Srinivasan, "Does CEO Charisma matter? An Empirical Analysis of the Relationships Among Organizational Performance, Environmental Uncertainty, and Top Management Team Perceptions of CEO Charisma," *Academy of Management Journal 49*, no. 1 (2006): 161–174.

8   Angela L. Duckworth and Christopher Peterson, "Grit: Perseverance and Passion for Long-Term Goals," *Journal of Personality and Social Psychology 92*, no. 6 (2007): 1087–1101.

9   This effect compares those who scored high (top 5 percent) on the forceful champion scorecard to those who scored low (bottom 5 percent). It is based on a regression analysis predicting the effect of the forceful champion scale on performance, holding other variables constant.

10 See Amy J. C. Cuddy, Peter Glick, and Anna Beninger, "The Dynamics of Warmth and Competence Judgments, and Their Outcomes in Organizations," *Research in Organizational Behavior 31* (2011): 73–98. Professor Frank Flynn at Stanford Business School conducted an experiment where he asked students to read a case study based on Heidi Roizen (www.heidiroizen.com), a well-known venture capitalist in Silicon Valley. He assigned half of the students to read the story of "Heidi" and the other half to read a version of the case in which he had changed the name to "Howard." Students rated Heidi and Howard as equally competent, but they regarded Howard as a more appealing colleague. They saw Heidi as selfish and "not the type of person you'd want to hire or work for." As these results suggest, women in the workplace are perceived as either competent or liked, but not both. Flynn wrote: "As gender researchers would predict, this seems to be driven by how much they disliked Heidi's aggressive personality. The more assertive they thought Heidi was, the more harshly they judged her." "Gender-Related Material in the New Core Curriculum," Stanford Graduate School of Business, January 1, 2007, accessed

February 24, 2017, http://www.gsb.stanford.edu/stanford-gsb-experience
/news-history/gender-related-material-new-core-curriculum.

11   In a review of research findings on the topic, Professors Laurie Rudman
     and Julie Phelan conclude that competent women at work face a backlash
     as a result of this categorization: "Although women must present them-
     selves as self-confident, assertive, and competitive to be viewed as quali-
     fied for leadership roles, when they do so, they risk social and economic
     reprisals." Laurie A. Rudman and Julie E. Phelan, "Backlash Effects for
     Disconfirming Gender Stereotypes in Organizations," *Research in Organi-
     zational Behavior 28* (2008): 61–79.

12   Mark C. Bolino and William H. Turnley, "Counternormative Impression
     Management, Likeability, and Performance Ratings: The Use of Intimida-
     tion in an Organizational Setting," *Journal of Organizational Behavior 24*,
     no. 2 (2003): 237–250.

13   Jonah Berger, *Contagious: Why Things Catch On* (New York: Simon &
     Schuster, 2016).

14   Jonah A. Berger and Katherine L. Milkman, "What Makes Online Con-
     tent Viral?" *Journal of Marketing Research 49*, no. 2 (2012): 192–205.

15   The name and certain details have been altered.

16   A November 2008 article by Mike Stobbe named Huntington the "fat-
     test" and "unhealthiest" city in America. Mike Stobbe, "Appalachian
     Town Shrugs at Poorest Health Ranking," *Herald-Dispatch*, November 16,
     2008, accessed February 24, 2017, http://www.herald-dispatch.com/news
     /appalachian-town-shrugs-at-poorest-health-ranking/article_c50a30c5
     -f55c-5a3a-8fad-2285c119e104.html. This statement was based on 2006
     data from the Centers for Disease Control and Prevention.

17   Obesity rate in Huntington 2005 (34.2 percent), 2006 (45.3 percent), and
     2007 (34.2 percent). Laura Wilcox, "Huntington Area Labeled as Nation's
     Most Unhealthy," *Herald-Dispatch*, November 16, 2008.

18   Jane Black, "Jamie Oliver Improves Huntington, W.Va.'s Eating Habits,"
     Washington Post, April 21, 2010.

19   Names, country, and other details have been altered.

20   This notion of corporate purpose was articulated well in *Built to Last*,
     which included the Disney example. Jim Collins and Jerry I. Porras, *Built
     to Last* (New York: HarperCollins, 1994).

21   The appearance of this story has been approved by Agilent Technologies.

22   "At Age 22, DNA Sequencing Put My Cancer on Pause," video with

Corey Wood, accessed February 24, 2017, http://www.forbes.com/video /3930262661001. The video is also available on YouTube, https://www .youtube.com/watch?v=G1ZLyGW8rKY.

23 We found a number of examples of junior employees and senior managers connecting purpose to tedious jobs.

24 Names and details have been altered.

25 Adam M. Grant, Elizabeth M. Campbell, Grace Chen, Keenan Cottone, David Lapedis, and Karen Lee, "Impact and the Art of Motivation Maintenance: The Effects of Contact with Beneficiaries on Persistence Behavior," *Organizational Behavior and Human Decision Processes 103* (2007): 53–67.

26 Vibeke Venema, "The Indian Sanitary Pad Revolutionary," BBC News, March 4, 2014, accessed June 23, 2017, http://www.bbc.com/news/magazine -26260978. See also "Launch Pad," by Yudhijit Bhattacharjee, *New York Times Magazine*, November 10, 2016. See also *Menstrual Man*, a film by Amit Virmani, Coup Production, 2013.

27 Sarah Kellogg interviewed Lorenza Pasetti and helped write these paragraphs on Volpi. All data on Volpi and Pasetti are from this interview.

28 See Adam Gerace, Andrew Day, Sharon Casey, and Philip Mohr, "An Exploratory Investigation of the Process of Perspective Taking in Interpersonal Situations," *Journal of Relationships Research 4*, no. e6 (2013): 1–12.

29 Jeffrey Pfeffer, *Power: Why Some People Have It and Others Don't* (New York: HarperCollins, 2010), 53.

30 It is unclear whether President Johnson really said this or whether the journalist David Halberstam quoted or paraphrased him. It was in reference to Johnson resigning himself to the difficulty of firing J. Edgar Hoover as FBI director. David Halberstam, "The Vantage Point; Perspectives of the Presidency 1963–1969. By Lyndon Baines Johnson. Illustrated. 636 pp. New York: Holt, Rinehart and Winston. $15," *New York Times*, October 31, 1971.

31 See https://en.wikipedia.org/wiki/Menstrual_Man.

SEVEN: FIGHT AND UNITE

1 See https://en.wikiquote.org/wiki/Cyrus_the_Great.

2 Frank Kappel, "BOP Invasion First Hand Account—May 1961," Cuban Information Archives, May 29, 1961, Dade County OCB file #153-D, accessed December 18, 2014, http://cuban-exile.com/doc_026-050/doc0041.html.

3 David Halberstam penned the book *The Best and the Brightest*, referring to the Kennedy administration's team. Halberstam's book covers the period from 1960 to 1965 and focuses on the Vietnam War. David Halberstam, *The Best and the Brightest* (New York: Ballantine Books, 1992). One of the best accounts of the Bay of Pigs invasion is Jim Rasinger, *The Brilliant Disaster: JFK, Castro, and America's Doomed Invasion of Cuba's Bay of Pigs* (New York: Scribner, 2012). It contains recently declassified information and as such is more accurate than previous accounts.

4 Arthur Schlesinger, Jr., *A Thousand Days: John F. Kennedy in the White House* (New York: Mariner Books, 2002).

5 Ibid.

6 Mann and the following Bundy quotes are from this source: Piero Gleijeses, "Ships in the Night: The CIA, the White House and the Bay of Pigs." *Journal of Latin American Studies* 27, no. 1 (February 1995):1–42, Cambridge University Press.

7 In Michael A. Roberto, *Why Great Leaders Don't Take Yes for an Answer: Managing for Conflict and Consensus* (Upper Saddle River, NJ: Wharton School Publishing, 2005), 40.

8 Schlesinger, *A Thousand Days*.

9 Elise Keith, "55 Million: A Fresh Look at the Number, Effectiveness, and Cost of Meetings in the U.S.," Lucid Meetings Blogs, December 4, 2015, accessed February 24, 2017, http://blog.lucidmeetings.com/blog/fresh-look-number-effectiveness-cost-meetings-in-us.

10 "Survey Finds Workers Average Only Three Productive Days per Week," Microsoft, March 15, 2005, accessed February 24, 2017, http://news.microsoft.com/2005/03/15/survey-finds-workers-average-only-three-productive-days-per-week/#sm.0000w6727617qoer8zudfzhklx956#zkx63Uq1t9OW2X20.97.

11 Minda Zetlin, "17 Percent of Employees Would Rather Watch Paint Dry than Attend Meetings," *Inc.*, January 30, 2015, accessed February 23, 2017, http://www.inc.com/minda-zetlin/17-percent-of-employees-would-rather-watch-paint-dry-than-attend-team-meetings.html.

12 Name and details have been altered.

13 Morten T. Hansen, Herminia Ibarra, and Urs Peyer, "The Best-Performing CEOs in the World." *Harvard Business Review* (2013); and Morten T. Hansen, Herminia Ibarra, and Urs Peyer. "The Best-Performing CEOs in the World." *Harvard Business Review* (2010).

14 Morten T. Hansen, Herminia Ibarra, and Nana von Bernuth, "Transforming Reckitt Benckiser," Case 5686 (Fontainebleau: INSEAD, April 2011).

15 Bart Becht, "Building a Company of Global Entrepreneurs, "My RB Opportunity Blog," June 18, 2010.

16 The Air Wick Freshmatic story is told by Sarah Shannon, "Britain's Reckitt Benckiser Goes Shopping," *Bloomberg Businessweek*, July 29, 2010, accessed June 23, 2017, https://www.bloomberg.com/news/articles/2010 -07-29/britains-reckitt-benckiser-goes-shopping.

17 "Leadership Principles," Amazon, accessed February 24, 2017, https:// www.amazon.jobs/principles.

18 Shana Lebowitz, "One of the Most Influential Silicon Valley Investors Reveals How His Firm Decides Whether to Back a Company," *Business Insider*, June 2, 2016, accessed February 24, 2017, http://uk.businessinsider .com/how-andreessen-horowitz-decides-to-back-a-company-2016-6?r= US&IR=T.

19 Katherine Phillips, "How Diversity Makes Us Smarter," *Scientific American*, October 1, 2014.

20 Scott E. Page, *The Difference: How the Power of Diversity Creates Better Groups, Firms, Schools, and Societies* (Princeton: Princeton University Press, 2007).

21 Schlesinger, *A Thousand Days*.

22 See Morten T. Hansen, Herminia Ibarra, and Nana von Bernuth, "Transforming Reckitt Benckiser," Case 5686 (Fontainebleau: INSEAD, April 2011).

23 Name and setting have been altered in the "Tammy" and "Donald" stories.

24 Author interview with Dolf van den Brink on November 12, 2014.

25 Reproduced with permission of Dolf van den Brink. Photo by Bruce Hamady.

26 Amy C. Edmondson and Kathryn Roloff, "Leveraging Diversity Through Psychological Safety," *Rotman Magazine* (Fall, 2009), 47–51.

27 Author interview and email exchange with van den Brink, January 16, 2015.

28 Susan Cain, *Quiet: The Power of Introverts in a World That Can't Stop Talking* (New York: Broadway Books, 2013).

29 Name and details have been altered in the "Tammy" and "Donald" stories.

30 As told in Richard M. Bissell Jr., *Reflections of a Cold Warrior: From Yalta to the Bay of Pigs* (New Haven: Yale University Press, 1996). See also H. Bradford Westerfield, "A Key Player Looks Back," May 8, 2007, last

updated August 3, 2011, https://www.cia.gov/library/center-for-the-study
-of-intelligence/kent-csi/vol42no5/html/v42i5a09p.htm.

31   The information for the *Columbia* shuttle disaster is taken from Richard
     Bohmer, Laura Feldman, Erika Ferlins, Amy C. Edmondson, and Michael
     Roberto, *"Columbia*'s Final Mission," Case 304-090 (Boston: Harvard Busi-
     ness School, April 2004). The accompanying simulation contains the quotes.

32   Scott Plous, *The Psychology of Judgment and Decision Making* (New York:
     McGraw-Hill, 1993), 233.

33   This exchange is reported in the epilogue section on "speaking up" in
     Richard Bohmer, Laura Feldman, Erika Ferlins, Amy C. Edmondson, and
     Michael Roberto, *"Columbia*'s Final Mission: A Multimedia Case," Teach-
     ing Note 305-033 (Boston: Harvard Business School, June 2005, revised
     January 2010).

34   Youchi Cohen-Charash and Paul E. Spector, "The Role of Justice in Or-
     ganizations: A Meta-analysis," *Organizational Behavior and Human Decision
     Processes 86*, no. 2 (2001): 278–321.

35   Names and settings have been altered in this example.

36   Quote from the video "1994 Bulls Knicks Game 3 Buzzer Beating Game
     Winner (The Story Behind)," Sole Records, accessed December 18, 2014,
     https://www.youtube.com/watch?feature=player_detailpage&v=c7SbG
     -8Bvgk.

37   Doug Sibor, "The 50 Most Unsportsmanlike Acts in Sports History,"
     Complex, July 5, 2013.

38   Quoted in Phil Jackson and Hugh Delehanty, *Eleven Rings* (New York:
     Penguin Books, 2014).

39   Name and demographic information have been altered.

40   In this example, I have altered the industry setting.

41   David Breashears, Morten T. Hansen, Ludo van der Heyden, and Elin
     Williams, "Tragedy on Everest," case 5519 (Fontainebleau: INSEAD,
     September 2014).

EIGHT: THE TWO SINS OF COLLABORATION

1   Amy C. Edmondson, Ashley-Kay Fryer, and Morten T. Hansen, "Trans-
     forming Care at UnityPoint Health—Fort Dodge," Case 615-052 (Bos-
     ton: Harvard Business School, March 2015).

 2   See Fred G. Donini-Lenhoff and Hannah L. Hedrick, "Growth of Spe-
     cialization in Graduate Medical Education," *JAMA: The Journal of the*

American Medical Association 284, no. 10 (2000): 1284–1289. Also see "Specialty and Subspecialty Certificates," ABMS, accessed May 29, 2017, http://www.abms.org/member-boards/specialty-subspecialty-certificates/.

3   Laurie Barclay, "Better Handoffs Cut Medical Errors 30% in Multicenter Trial," Medscape, November 6, 2014, citing Amy J. Starmer, Nancy D. Spector, Rajendu Srivastava et al., "Changes in Medical Errors after Implementation of a Handoff Program," *New England Journal of Medicine* 371 (2014): 1803–1812.

4   The management literature is full of articles talking about breaking down or busting silos in companies. Here are a few examples from well-known professors using the language of silo busting: Vijay Govindarajan, "The First Two Steps Toward Breaking Down Silos in Your Organization," *Harvard Business Review*, August 9, 2011, accessed February 24, 2017, https://hbr.org/2011/08/the-first-two-steps-toward-breaking-down-silos/; Ranjay Gulati, "Silo Busting: How to Execute on the Promise of Customer Focus," *Harvard Business Review 85*, no. 5 (2007): 98–108; and Kotter International, Contributor, "Leadership Tips for Cross-Silo Success," *Forbes*, April 15, 2013, accessed February 24, 2017, http://www.forbes.com/sites/johnkotter/2013/04/15/leadership-tips-for-cross-silo-success/#6749fa2a6718. Some books exist on the topic too: Heidi K. Gardner, *Smart Collaboration: How Professionals and Their Firms Succeed by Breaking Down Silos* (Boston: Harvard Business Review Press, 2017) and Gillian Tett, *The Silo Effect: The Peril of Expertise and the Promise of Breaking Down Barriers* (New York: Simon & Schuster, 2015).

5   General Electric 1990 annual report, cited in Larry Hirschhorn and Thomas Gilmore, "The New Boundaries of the 'Boundaryless' Company," *Harvard Business Review 70*, no. 3 (1992): 104–115.

6   These results were reported in Martine R. Haas and Morten T. Hansen, "When Using Knowledge Can Hurt Performance: The Value of Organizational Capabilities in a Management Consulting Company," *Strategic Management Journal 26* (2005):1–24.

7   It might seem odd to regard excessive collaboration as a problem, but other evidence confirms it. Professors Rob Cross, Reb Rebele, and Adam Grant found that managers and employees across a number of organizations have seen a 50 percent jump in collaborative activities. In a survey they undertook at one Fortune 500 company, three in five employees reported wishing that they spent less time responding to requests for collaboration.

Rob Cross, Reb Rebele, and Adam Grant, "Collaborative Overload," *Harvard Business Review 94*, no. 1 (2016): 74–79.

8 Name and details have been altered.

9 In this analysis, the top 10 percent were compared to the bottom 10 percent, with all other variables held constant at their average values.

10 The author interviewed and exchanged emails with Mike McMullen for the LC triple quad case study. Agilent Technologies approved the text for this case.

11 Names and details have been altered.

12 I first presented this equation in my book *Collaboration*, 2009, p. 41. I have since used this in numerous executive education classes and consulting assignments to great effect. Morten T. Hansen, *Collaboration: How Leaders Avoid the Traps, Build Common Ground, and Reap Big Results* (Boston: Harvard Business Press, 2009): 41.

13 Ibid., p. 41.

14 Names and details have been altered.

15 While there was potential for conflict of interest because verification could not verify DNV's own consulting services, the business case took these third-party conflicts into account and excluded them from calculations. Morten T. Hansen, "Transforming DNV: From Silos to Disciplined Collaboration Across Business Units—Food Business in 2005," Case 5458 (Fontainebleau: INSEAD, August 2007).

16 "Transcript of presidential meeting in the cabinet room of the White House; Topic: supplemental appropriations for the National Aeronautics and Space Administration (NASA), 21 November 1962," accessed December 18, 2014, http://history.nasa.gov/JFK-Webbconv/pages/transcript.pdf. The transcripts were first released in 2001. Andrew Chaikin, "White House Tapes Shed Light on JFK Space Race Legend," *Space & Science*, August 22, 2001.

17 See for example the Web page for the nonprofit organization "Malaria No More," accessed April 15, 2016, https://www.malarianomore.org.

18 Steven Kerr, "On the Folly of Rewarding A, While Hoping for B," *The Academy of Management Executive 9*, no. 1 (1995): 7–14.

19 Names and details have been altered.

20 Names and setting have been altered.

21 For an overview of trust in academic research, see Roderick Kramer, *Organizational Trust: A Reader* (New York: Oxford Management Readers, 2006).

22 Name and setting have been altered.

23   For details, see, Amy C. Edmondson, Ashley-Kay Fryer, and Morten T. Hansen, "Transforming Care at UnityPoint Health—Fort Dodge," Case 615-052 (Boston: Harvard Business School, March 2015).

NINE: GREAT AT WORK . . . AND AT LIFE, TOO

1   Well-being, of course, has many dimensions, including physical health, happiness, meaningful relationships, a sense of purpose in life, and so on. But work-life balance, job burnout, and job satisfaction seemed like the most promising metrics to assess. Of all the areas of well-being, they pertained most directly to people's experience at work.

2   Personal communication with author, June 4, 2013.

3   Name and location details are disguised.

4   Jonathon R. B. Halbesleben, Harvey Jaron, and Mark C. Bolino "Too Engaged? A Conservation of Resources View of the Relationship Between Work Engagement and Work Interference with Family," *Journal of Applied Psychology 94*, no. 6 (2009):1452–1465.

5   Lewis Garrad and Tomas Chamorro-Premuzic, "The Dark Side of High Employee Engagement," *Harvard Business Review*, August 16, 2016, accessed February 24, 2017, https://hbr.org/2016/08/the-dark-side-of-high-employee-engagement.

6   Mayo Clinic Staff, "Job Burnout: How to Spot It and Take Action," September 17, 2015, accessed February 24, 2017, http://www.mayoclinic.org/healthy-lifestyle/adult-health/in-depth/burnout/art-20046642.

7   Samuel Melamed, Arie Shirom, Sharon Toker, Shlomo Berliner, and Itzhak Shapira, "Burnout and Risk of Cardiovascular Disease: Evidence, Possible Causal Paths, and Promising Research Directions," *Psychological Bulletin 132*, no. 3 (2006): 327–353; Ronald J. Burke and Esther R. Greenglass, "Hospital Restructuring, Work-Family Conflict and Psychological Burnout Among Nursing Staff," *Psychology and Health 16*, no. 5 (2001): 583–594, and Armita Golkar, Emilia Johansson, Maki Kasahara, Walter Osika, Aleksander Perski, and Ivanca Savic, "The Influence of Work-Related Chronic Stress on the Regulation of Emotion and on Functional Connectivity in the Brain," *PLoS One 9*, no. 9 (2014), doi: 10.1371/journal.pone0104550. See also Sharon Toker and Michal Biron, "Job Burnout and Depression: Unraveling Their Temporal Relationship and Considering the Role of Physical Activity," *Journal of Applied Psychology 97*, no. 3 (2012): 699–710.

8   See for example Kathleen M. Eisenhardt and Mark J. Zbaracki, "Strategic
    Decision Making," *Strategic Management Journal 13*, no. 52 (1992): 17–37.
    See also, Allen C. Amason, "Distinguishing the Effects of Functional and
    Dysfunctional Conflict on Strategic Decision Making: Resolving a Para-
    dox for Top Management Teams," *Academy of Managers Journal 39* (1996):
    123–148.

9   Ann C. Mooney, Patricia J. Holahan, and Allen C. Amason, "Don't Take It
    Personally: Exploring Cognitive Conflict as Mediator of Effective Con-
    flict," *Journal of Management Studies* 44, no. 5 (2007): 733–758.

10 In one study of 271 working adults, higher passion at work was highly
    correlated (0.82) with vocational satisfaction. Another study of 370 uni-
    versity employees demonstrated that those who felt their working con-
    tributing to the greater good also reported much higher job satisfaction.
    Patricia Chen, Phoebe C. Ellsworth, and Norbert Schwarz, "Finding a Fit
    or Developing It: Implicit Theories About Achieving Passion for Work,"
    Personality and Social Psychology Bulletin 41, no. 10 (2015): 1411–1424, and
    Michael F. Steger, Bryan J. Dik, and Ryan D. Duffy, "Measuring Meaning-
    ful Work: The Work and Meaning Inventory," *Journal of Career Assessment*
    20, no. 3 (2012): 322–337.

11 Michael P. Leiter and Christina Maslach, "The Impact of Interpersonal
    Environment on Burnout and Organizational Commitment," *Journal of
    Organizational Behavior 9*, no. 4 (1988): 297–308.

12 Dustin Moskovitz, "Work Hard, Live Well," Building Asana, August 19,
    2015, accessed February 24, 2017, https://medium.com/building-asana
    /work-hard-live-well-ead679cb506d#.c0k0etr2a.

RESEARCH APPENDIX

1   This is a weighted sum of the standard scores (z-scores) for each item in
    the dimension. The weights for each item are computed to maximize the
    correlation between the item value and the resulting factor score. This
    represents the optimal combination of items to measure the general con-
    cept represented by the dimension.

2   The responses on some questionnaire items were incomplete for some of
    the 4,964 respondents. There were N=4958 fully complete questionnaires
    available for regression models.

3   The tolerance value for these two variables is too low to allow separate
    interpretation of the linear and curvilinear quadratic effects, but we are

simply using them as a pair to represent and control for the single construct of hours worked.

4   This was done with a polynomial regression in which successive models minimizing mean squared error are fit to the data. At each step, an additional power of the predictor variable is added. In words, the first model says "x predicts y in a straight line (the linear model)." At the next step it says "now add x^2 (a U-shaped parabola, the quadratic component) and see if it lowers the error." This process continues until there is no improvement in prediction.

5   Further testing of the decreasing portion of the curve at high hours worked beyond the quadratic maximum showed that the quadratic model predicted a decline in performance at these high values that was significantly more rapid than what actually appeared in the data. After reaching the maximum, the falloff in performance was linear, not quadratic.

6   It is explained in much more mathematical detail in John Pencavel, "The Productivity of Working Hours," *Economic Journal 125*, no. 589 (2015): 2052–2076.

7   The criteria for accepting a model as plausible are the Root Mean Square Error of Approximation (RMSEA) and a significance test (the conventional p-value). RMSEA is average error between the predicted values and the actual values of all the correlations between pairs of variables in the model. The smaller it is, the better the model fits the data. Low RMSEA means the predicted correlations from the model match the actual correlations found in the data. A conventional value for accepting a model as plausible is RMSEA of less than 5 percent.

The p-value is the probability that the error between predicted and actual correlations is due to random noise and not to errors in the hypothesized structure of cause and effect. In conventional hypothesis testing between a null effects model and a hypothesized model, one looks for low values of p, typically $p < .05$, to indicate the results were unlikely to be due to chance. In SEM, this logic is reversed. A higher p-value indicates that differences between predicted and actual correlations are more likely to be random effects than to be an incorrect model structure.

A typical criterion for a plausible model is $p > .05$. This value is computed from the Chi Square statistic that summarizes differences between expected and actual correlation values according to the number of these values that are free to vary (the degrees of freedom, or d.f.).

Acknowledgments

Many people generously provided help and support to conduct this study and create the book. I would like to thank all the people who helped in various ways with the research, case studies, and production of the manuscript: Lucy Berbeo, Thomas Boyd, Philip Bradock, Warren Cormier, Shirish Dhar, Katie Findley, Rachel Gostenhofer, James Gordon, Andrea Ichino, Michelle Kossack, Yifei Liu, Dave Paunesku, Charlie Schaub, Stephanie Snipe, Lazar Stojkovic, Robert Tafet, John Toussaint, David Volpe, James Watt, and Andy Young.

I also want to thank the number of people who gave of their precious time for the case studies for this study: Espen Agdestein, Claudia Bach, Bart Becht, Steven Birdsall, Susan Bishop, Marie-Claire Blackburn, Carl Blake, David Breashears, Margaret Bree, Clay Caldwell, Freddy Caspers, Bill Davidow, Andreae Dawson, Alejandra de Obeso, Massimiliano Dotti, John Everett, Laurent Faracci, Roberto Funari, Brittany Gavin, Hartmut Goeritz, Dominique Grau, Terry Grote, Genevieve Guay, Ian Hutchinson, Liz Jones, Ofer Kolton, Isabelle Lomba, Dan McLaughlin, Mike McMullen, Dmitry Melnik, Simon Nash, Arantxa Olivares, Lorenza Pasetti, Gard Steiro, Ian Telford, Dolf van den Brink, Bård Viken, and all the people we interviewed from the 5,000 person study whose real names remain anonymous throughout the book. I also thank Greg Green at the Clintondale High School and all the other staff we interviewed when we visited, including Meloney Cargill, Len Lewandowski, Dave Schindler, and Rob Townsend, and also the students we interviewed, including Desmond Cribbs, Imani Moore, Isaac Van Eeckhoutte, Faith Young, and Dionya Williams. I thank Bill Leaver, Pam Halvorson, Deb Shriver, Sue Thompson, and other interviewees at UnityPoint Health (Fort Dodge) for their participation in their hospital's case study.

A number of people read and commented on drafts of the chapters, and I thank them all for their valuable feedback: Ron Adner, Osvald Bjelland, Philip Braddock, Alex Budak, Bertil Chappuis, Jim Collins, Patrick Forth, Charles Fuller, Josef Gorek, Boris Groysberg, Egill Hansen, Marianne Hansen, Chip Heath, Herminia Ibarra, Erling Kagge, David Kang, Frank Ketcham, Mats Lederhausen, Carista Luminare, Mac MacLaren, Birger Magnus, David Ruben, Jeffrey Pfeffer, Tom Rath, Arne Selvik, Jim Phills, Joel Podolny, Peter Sims, Don Sull, Sissel Sundby, and Mary Anne Veldkamp. In addition, I am thankful to a number of academics who provided useful insights and information to concepts and examples or with whom I have collaborated: Amy Edmondson, Cynthia Emrich, K. Anders Ericsson, Ashley-Kay Fryer, Catherine Lewis, Leslie Perlow, Jason Steffen, Ludo van der Heyden, and Freek Vermeulen.

I also thank several people who helped with editing or with the writing of paragraphs and sections of the book: Nell Casey, Craig Good, Connie Hale, Sarah Kellogg, Emily Loose, and Dan Lyons. I especially thank Seth Schulman and his collaborator Marc Dunkleman. Seth's contribution was magnificent.

Over the past five years, many of my students at UC Berkeley and numerous executives in different companies have been exposed to early ideas and more developed formulations, and their reactions and discussions have been very helpful in improving the material.

I owe a tremendous debt of gratitude to my agent Christy Fletcher and her staff at Fletcher & Company. Christy believed in this project early on and helped shape and improve the manuscript numerous times. Sylvie Greenberg joined at a later stage and has been very helpful with the launch of the book.

I am also tremendously grateful to my publisher, Jon Karp, and my chief editor, Ben Loehnen, whose insightful comments and edits pushed me to improve the book. The rest of the team at Simon & Schuster have been very helpful in launching the book: Many thanks to Larry Hughes, Amar Deol, Dana Trocker, Jessica Breen, Richard Rhorer, and Marie Florio.

In addition, several people have been helping with launching and marketing the book. Many thanks to Ken Gillet and his team at Target Marketing Digital and Mark Fortier and Pamela Peterson at Fortier Public Relations.

I would also like to express my profound gratitude to Jim Collins, Carol Dweck, Adam Grant, Chip Heath, Herminia Ibarra, and founders Stuart Crainer and Des Dearlove at Thinkers50. They gave of their time to review and endorse the book.

My project manager and long-time collaborator, Nana von Bernuth, deserves special mention. She has worked on about every part of this project, including editing numerous manuscripts and chasing data and leads. I am extremely grateful for all her valuable ideas and contributions.

Finally, I could not have accomplished this project without my lovely family, my two daughters, Alexandra and Julia, and my wife, Hélène. They have supported me emotionally and let me take family time away to work on the book. Hélène has provided feedback on far too many iterations and helped with all sorts of other tasks. I thank them from the bottom of my heart.

Index

About the Author

MORTEN T. HANSEN is a management professor at University of California, Berkeley. He is also a faculty member at Apple University, Apple. He is the coauthor (with Jim Collins) of the *New York Times* bestseller *Great by Choice* and the author of the highly acclaimed *Collaboration*. Formerly a professor at Harvard Business School and INSEAD (France), Professor Hansen holds a PhD from Stanford Business School, where he was a Fulbright scholar. His academic research has won several prestigious awards, and he is ranked one of the world's most influential management thinkers by Thinkers50. Hansen was also a manager at the Boston Consulting Group, where he advised corporate clients worldwide. Born and raised in Norway, he lives in San Francisco with his wife and two daughters, and he travels the world to give keynotes and help companies and people become great at work.